THE CHEROKEE FRONTIER

Conflict and Survival, 1740–62

The Cherokee Frontier

CONFLICT AND SURVIVAL, 1740–62

By David H. Corkran

The Three Cherokees came over from the head of the River Savanna to London 1762.

UNIVERSITY OF OKLAHOMA PRESS : NORMAN

To Marion

Foreword

THIS IS A BOOK about the Cherokees in the Colonial period—
how they behaved and why. It was conceived in the belief that
other works dealing with the tribe in this era had not given
adequate consideration to Indian motives and objectives. The
Cherokees were not only an Indian tribe sustained by a strong
cultural tradition; they were a people struggling for nationalism and survival. Their behavior, then, derived from these circumstances. The problem of the historian is to understand their
culture, their intra-tribal problems, and their international situation. It is not sufficient to approach their story from the point
of view of the advancing and victorious whites. The records
available for the period are, of course, those of the Colonials.
From them I have attempted where possible to sift the purely
Indian material and to permit it to speak for itself.

It is clear from the record that the southeastern Indian cus-
toms, politics, and policies had much to do with Indian attitudes
toward the English colonies than did the feeble machinations of
the French, which were so often alleged by excitable and not
disinterested parties in Carolina as the reason for apprehension
on the Cherokee frontier.

David H. Corkran

Chicago, Illinois
July 2, 1962

Acknowledgments

THE PREPARATION OF THIS VOLUME has not been a solitary venture. I am obligated to many libraries and librarians: Miss Margaret Ligon and Miss Ida Padelford of Pack Memorial Library, Asheville, North Carolina, made unsparing efforts to obtain necessary materials from other collections. Elizabeth Peterson, Manuscripts Division of the Library of Congress, called my attention to previously unexplored documentary materials concerning the Cherokees. Harold Easterby, director of the Historical Commission of South Carolina, and his assistant, Francis M. Hutson, guided me through their collection. Stanley Pargellis of the Newberry Library, Chicago, and Howard Peckham, Clements Library, Ann Arbor, Michigan showed me every courtesy. Miss Helen G. McCormack, Gibbes Art Gallery, Charleston, South Carolina, did a tremendous amount of research, and was finally able to uncover the portrait of James Glen which appears in this book.

The following libraries were visited and used: The Sondley Collection, Pack Memorial Library, Asheville, North Carolina; the Library of Congress; the Historical Commission of South Carolina, Columbia, South Carolina; the Library of the University of North Carolina; the Library of the University of South Carolina; the Library of the University of Georgia; the Library of the University of Virginia; Widener Library, Harvard University; the Library of the University of Michigan; the Huntington Library, San Marino, California; the Clements Library, Ann Arbor, Michigan; the Newberry Library, Chicago, Illinois; Manuscripts Division, New York Historical Collection, Albany, New York; the Charleston Library Society, Charleston, South Carolina; the Georgia Department of Archives and History, Atlanta, Georgia; the New York Public Library; and the Boston Public Library.

Mr. George Stephens, Asheville, North Carolina, gave initial impetus to this work. Mr. Dennison B. Hull, Winnetka, Illinois, read the manuscript and has been a major source of stimulus and encouragement. Mrs. Lake H. Bobbitt, Jr., kindly read the proofs.

D.H.C.

Contents

Illustrations

THE CHEROKEE FRONTIER
Conflict and Survival, 1740–62

Introduction: The Cherokees

IN THE EIGHTEENTH CENTURY the Cherokee was the largest Indian tribe on the frontiers of English America. A mountain people, the Cherokees lived near and among the high Appalachians on the inland borders of North Carolina, South Carolina, and Georgia. In 1755 they numbered upward of 10,000 persons, of whom 2,500 or 3,000 were fighting men.[1] Their forty or more villages were organized into three great regional communities, each of which spoke its own variant of the mother tongue. Beneath the Blue Ridge escarpment in the upper Piedmont of South Carolina stood the five or six Lower Towns, their fortunes governed by Keowee, gateway to the Carolina trade, and Estatoe, large and belligerent. Sixty miles westward in the mountain valleys began the Middle Settlements, a group of four village clusters, the parent aggregate situated on the headwaters of the Little Tennessee and the others on the Tuckaseigee, Cheoah, and Valley rivers. The farthest inland Cherokee segment was the Overhill on the Lower Little Tennessee. The nine Overhill towns represented two colonizations: the first, that of Great Tellico and Chatuga from the Valley cluster, and the second, that of the seven Chota towns, or the Overhills proper. This latter group, the last of all the Cherokees to migrate into the South, was the parent nucleus of the tribe.

Though regionally divided, the Cherokees were not a confederation but a nation. They were one people descended from

[1] S. C. Council Journals, Sept. 1, 1755, p. 319; J. H. Payne, MSS, VII, 2–3.

one council fire, that of Chota, capital of the Overhills. All Cherokees acknowledged the prestigial ascendancy of the one King, or Uku, the First Beloved Man of Chota. Bound to each other by clan ties which cut across the regions, the various regional peoples were governed by councils of headmen, all of whom were members of the historic ruling family of the nation. From among the main line of that family resident in the Overhills, these headmen elected the Uku, who presided for life at Chota assisted by his Right Hand Man, and the Great Warrior, who were his relatives.[2] The Uku's word was "awful" or holy among the towns, and traditionally no major transactions of peace or war had validity without his consent. Nevertheless, his authority sat lightly; for the regional councils were semiautonomous, and rivalry of interests among them frequently forced situations which Chota could only tolerate. Though Chota itself was not above using its national prestige to promote interests primarily Overhill, in the mid-eighteenth century it was engaged in a bitter struggle to assert its ascendancy over the centrifugal forces in the nation.

Governed by substantial traditional institutions and with their economy based upon agriculture, the Cherokees were a relatively stable people. Their towns situated on bottom lands by clear, rushing streams were neat and attractive.[3] Their small gabled houses built of white clay and cane stood irregularly among their cornfields. As many as two hundred houses might make one community, and but twenty-five another. Scattered among them were slatted corn cribs, set on posts a foot or more above the ground, and compact cone-shaped winter houses formed with earth-covered hides where in the cold months families would lie in close naked warmth around a smoldering fire, the smoke having no vent save when the flap covering the doorway was lifted. Central in each town but near the river was the community center, or town house. A great domelike structure perhaps fifty feet in diameter and fifteen feet high at the smoke

2 Payne, MSS, III, 32.
3 Christopher French, "Journal," Bk. II, 140, 143.

hole, it stood on a low earthen mound. In its dark interior, lighted only by the daylight entering the smoke hole or at night by the central fire, a cane bench hugged the low wall about the circumference. On the bench and the floor could be seated in concentric rings almost the entire adult population, focusing upon the arena made by the seven central pillars which supported the roof and surrounded the sacred fire. Here occurred the formal councils of the rulers, the rituals of certain religious ceremonies, and, in winter, the circling dramatic dances of a gregarious and expressive people. The town house was never vacant, for on its bench reclined the retired ancients of the town, the patriarchs who had served their time in the offices of peace and war. Now at ease they smoked their pipes and reminisced of the past, welcomed visiting strangers, or instructed the young of the ruling family in their people's traditions.[4] Next to the town house stretched the gaming yard, where the maturer spirits occupied their leisure hours with the chunky game, a stick-and-disk contest suggestive of lawn bowling. Near by was the flat ceremonial field on which the entire town paraded and danced at festival time and where at other times young men who had staked their all on the outcome played a frenzied lacrosse-like ball game.

Ceremonially, the Cherokees celebrated and propitiated in periodic festival the Creator God, The Great White Being Above, whose divinity entering water and fire gave fertility to earth and man.[5] To him they sacrificed food in fire and offered themselves in the waters which flowed ceaselessly beside the towns. His being was symbolized, and perhaps incarnated, in the white-robed Uku, who on ceremonial occasions was paraded on a platform in his awful majesty in the most loved communion of the nation. Before him and his resplendent symbolism the people danced with a mystic joy they knew at no other time.

In spring and summer, young and old, male and female, worked the cornfields allotted them by the town councilors. In

---

[4] Edmund Atkin to Board of Trade, n.d., Loudoun Papers, p. 5.

[5] Alexander Long, "A Small Postscript to the Ways and Manners of the Nashon of Indians Called Cherikees," 1.

fall and winter they hunted the deer for periods of as much as a month at a time—entire families moving off to predetermined areas. Originally necessary for subsistence, by 1750 deer hunting had become the chief industry of the Cherokees for they had become dependent upon the white man's manufactured goods. Formerly clothed merely in a deerskin flap or breechcloth and a loose mantle of furs or deerskin, the men now wore woolen matchcoats and flaps of British make.[6] Although the women still wore the short deerskin skirts, which, as one white observer remarked, were designed to display their pretty legs, they increasingly demanded that their men provide them with calicoes. Glass beads had displaced those of shell, and brass earrings were common. Brass arrowheads, iron axes, hoes, and kettles, and steel knives had replaced flint points, stone tools, and earthen pots. Though bows and arrows were still made, and sometimes beautifully, all men aspired to guns, powder, and ball. Indeed, without them, survival amidst other Indians thus equipped would be impossible. All these articles could be had only by trading deerskins to the whites. To obtain them, the Cherokees supplied the Charlestown merchants with over fifty thousand deerskins annually. Long since, they had become perennial debtors to the traders who staked them in their winter hunts. The Cherokees roamed the forests almost as employees of a trading system built around the faraway demands of European society.

The Cherokee economy was thus essentially one of peace and industry. But by tradition and necessity the Cherokees were warriors. No young man could arrive at accepted adulthood until he had achieved a war name by action against the enemies of his people. No member of the ruling family could be promoted to effective headship unless he had proved himself in war—a possible exception being proficiency in the occult mysteries of shamanism which could only be achieved by training from early youth.[7] This war cult had grown up from the necessity of pro-

---

[6] Lt. Henry Timberlake, *The Memoirs of Lt. Henry Timberlake*, 51.
[7] W. H. Gilbert, Jr., *The Eastern Cherokees*, 341–42, 356.

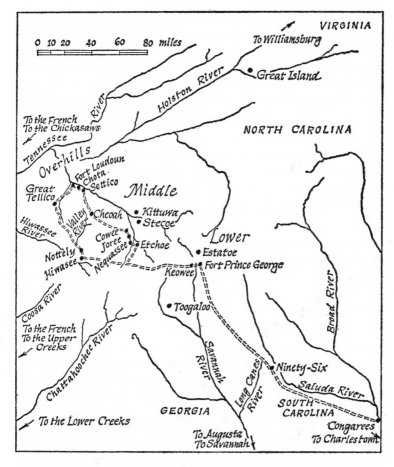

The Cherokee country, 1740–62. Dotted line marks the main trail across the Cherokee nation.

tecting the nation's food supply. Indian population bore a direct ratio to food resources, and a diminution of tribal hunting
grounds by an invasion of aliens meant disaster. But war from
time immemorial had become ritualized into the social fiber of
the nation. It had its own mysteries and incentives. If no immediate neighbor threatened, the young men and warriors sought
far fields of action. On occasion Cherokee war parties fought
several hundred miles from home in Illinois, Arkansas, New
York, and Florida. But by the mid-eighteenth century the Cherokees had little need for mere adventurous war. Continued
involvement as allies of the Chickasaws in war against the Choctaws, frequent conflict with the neighboring Creeks to the south,
and the raids of the French-inspired northern Ottawas and
Iroquois made war a constant and bitter fact of Cherokee life.

Cherokee women abetted the young men's war lust. The seven
or nine Cherokee clans were matrilineal. Since blood vengeance
was a rigid rule of Cherokee life, all male members of a killed
or wounded man's clan were obliged to avenge his blood. Scalps
of enemy dead were presented to women whose bloodlines had
suffered.[8] Women appear to have had an active war role. In pre-
historic times War Women were said to have accompanied war
parties to perform menial tasks about the encampments. The
War Women also had the disposition of captives.[9] Women's
councils may have had a voice in the decision for war.[10] Certainly they had a peace role, for official women accompanied
peace missions. Although no white man appears ever to have
heard a Cherokee woman speak in council, women were un-
doubtedly present at treaty-making as official observers, perhaps
even as behind-the-scenes councilors. The titles War Woman
and Beloved Woman suggest war and peace organizations
among the women similar to those of the men. Holders of these
titles, like their male counterparts, probably were women of the

8 Coytmore to Lyttelton, July 23, 1759, Lyttelton Papers.
9 William De Brahm, *Philosophico-Historico-Hydrogeography of South Carolina, Georgia, and East Florida*, 220.
10 J. P. Brown, *Old Frontiers*, 18.

regal line. There must also have been women's mysteries and ceremonials, but the only evidence of these appears in occasional organized public demonstrations by the women.

Though in historic times the Cherokees never had a woman ruler, Cherokee women enjoyed a clearly defined supremacy in domestic life. An early eighteenth-century observer noted that in the household "the women rules the rost and weres the britches and sometimes will beat thire husbands within an inch of thire life. The man will not resist their poure if the woman was to beat his branes out."[11] James Adair, writing fifty years later, remarked that the Cherokees "have been a considerable while under petticoat government, and allow their women full liberty to plant their brows with horns as often as they please without fear or punishment." Companionate marriages and easy separations were not infrequent; nevertheless, the housing of the tribe by family units indicates that most marriages were long sustained and that families were stable despite both male and female license. The demands of the women for dresses, ornaments, and subsistence were powerful motives of the men's hunting and trading activities and the warriors' insistence upon rewards from the English for their services.

Cherokee children brought up to respect tribal prestiges and taboos were not undisciplined. Misbehavior in sacred matters ordinarily brought punishment by dousing in cold water, or more seriously by scratching with a snake's tooth comb. Children of the ruling family went to school to certain elders to learn their lore and duties, and those destined to shamanism were apprenticed to shamans.[12] Children had duties working in the fields and helping in the deer drives which featured the family hunt. But in their early childhood, Cherokee children, like children from time immemorial, gamboled in unrestrained play. Like children of all peoples, they were loved by their parents, who gave them such endearing names as "the Pretty One," "The Little War Captain," "the Tree Climber."[13]

11 Long, *op. cit.*, 22.
12 Gilbert, *op. cit.*, 341–42.
13 Long, *op. cit.*, 24.

Although sociability, sentiment, and gaiety colored the surface of Cherokee life, beneath its sparkle operated deep currents of fear. With the heavy force of tradition, mysticism, and taboo, the Cherokee shamans taught that omens and spirits governed man's world. Dreams were portents; a personal enemy could fix a spell on one; the hoot of the owl presaged death; to step on lightning-struck ground was fatal; the favor of the Great Being Above had always to be invoked and his wrath stayed or propitiated. These and a hundred other superstitious beliefs made a world in which the terrible could always occur at the will of the great power brooding over human destinies.

The world of Cherokee human contacts also held terrors. A trespass, a passionate blood incident, and retaliation would strike. Always apprehensive, the Cherokee readily believed the worst of any wild rumor. He feared, too, that failure to act upon a menacing report meant disaster. Under the circumstances, the tribal requirement that the young men be bold to distinguish themselves created frequent crises. In times of panic all the patience and wisdom of the elders were taxed to prevent premature violence; and, frequently, even these could not curb the madness of the young men and the frenzy of the women.

Cherokee retaliatory violence was morbidly sadistic. When the warriors of Nottely in 1760 assaulted trader John Kelly to avenge the imprisonment of their chiefs, they not only scalped him, but slowly dismembered him while he was yet alive and conscious.[14] In 1761 the Overhills scalped and mutilated Captain Paul Demere and then made him dance.[15] Outraged by a Catawba protest of grievance, the Keowees beat a Catawba woman to death, hacked up her body, and fed it in utmost contempt to the dogs. The genitals of enemy dead were fit accompaniments of their scalps. Ceremonial cannibalism featured the sealing of alliances between tribes—the allied headmen feasting upon the flesh of enemy dead. Cherokee women mocked the manhood of prisoners burned at the stake.

[14] Enc. No. 30, Amherst to Pitt, Mar. 8, 1760, B.P.R.O., C.O. 5/58.
[15] *Maryland Gazette*, Nov. 6, 1760.

But in peacetime Cherokees enjoyed trading. Prehistorically the trading path had been almost as important as the war path; and the war leaders appear also to have had control of trade. Cherokee traders went far places to offer pipes, quartzite arrowheads, and perhaps even baskets, for conch shells from which to make trumpets, pieces of copper for ornaments, or other useful or talismanic objects. Diplomacy was also a form of trade. When Cherokee diplomats faced the English, they always sought a specific *quid pro quo*. They demanded high and offered low and so worked out a bargain which they expected to be carried out to the letter. The sanctity of the given word among them led to sophistry, craftiness, and narrow literalness; for the Indian realized that his insistence upon the inviolability of the word made him also vulnerable. An Indian headman who failed to hold a bargainer to his word or to keep his own word was subject to verbal and sometimes actual assault from his fellows.

In some thirty of the Cherokee towns lived licensed Carolina traders, most of whom had marriage ties with leading headmen. These traders maintained homes after the English mode, setting fashions to which the headmen frequently aspired. Their log storehouses were separate structures in which they kept their goods and from behind the counters of which they carried on their daily traffic. Always the Indians were in debt to them, for the traders outfitted their customers on credit charged against each man's anticipated take of deerskins. Often a hunter's take proved too little to cover his account, and the situation provoked a not always unjustifiable suspicion on the part of the debtor.

The traders were official Carolina's contact with the Cherokee nation. Their reports, be they rumor or grim truth, formed the fibers from which colony and crown wove the fabric of their Indian policies. In their dual role of reporters and agents not all traders could be trusted, for alienation of the natives or untimely war could mean heavy financial loss. However, such men as Cornelius Dougherty of Hiwassee, Ludovic Grant of Cheoah, Robert Bunning of Tuckaseigee, and James Beamer of Estatoe formed the very pillars of English strength in the nation. The confidence they commanded, their intimacy with the headmen, and their good judgment enabled them to exert great influence in Indian councils. Often in time of stress they had only their patient understanding of Indian ways and their bold courage to stay the deadly hand of savage anger. Their craft and diplomacy frequently shaped the agenda of the great missions the Cherokees annually undertook to Charlestown.

CHAPTER ONE

The Great Alliance

IN APRIL, 1745, two hundred Cherokees entered the little Colonial city of Charlestown to greet the new royal Governor of South Carolina, James Glen. With them they brought the Carolina-commissioned Young Emperor, Ammonscossittee of Great Tellico, a boy of fourteen or fifteen years. Flashing cannons boomed from walls, forts, and ships, while, led by the Governor's coach and six bearing the regal Indian youth, the warriors, painted and bedecked as garishly as their native mountains in azalea time, marched proudly down Broad Street to the stately council house.[1] In the spacious council room the Young Emperor knelt before the redcoat Governor and, taking from his head a rude crown of silk and furs, placed it at the Governor's feet. Rising, he displayed for all to see the parchmented treaty of trade and alliance which Cherokee deputies had made in London in 1730, and in formal oration he stutteringly promised to maintain its provisions. When the Governor had made his gracious reply, the headmen of the various towns and regions came forward to receive from his hand new commissions as captains, lieutenants, and ensigns in the service of the great King George over the seas, whose majesty they were to represent among their people. There were probably more speeches in which the two peoples expressed their love and friendship for each other. Finally the Governor brought the ceremonies to a close with a reminder that the Cherokees should be on their good behavior and cease harboring the

[1] Peter Henry Bruce, *Memoirs*, 519–20.

13

wild northern Indians who made war upon their neighbors, the English-allied Creeks and Catawbas.[2] The ceremonial offerings of presents requisite to such a meeting between Indians and whites is not enumerated, but it no doubt included gay clothing for both men and women, plenty of brass wire for the great earrings Cherokees loved to wear, utilitarian pins, needles, pots and pans, even guns and ammunition, and perhaps special novelties for important headmen. For a few days the Cherokees lingered in the city, visiting those awe-inspiring symbols of the white man's power: the white-steepled churches, the bristling forts, the dark-hulled ships. Then, their hearts at peace, they departed through the flower-scented countryside on the three-hundred mile journey to their wilderness homes.

For all its pageantry the visit represented harsh reality. The Cherokees were dependant upon Carolina. On the American frontier of the industrial revolution, the Cherokees had lost their old self-sufficient forest economy. As Skiagunsta, the old head warrior of the Lower Towns, stated it:

> My people . . . cannot . . . live independent of the English . . . .
> The clothes we wear we cannot make ourselves. They are made for us. We use their ammunition with which to kill deer. We cannot make our guns. Every necessary of life we must have from the white people.[3]

Living in a competitive wilderness inhabited by probable enemies similarly dependent upon the English or French, every Cherokee knew the force of Skiagunsta's argument.

Yet Carolina's position was almost as difficult. The twelve thousand Cherokees lived astride the shadowy boundary between French and English claims in the south. Their nearest communities, the Lower Towns on the branches of Keowee River, a Blue Ridge affluent of the Savannah, lay but one hun-

[2] S. C. Council Journals, May 4, 1745.

[3] "Indian Books of South Carolina" (hereinafter referred to as IBSC), III, 321–23.

dred miles beyond the farthest west of the English settlements. From their mountains the Cherokees could pour torrents of warriors eastward against Virginia, the Carolinas, and Georgia. Governor Glen stated the case pointedly in 1751:

> It is absolutely necessary for us to be in friendship with the Cherokees in particular . . . . They are reckoned to be about three thousand gunmen, the greatest nation we know of in America except the Choctaws and while we call them friends we may consider them a bulwark at our backs; for such numbers will always secure us in that quarter from the attempts of the French.[4]

Furthermore the Cherokee trade in deerskins for English strouds and duffels in which English and Carolina capital invested heavily to support ships, pack trains, and a score of trading depots formed a monopoly important in the Carolina economy.

Through fifty years of facing frontier dangers, Carolina had developed mutually satisfactory arrangements with the Cherokees. The system, ignoring the primary council at Chota among the Overhills, looked to the village and regional head warriors who in Cherokee tribal organization had charge of trade as well as war. Recipients of generous English presents to distribute among their retainers, these officials became increasingly dependent upon English traders, thus emphasizing their natural tendency toward regional and local automony from Chota. By 1740 circumstances had forced the English to augment their trade practices with a rudimentary form of centralized control of the Cherokees, built around the warrior hierarchy instead of the native political and religious officials whom tradition decreed to be the heads of the nation. The English puppet government had its genesis in Moytoy of Great Tellico, probably Great Warrior of the Overhills, in 1730 designated emperor of the Cherokees by that mysterious and irresponsible visitor to the Carolina mountains, Sir Alexander Cuming. The office logically belonged to the Uku of Chota, but Moytoy eagerly reached for it and in-

[4] S. C. Council Journals, May 28, 1751.

duced Chota to send deputies with Cuming to England to make the famous treaty. Carolina did not recognize the emperorship until 1738, and then only after another eccentric European, Christian Prieber, who styled himself secretary of state to the Emperor, had begun to advocate a centralized Cherokee state independent of the English.[5] Fearing such a state and needing Cherokee help in King George's War, Carolina issued a commission to Moytoy as Emperor in return for his acting against the French-allied Choctaws. In 1741, Moytoy died in battle.[6] To retain the advantage it enjoyed at Great Tellico, Carolina disregarded the passing of the Great Warriorship to a town near Chota on the Little Tennessee, and commissioned Moytoy's thirteen-year-old son Ammonscossittee emperor, and set over him as guardian the Raven of Hiwassee, who was the head warrior of the Valley.[7] Thus the anomalous emperorship functioned through the Raven of Hiwassee and the Tellico council where sat the two Tacites, Johnny and Osteneco, the Judd's Friend of the Carolina records; and Old Caesar, headman of near-by Chatuga, who in his youth had been an English slave and was the only full-blood Cherokee in all the nation who spoke English well.

The emperorship of Ammonscossittee, save as it formed the English trading contact, had little standing at Chota, the mother town of all the Cherokees, where ruled Connecorte, called by the English Old Hop because of his lameness, and Johnny of Tanase, Moytoy's successor as Great Warrior. To Chota, Great Tellico, twenty miles away, was upstart. Great Tellico was a duly constituted mother town colonized from the Valley to the southeast to spawn a new regional group on the flats of Tellico Creek. But its title was inferior to Chota's for Chota, the town of shelter, contained the eldest of Cherokee councils. From it in the fourteenth or fifteenth centuries or earlier all the Cherokee

[5] S. C. Commons House Journals, 1738, p. 116.

[6] Allen D. Chandler, ed., *Colonial Records of the State of Georgia*, XXIII, 224.

[7] *South Carolina Gazette*, June 23, 1756; Chandler, *op. cit.*, IV, Supplement, 81–82.

regional councils had been directly or indirectly colonized. Migrating late from the northeast to join the great nation that had grown from its seed in the high southern Appalachians, it had settled in the Great Tellico–Little Tennessee area, where it formed the outpost of the Cherokee nation against all the western Indians and absorbed the lands and authorities to which Great Tellico aspired. Thus until Moytoy's time Great Tellico had remained an enclave of lost potentiality, its officialdom but participants in the Chota council and holding high office only as the chances of heredity by Chota paternity offered. That the Valley colony should be raised to *de facto* superiority over Chota by the English influence stimulated Chota to reassert its native authority. Nearly a decade passed after the ascension of the Young Emperor before Chota entirely supplanted the Hiwassee-Tellico coalition and eliminated it as a divisive force in the nation. Chota's reassertion of its primacy began to take shape in 1742. Because Moytoy had led the Cherokees into King George's War, the nation was in distress. Not only had it lost heavily in a smallpox epidemic brought home from the English camps about St. Augustine in 1740, but it was confronted by the most formidable array of enemies that it had encountered in historic times. To prevent the English-allied Cherokees from moving against Spanish Florida as they had in 1739–40, the French had set the Creeks upon the Lower Cherokees and had sent the Canadian Iroquois, the Senecas, Shawnees, and Ottawas from above the Ohio against the Overhills.[8] With the Valley and Great Tellico committed to fight beside the English, Chota believed the nation had more war than it could handle and that it must break out of its entanglements with friend and foe.[9]

Governors Clarke of New York and Glen of South Carolina unwittingly lent aid to Chota's designs. Laboring for an English-oriented peace among their Indian allies, they succeeded in bringing the Cherokees and Iroquois together at Onondaga and

[8] Chandler, *op. cit.*, XXV, 474–75.

[9] Sainsbury Transcripts (Public Records of South Carolina; hereinafter referred to as PRSC), XXIII, 169–75.

caused an exchange of peace talks and tokens between the Cherokees and the Creeks.[10]

But after five years of total war Chota desired nothing less than total peace. It sent emissaries to Fort Toulouse[11] in Alabama and Fort Chartres in Illinois to induce the French to draw off their western allies. In these negotiations the Cherokees held an important card. Their raids on the French Mississippi and Ohio River convoys not only interrupted communications between New Orleans and Illinois but threatened the very existence of Louisiana, which depended upon Illinois for some of its food supply. For years past the governors of Louisiana had besought France to fortify the mouth of the Tennessee in order to halt the Cherokees; but the parsimonious home government not only had rejected the plea but also had refused the governor's permission to end the costly war between the French Indians and the Cherokees. Paris believed that intertribal wars weakened the Indians and hastened the day of French occupation of the entire Mississippi Valley. Moreover, the governors of Canada held that fighting against the far-off Cherokees kept the Canadian Indians from causing trouble near home. But by 1745 the Ministry of Marine had begun to perceive advantages in detaching the Cherokees from the English and ordered Vaudreuil to make the peace.[12] French emissaries then went to the Cherokees.

Isolated from Chota's thinking, the Carolina trading interest failed to realize that Chota did not intend a break with the English and reported to Charlestown that Chota conspired with the French.[13] Chota thus won a reputation for hostility toward the English which, though eventually becoming a source of strength, presently caused the Carolinians to support the pro-English Young Emperor more firmly.

[10] E. B. O'Callaghan, ed., *Documents Relating to the Colonial History of New York*, VI, 210–11.

[11] Dunbar Rowland and A. G. Saunders, *Mississippi Provincial Archives*, III, 772–73.

[12] Paris, France, Archives Nationales Colonies, A.C. C13, 28:49; C13, A28:86–91; C11, A97; B81, 358–59.

[13] S. C. Council Journals, 1746, pp. 69–71.

Chota's peace with the French Indians also backfired. Once-hostile northern Indians flocked into the Cherokee towns to take advantage of the English traders' low prices, and based in the Cherokee country to annoy the Carolina frontier.[14] From the Cherokee towns the Iroquois warred against the Catawbas, while northern Shawnees encouraged young Cherokees seeking war names to join them against the Creeks.[15]

In this situation Glen trod a narrow path between Carolina's need for Indian allies and customers and the complaints of the angry Creeks, Catawbas, and Carolina frontier settlers.[16] He worked through the Young Emperor and his advisers to rid the Cherokee nation of both Frenchmen and French-allied Indians. In May, 1746,[17] he met the Cherokees in conference at Ninety-Six and won their promise to drive the northern Indians from their midst.[18]

But the Young Emperor's party lacked power to keep its promise. Though the Raven of Hiwassee's henchmen assassinated one French emissary and wounded another, the Hiwassee-Tellico coalition could not prevent Chota's completing its French peace. Nor could it drive out the northern Indians. To have done so would have broken Chota's peace or split the nation, for the price of her peace had been tacit alliance with the northerners.

Confronted by the failure of the English party to check the French, late in 1746, Glen sent George Pawley to work on the Overhills and incidentally to purchase land from the Lower Cherokees.[19] At Keowee, Pawley obtained the lands below Long Canes Creek; but at Chota he found his mission blocked by nationalistic headmen who used his failure to recognize their authority in the land purchase to excuse their unwillingness to drive away the Frenchmen.[20]

14 PRSC, XXIV, 434–35.
15 *South Carolina Gazette*, June 9, June 23, 1746.
16 S. C. Council House Journals, March 27, 1746.
17 PRSC, XXII, 149–50.
18 *South Carolina Gazette*, June 23, 1746.
19 S. C. Council Journals, Jan. 22, 1747.
20 *South Carolina Historical and Genealogical Magazine*, Vol. X (1910), 54–63.

Pawley attempted to seize the Gauls; but in a fracas with Logstown Shawnees and Senecas several of his party were badly battered while Chota looked blandly on.[21] More circumspect with failure, Pawley visited privately around the Overhill towns and heard that for them to turn away the Frenchmen would mean a renewal of war. Before the Overhills would undertake that risk, the English must build a fort near Chota and Tanase.[22]

This proposal consisted with Chota's drive for ascendancy. Such a fort had been discussed at the Ninety-Six meeting. Both Chota and Great Tellico doubtless knew its prestige and political values. At Chota or Tanase it would enable Chota to undercut the Young Emperor's clique by direct contact with the English. The trading capital and the national capital would be combined in the hands of Chota-Tanase where they rightfully belonged.

However, the Chota-Carolina *rapprochment* failed. Pawley, calm enough at Chota over injuries to members of his party wrote indignantly to Glen. Glen responded with demands upon Chota for compensation and an immediate cessation of northern Indian raids upon the Creeks and Catawbas. Though he also promised the Overhills a fort, his demands created bad feelings, and Chota took no action. The fort was not built.

Having failed to extract from Carolina what it desired, Chota tacitly sanctioned the rising anti-English sentiment elsewhere in the nation. Hostility mounted, particularly among the Lower Towns which provided the most convenient rendezvous for Senecas and Shawnees raiding the Lower Creeks and the Catawbas. In the spring of 1748 northern visitors supported Lower Cherokee resentment that Carolina required the Lower Towns to punish a prominent headman who had murdered a ruffian packhorse man. Only when pro-English Middle Settlements headmen, aligned with Hiwassee-Tellico, threatened to split the nation and burn the offending towns did the Lower Townsmen execute the offender.

Bitterness in the Lower Towns rose to new heights. Logstown

[21] S. C. Commons House Journals, June 20, 1748.
[22] PRSC, XXII, 173, 272–79.

Senecas, probably those Pawley had encountered at Chota the year before, captured Carolina surveyors Haig and Brown and brought them to Keowee where no headman would help them. Indeed, when the English traders gathered to effect a rescue, Wawhatchee of Conasatchee, young head warrior of the Lower Towns who had once been a prisoner in Canada, proposed killing all the traders in the nation.

Again Carolina pressed, opportunely and forcefully, by embargoing the Cherokee trade. Glen summoned headmen from both Hiwassee-Tellico and Chota. He demanded the surrender of the headmen who advocated war with the English, hostages for Haig and Brown, whose release the Cherokees must effect, and the expulsion of northerners from the Cherokee villages, on pain of continuance of the embargo.[23]

At another time these demands would have consolidated nativist sentiment behind Chota, but Chota's prestige was low. Chota's northern peace had brought a Creek war to the Lower Towns when Creeks had detected young Cherokees in a Shawnee war party. Furthermore, the freedom of the northerners in the nation had caused the embargo. But because the embargo denied them ammunition with which to fight the Creeks, the Cherokees assented to the Carolina demands. Wawhatchee was delivered in Charlestown to be disciplined; and for the time being the Chota drive toward national leadership was checked.

The strength of Hiwassee-Tellico thus renewed, Chota bided its time, content that those who accepted the English yoke should have trouble. The Overhill towns, free from Creek assaults, entertained northern warriors, some of whom went against the Creeks. In the Lower Towns resentment now grew against Chota's peace with the French as it became evident that the French supplied the Creeks with ammunition. Encouraged by the English, Hiwassee-Tellico planned to force a French war upon the Overhills by attacking Fort Toulouse and sending war parties down the Tennessee against French convoys upon the

23 S. C. Commons House Journals, 1747, pp. 478–79; 1748, pp. 602–603, 642–44.

21

Mississippi. But the peace of Aix-la-Chapelle intervened, and Glen ordered the Raven of Hiwassee to restrain his warriors.

The Creek war, too, was interrupted. Preferring the profits of the winter hunt to the glory of war, both Creeks and Cherokees in the winter of 1748–49 asked Glen to arrange a peace, and on his mediation exchanged deputies. When it developed that the Creek terms required the Cherokees to drive out or kill the northerners, Chota objected, and Frenchmen induced the notorious Creek headman, Acorn Whistler, to renew the war. Urged by Hiwassee-Tellico and the traders Cornelius Dougherty and Anthony Dean, Chota finally compromised, agreeing to keep the northerners from warring on the Creeks and proposing a geographical line to divide Creek from Cherokee hunting grounds. Encouraged, Glen called on the two nations to meet in August, 1749. Leading Creeks, in the haughty spirit of Indian victors, refused to attend. After some delay a group of lesser Creek headmen met with the Raven of Hiwassee and the Young Emperor in Charlestown in September. They agreed that Carolina should punish whichever party violated the peace and that the aggrieved should consult with Glen before taking vengeance. Tragic aftermath of the meeting was that on their way home Creeks and Cherokees, including Johnny, the Great Warrior of Tanase, fell victim to a fatal fever, incidentally lending color to French propaganda that the meeting was an English plot to destroy the Indians.

The peace of 1749 was Carolina's and therefore Hiwassee-Tellico's triumph. Had it been maintained, Chota might have failed in its ambitions; but shortly the war broke out anew. As the two nations began their winter hunts, Frenchmen stirred the Cowetas with a story that Lower Cherokees had attacked a Cussita hunting party. The angry Cowetas sent warriors into the neutral grounds between the two nations to kill Cherokee hunters. Keowee retaliated by inducing a large party of northerners to join the Lower Towns in an attack on Creek hunters.

When Skiagunsta, as elder statesman of Keowee, demanded that Glen enforce the promised embargo against the aggressor

Creeks, the Carolina Governor refused. He said that by again embracing the northerners the Cherokees had broken their part of the bargain. He determined to go into the Cherokee country to build a fort to check the Senecas and Shawnees. However, his assembly balked at the expense, and he was compelled to resort to diplomacy. His emissary, James Maxwell, kept the Valley and the Overhills at peace with the Upper Creeks by granting the Gun Merchant, a leading Creek, illegal trading privileges with the Carolina traders among the Cherokees. This move confined the war to the Cowetas under French-inspired Malatchi and the Lower Cherokees, a situation not unwelcome to Chota. Chota needed Lower Towns' disillusionment with the English to force Skiagunsta's people to accept its leadership against Hiwassee-Tellico.

Disillusionment was not long in coming. On the morning of April 14, 1750, Malatchi and five hundred Creeks attacked and destroyed Echoi and Estatoe, with heavy loss to the Cherokees. Glen proposed punishing the Creeks with an embargo.[24] Malatchi, however, entertaining a French mission, refused to be impressed even by the pleas of the Gun Merchant, who was unwilling that all the Creeks should suffer.[25] The war should go on until the Cherokees had ousted the northerners. But when Glenn learned that Georgia traders would not respect a Carolina embargo and that the French supplied Malatchi with arms and ammunition, he hesitated.[26] Thereupon anti-English nativism flared among the Lower Cherokees. Chota then stepped in, inviting Senecas and Mingos from western Pennsylvania into the Overhill towns and sending them to Keowee where anti-Carolina sentiment undermined Hiwassee-Tellico influence.[27]

The northern Indians had a freedom to annoy the Carolinians denied the Cherokees, for they could not be curbed by Carolina

---

[24] S. C. Council Journals, 1749, pp. 399–400, 468, 483, 585–89, 592; 1750, pp. 67, 99, 174.

[25] S. C. Council House Journals, 1750, p. 124.

[26] Chandler, *op. cit.*, VI, Oct. 4, 1750.

[27] IBSC, II, 77–79, 116–18.

embargoes. French influence among them was strong. Some were Caughnawagas from near Montreal in Canada. Still others were Logstown Shawnees and Mingos ruled by Seneca proconsuls and wooed by Pennsylvania and Virginia. From the Illinois and the Wabash came pro-French Miamis and Ottawas. In the spring of 1750 northern warriors ambushed a traders' pack train in the Cherokee mountains, killing several white men. On Broad River in northeast Carolina, Senecas accompanied by young Cherokees forced a trader to run for his life.[28] In mid-January, 1751, one hundred northern Indians who had entered the Tuckaseigee Valley near the high Smoky Mountains marched into the Middle Settlements, broke open traders' houses, stole goods, and rioted on plundered rum. Arriving in Tomasee in the Lower Towns, they talked of going against the Catawbas and announced a willingness to fight whoever attempted to stop them. Thus a major challenge to the pro-English faction among the Cherokees had developed. To maintain control over the nation Hiwassee-Tellico must force the Overhills to halt the northerners.

[28] S. C. Council House Journals, 1750, p. 124.

CHAPTER TWO

The Embargo of 1751

IN THE SPRING OF 1751, Cherokee-English relations broke down. The trouble came to a head when Carolina thieves stole over three hundred deerskins from a Toogaloo hunting party and the Toogaloos believed that Justice James Francis of Ninety-Six protected the suspects, among whom was the famous James Adair.[1] Already angry that Glen did not punish the Creeks who warred on them, the Lower Towns retaliated. Near Ninety-Six young Cherokees concealed among roving bands of Senecas trampled settlers' crops, killed hogs, maimed cattle, and threatened isolated farmers. One night on Oconee River in Georgia, Cherokees and Senecas, ostensibly in pursuit of enemy Creeks, attacked a trader's store, killed two whites and a Chickasaw, and carried a Chickasaw prisoner back to Keowee. Quietly pleased with the episode, the Keowee headmen sent the captive home to the Chickasaw town near Silver Springs with a Cherokee deputy bearing apologies to Squirrel King, the Chickasaw headman.[2] But they awaited Carolina's reaction with the anxiety born of guilt. When the Little Carpenter, Right Hand Man of the Chota Uku brought into Keowee a report he had heard from the Iroquois that Carolina and New York talked of a joint expedition with the Iroquois to chasten the Cherokees, fears began to mount. Then late in April a rumor came from the settlements that a thousand whites would soon march against the

[1] IBSC, II, 17–30, 133.
[2] S. C. Council Journals, 1751, pp. 1, 28–29, 174–75.

Lower Towns. With no way of knowing that both stories stemmed from mendacious frontier gossip, the frightened Keowee headmen dispatched runners to the Valley and to Chota to urge that the Cherokees strike first by killing all the traders in the nation.

More than ever that spring, killing traders seemed justifiable. The Creek war had caused two years of bad hunting, and Cherokee trading debts had mounted.[3] The Cherokees knew that the hard-pressed and nearly bankrupt traders cheated them with false weights and measures, and they had begun to believe that all Englishmen were bad.

Serious trouble was not long in coming. Stecoe, among the Out Towns on Tuckaseigee River, frequented by northern Indians whom its young men accompanied on raids against the Catawbas, had a hard core of anti-English sentiment. Following the Keowee cue, in Stecoe town house the Slave Catcher of near-by Kituhwa demanded the death of Stecoe trader Bernard Hughes. Warned by his Indian mistress, Hughes fled up the river to Robert Bunning's trading house at Tuckaseigee while maddened Stecoes looted his store. One of the most respected of traders and an old Cherokee hand, Bunning took Hughes to Tuckaseigee town house and, invoking the Treaty of 1730, placed him under the protection of the headmen. Then he rode sixty miles in the night through dark mountain gorges to seek the help of the Raven of Hiwassee.

Swift-spreading rumor magnified the Stecoe incident into the murder of Hughes and three other whites. Traders from all over the nation stampeded to Augusta in Georgia and to Ninety-Six. Terrified by the traders' lurid stories and by the report that a trader had been shot near by, settlers in the Ninety-Six region streamed down-country while the more hardy fortified their homes.[4] The great Cherokee uprising which Carolina had long feared seemed at hand.

But suddenly the disturbance subsided. The Raven of Hiwas-

[3] IBSC, II, 17–20, 52–53, 117–18, 131–33.
[4] S. C. Council Journals, 1751, pp. 63–65, 158.

see stepped in. He sent his son with several warriors and Bunning to order the offending Stecoes to stop their foolishness or be disgraced by his bringing his awful presence among them. The messengers found Stecoe deserted, the British flag, a plea for mercy, flapping idly over its town house. Perceiving that they had acted alone in an abortive enterprise, the appalled Stecoes had run into the mountains to hide. The Raven's son hauled down the flag with the remark that the people were not worthy of it and went over Cowee Mountain to wait at Joree for the Stecoes to emerge from hiding. Soon he received their abject message that "their doggs, their hoggs, and themselves were mad and it was by a lying talk from Keowee that they did what they did," that they were sorry and would pay for Hughes' looted goods.

Keowee, too, calmed down. No responsible regional headmen had responded to its war overture. The Raven of Hiwassee had refused to listen to one Keowee runner, and the headman of Watauga had disarmed the other and sent him back to Keowee divested of his official symbols. At Chota, where irresponsibles looted trader Anthony Dean's store, Old Hop took Dean into his own home and ordered the looters to surrender all the stolen goods. Keowee perceived that whatever action had been intended —and Skiagunsta was later to insist that no harm had been meant—had failed. In a few days the Lower Towns headmen gravely demanded that Stecoe return trader Hughes's goods. From Chota, Old Hop sent out word that no white man was to be hurt. The Stecoes returned Hughes's goods, all but four hundred pounds of deerskins held perhaps as reprisal for the Toogaloos' losses in the January theft, and about £50 or £60 worth of damaged goods. Headmen from all over the nation sent Glen assurances of their friendship.[5]

But trouble with Carolina could not be avoided. As soon as Glen heard of the upcountry panic, he ordered all the traders to leave the nation. Then he faced an angry Commons House bent on punishing the Cherokees. In vain did he protest that an embargo on the Cherokee trade and supplies of arms and ammu-

[5] IBSC, II, 51, 55–56, 78–79, 81–84, 116–18; III, Apr. 13, 1752.

nition would enable the Creeks to destroy them. The Commons had read a petition headed by the name of Justice Francis of Ninety-Six complaining that the Governor neglected the back-country people.[6] It threatened to inform the crown if the Governor did not act.[7] Glen, knowing that the trouble originated in the theft of the Toogaloos' deerskins, countered by sending to the Commons reports discrediting Justice Francis and by removing Francis from his militia command. But the opposition was too strong. Spurred by panic-stricken traders who hysterically proclaimed that the Cherokees intended war, the Commons embargoed the Cherokee trade until the Indians should give full satisfaction for their various outrages.[8] There was nothing Glen could do but enforce the measure. On June 6 he wrote to the faithful Raven of Hiwassee commending his conduct in the Stecoe matter but informing him of the embargo. He required that the Cherokees surrender the Slave Catcher of Conutory, who was accused of wounding a white man; those guilty of the Oconees' murders; and the Little Carpenter, Second Man of the Overhills, who, according to Glen, had declared himself hostile to the English. Finally he warned that if the demands were not complied with, he would use force.[9]

The developing crisis had already sharpened the conflict between Chota and Hiwassee-Tellico. The pro-English faction decided, as it had in 1748, to force Chota's compliance with Carolina's demands by breaking Chota's French peace. In June, Tellicoes took two French scalps on the Mississippi to provoke French retaliation.[10] Chota countered with moves to fill the gap left by the flight of the Carolina traders. Old Hop's councilors determined to try to interest both the French and the Virginians in their trade. Late in June, 1751, the Little Carpenter with Long Jack of Tanase (Johnny's successor as Great Warrior) and the

---

[6] S. C., Journals of the Upper House of Assembly, 1751, pp. 57, 80–81.

[7] IBSC, II, 58–59.

[8] S. C. Commons House Journals, 1751, pp. 28–29, 585–86.

[9] S. C. Council Journals, 1751, pp. 47–48, 164–66.

[10] IBSC, II, 124–25.

Smallpox Conjurer, headman of Settico and an influential member of the Chota council, set out for Williamsburg. At the same time Old Hop sent a friendly message through the Upper Creeks to the French at Fort Toulouse.[11]

When, in July, Glen's embargo message reached the Raven of Hiwassee, the Hiwassee-Tellicoes agreed to accept Carolina's terms. Meeting at Cornelius Dougherty's house near Hiwassee, the Raven and the leading Tellico and Chatuga headmen promised to take the anti-English Slave Catcher of Conutory and the other offending headmen to Charlestown as soon as the accused should return from their summer hunts. The Little Carpenter they would have apprehended also, but he was safely departed for Virginia. They requested a meeting with Glen at Saluda on the Carolina frontier on August 21 and promised to bring the scalps of the two Frenchmen the Tellicoes had killed in June. Apprising Chota of the intended meeting, they sent Johnny and Osteneco, the two Tacites or war leaders of Great Tellico, to sound out the Lower Towns.

Chota, suffering with the others from the embargo, appointed deputies to the Charlestown meeting, but, as comported with its bid for ascendancy, had reservations. It held trader Anthony Dean hostage. Early in August a Shawnee brought into Chota a story from the Upper Creeks that Carolina had formed a coalition with Creeks, Catawbas, and Chickasaws to make war upon the Cherokees. The extreme nativists, Willinawaw (the Little Carpenter's cousin) and Ukanta of Chota, talked violently against Carolina, and Chota required Dean to inscribe a letter to Glen demanding to know his intentions and insisting on the reopening of the trade. They threatened vengeance on Dean and Dougherty if the governor refused their demands. This was blunter talk than Glen had ever before received from the Cherokees. Chota also sent the Shawnee story of imminent attack through the nation, thus blocking the Saluda meeting. In alarm Great Tellico recalled the two Tacites from the Lower Towns. Panic ruled the Lower Towns; and Keowee, Estatoe, Cheoah,

[11] S. C. Council Journals, 1751, pp. 414, 427.

Toxaway, and Oconee talked gloomily of breaking up and moving over the mountains to be near Overhill protection.

Only the Raven of Hiwassee and Osteneco of Great Tellico were unfrightened. These stalwarts of the pro-English faction did their utmost to discount the Chota moves. The Raven refused to break with Carolina and sent a talk to Glen assuring him that Dean's letter contained only the minority sentiment of the Overhills.[12] Osteneco in the same spirit disregarded Tellico timidity and went to Charlestown to see Glen. The resolution of these headmen had its reward; for Osteneco learned that on the basis of the Hiwassee-Tellico compliance with Carolina demands the embargo would be lifted. James Beamer, the trader at Lower Towns Estatoe, and Robert Goudy, the Great Tellico trader, would return to the nation with Osteneco as evidence of Carolina friendship, and to urge the Cherokees to go to Charlestown to discuss their grievances and draft a new trade treaty.[13]

Forces now operated which would cause Carolina to reappraise its Cherokee contacts. Chota's independence of and hostility to Hiwassee-Tellico, which Carolina had long regarded as mere nuisance, would soon stand revealed in its true import as a major drive to dominate the nation and to force Carolina's recognition. It was the genuine core of Cherokee nativist and nationalist leadership.

While Tellico's Osteneco talked conciliation in Charlestown, Chota's Little Carpenter presented the Cherokee cause in Virginia.[14] He informed the Virginians that the Treaty of 1730 guaranteed the Cherokees a trade in return for alliance with England. Carolina, he said, had now violated that treaty by denying the Cherokees a trade and supplying arms and ammunition to their enemies, the Creeks. He demanded that in Carolina's default, Virginia act. This bold bid laid the train of an explosive situation between the colonies of Virginia and Carolina, though at the moment the Virginians could not see their way to breaking their

[12] IBSC, II, 114, 123–24, 135, 139, 146.
[13] S. C. Council Journals, 1751, pp. 283, 292.
[14] *Virginia Gazette*, Aug. 16, 1751.

twenty-year understanding with Carolina that the Cherokees were Carolina's province. Council President Burrell, awaiting the arrival of a new royal governor, could only tell Old Hop's Right Hand Man that he would inform private traders of Cherokee desires. The Little Carpenter went home unsatisfied. Nevertheless, his Virginia mission bore valuable fruit for Chota. News of it in Charlestown alarmed Glen with the specter of Virginia competition in the Cherokee trade. Ignorant of the Little Carpenter's position in the nation, Glen wrote Burrell that the Little Carpenter had no standing and that Carolina would seize Virginians attempting to trade in the Cherokee country. The impressionable Burrell promptly informed the Virginia public that the Cherokees had perpetrated a fraud and that Virginia traders should not go to them.[15] But Glen realized that he must take strong measures to counter Overhill influence in the nation.

On September 22 the return of Osteneco from Charlestown with Beamer and Goudy brought joy to Keowee.[16] The exodus of Lower Towns people to remote regions halted, except from Ustanali which was guilty of depredations in Carolina. On rumor of approaching retaliation the Ustanalis had fled and settled permanently one hundred miles and several mountain ranges westward. But Keowee, hearing Osteneco's strong pro-English talk, basked in the light of renewed Carolina favor and prepared a delegation for the projected Charlestown conference.

However, the conference encountered renewed Chota opposition and materialized slowly. Though homeward-bound Osteneco's speeches in the Middle Settlements won acceptance, Overhill Chota, Tanase, and Settico ignored Glen's invitation. They had learned that French traders would come to them in the spring, and they had yet to hear the Little Carpenter's report. They continued to urge the Lower Towns to come over the hills and join them. Weary of Chota's delay, the Raven of Hiwassee, the Young Emperor, and the Tellicoes finally went off to Charlestown without them.

15 S. C. Council Journals, 1751, pp. 297–98, 302–303, 472.
16 IBSC, II, 146.

Hardly had the Carolina-bound headmen departed when the Little Carpenter, as if informed that his enemies had gone, arrived in Chota. But he did not linger. Disappointed in Virginia and dedicated to rescuing his people from the Carolina monopoly, he set off in a few days with a handful of followers toward the Ohio to find another trade source, possibly the Pennsylvanian George Croghan. With Glen feeling as he did about him, he was wise to seek far places.

When the Charlestown conference opened on November 13, 1751, 160 Cherokees were present, representing all the nation save truculent Chota. The Lower Towns deputies, led by Old Skiagunsta of Keowee and the Good Warrior of Estatoe, numbered more than at any time since 1745. Hiwassee-Tellico's greatest personality, the Raven of Hiwassee; the Raven's son Moytoy; and Old Caesar of Chatuga embodied the strength of the pro-English axis. The Young Emperor, taken sick, had turned back; and Osteneco, convalescent, had remained at home. The Middle Settlements, led by Kittagusta, the Prince of Joree, vitally concerned in the Stecoe matter, had strong representation. Indeed, from the Carolina point of view the only weakness of the delegation was that it had failed to bring any of the culprits in the late disorders. Such a surrender, which involved the breaking of sacred clan ties, was more than even Hiwassee-Tellico could manage at this time. Blandly the Raven informed Glen that the mixed blood, Andrew White, principal offender in the Oconees' murders, had gone to war against the Creeks; that the anti-English headmen of Kituhwa, Conutory, and Stecoe followed faraway game trails; that the Little Carpenter had gone from the nation on business. Under the circumstances Carolina justice must exercise patience. Indeed, forgetfulness might be the better course.

Glen put on his boldest front and read the headmen a stern lecture. He charged them with treaty-breaking, misdemeanors, and sundry crimes, and dwelt ominously on the importance of the English to the nation. Without the English, he declared, the

Cherokees would be using "bad bows, wretched arrows headed with bills of birds and knives of split cane and hatchets of stone." The headmen replied with wily sycophancy. The Raven avowed that he could weep at the crimes but that not all Cherokees were bad, that his town had been good, that in the bad time he had supported the English. The headmen of Stecoe and Tuckaseigee disclaimed responsibility for the Out Towns trouble, saying it would not have happened had they been at home at the time. Skiagunsta of Keowee referred to the Oconees' killings as accidental, admitted inability to control the Senecas, blamed Chota for Seneca visits to the nation, and asked Glen to build a fort among his towns to keep the northerners away. After seven days of this kind of talk and many consultations with the traders the Governor became convinced that only a fort in the Cherokee country would block the northerners and prevent Virginia intrusion on the trade, and that he must make concessions to the Cherokees.

The Treaty of November 29, 1751 reduced Carolina demands to four: Andrew White must be given up; Bernard Hughes's losses must be made good; the Little Carpenter must come to Charlestown; and the Cherokees must deny the northerners ammunition and prevent their molesting the settlers. The traders would return to the nation immediately, and Carolina would attempt a Creek peace. Privately Glen promised Skiagunsta a fort and sent a message to the Commons House asking immediate authorization. Finally, a new regulation of the trade was made.

The trade regulation contained two sets of rules: one to protect the traders from each other, and the other to protect the Indians from the traders. To prevent the Indians from pitting one trader against another, the Indians were permitted to trade only in their home towns and each trader was confined to his assigned town. Price schedules for goods and specifications for skins were established, and traders were forbidden to allow Indians to contract debts of over twenty-four pounds weight of deerskins. Twenty-one traders were licensed for thirty-eight towns, and the sale of rum was prohibited.[17]

Implementing the treaty terms and trade regulations proved difficult. The Cherokees were a temperamental and guileful people, the traders hardy and unscrupulous. Moreover, the Carolina assembly hesitated to authorize the promised fort. The course of trade proved thorny, and the prohibition of rum sales impossible. Headmen, though approving the rum ban, felt that it should be mitigated in their own favor; and traders needed rum to combat the "fatigues and alarms" of their business. What liquor Carolina traders could not purvey, Georgia traders smuggled in.

Cutthroat competition continued in the goods-hungry nation. From Augusta in Georgia, quite outside Carolina law, Rae and Barksdale sent pack-horse men into towns for which Carolinians held licenses.[18] Virginians also began to come into the towns, among them Enoch Patterson who traded in Great Tellico.[19] Trading establishments developed beyond Carolina law to the north and the northeast of the Cherokee nation. Most famous of these was Eskippakithike, the site of Peter Chartier's temporary Shawnee settlement on Lulbegrud Creek in Kentucky. Though abandoned by Chartier in 1748, in 1752–53 it was revived as a rendezvous for Virginia-Pennsylvania trade with the Cherokees.[20] Two trading settlements were established in western North Carolina: Daniel Murphy's Aurora (site unknown) and John Anderson's post on the south fork of the Catawba in Anson County, North Carolina. Murphy's place proved short-lived; in his absence in Virginia to procure goods, northern Indians, perhaps inspired by Carolina traders, attacked the Cherokees settled around it and later killed Murphy. Anderson's business flourished at first, but declined after 1752.

---

[17] S. C. Council Journals, 1751, pp. 104–105, 389, 403, 414, 421, 432, 451–53, 512.

[18] IBSC, III, 10, 18.

[19] Draper MSS, QQ 71, Deposition of John Watts, Jan. 2, 1753.

[20] Charles A. Hanna, *Wilderness Trail*, I, 147; II, 213, 230–31.

The Treaty of 1751 failed to bring immediate peace with the Creeks, for the Creeks had taken advantage of the embargo to press their attacks upon the Cherokees. While Cherokee deputies talked in Charlestown, Oakfuskee Creeks attacked Hiwassee; and, as the conferees went home Creek warriors ambushed and killed in Carolina a Cherokee messenger accompanied by Carolinians.[21] Holding Carolina responsible, the Cherokees now in their turn demanded reparation. After January, 1752, the war raged from Great Tellico to Keowee. Suffering heavy blows and losing many of its older warriors, Great Tellico fortified with a stockade around its town house. Five times the Creeks hit Hiwassee, and the Raven complained bitterly to Glen. In April the Cowetas forced the abandonment of all the Lower Towns save Toxaway and Estatoe.[22] In sharp retaliation the Hiwassees and Tellicoes raided the Upper Creeks with success and ruined the Creek winter hunts in the woods between the two nations. Even Chota, unharmed by Creek depredations, planned to take the field but, deterred by a cry for help from their allies the western Chickasaws who warred against the Choctaws, finally sent its warriors under Oconostota down the Tennessee.[23] Attempts at a Creek peace were frustrated by Creek distrust and Glen's determination not to move until the Cherokees had fulfilled their treaty obligations.

The Cherokees, seeking to force Glen's hand, procrastinated. They joined Senecas in a raid on the eastern Chickasaws, only to be forced by the Chickasaw Squirrel King to apologize. Though Overhill Telassie rebuffed Senecas begging ammunition, Chota received them. Instead of surrendering Andrew White, Skiagunsta of Keowee advised Glen that, since the offender had risked his life in war against the Creeks, he be forgiven.[24] He also asked that the fort be built soon.

Glen's Commons House was reluctant to appropriate for the

21 S. C. Council Journals, 1752, pp. 147–48, 520.

22 IBSC, II, 12; III, Apr. 26, 1752, pp. 1, 13.

23 S. C. Council Journals, 1752, pp. 248, 520.

24 IBSC, III, 3–4.

fort. Some members wanted the Cherokees thrashed; others demanded a large land cession. Left to his own resources, Glen concluded that he could bring the Cherokees to terms only by ending the Creek war. Sending the Creeks a threat of countenancing the Seneca raids upon them, he demanded the surrender of the warrior who had killed the Cherokee messenger in the fall. The threat failed. Only when the Creeks carried their warfare to the neighborhood of Charlestown was Glen able to bring them to terms. Cherokee hunters, blocked from home by venomous Creeks, took refuge in Charlestown, at that time visited by thirty Creeks under the Acorn Whistler. A tool of the French, Acorn Whistler, after having promised Glen not to molest the refugee Cherokees, conspired with their pursuers who camped outside the town to have them murdered just beyond the city gates.[25] A few survived the attack to report the outrage to the Governor, who hurried apologies to the Cherokee nation and promised punishment. As a result, in October, under threat of complete embargo, the Creeks tentatively agreed to a Cherokee peace and quietly assassinated Acorn Whistler.

The peace came none too soon for Carolina to save her Cherokee buffer. The Lower Towns had been crushed. Keowee, Echoi, Toogaloo, Aquone, and Tomassee had broken up, some of their harrowed people joining Toxaway and Estatoe, others moving to the Middle Settlements or the Overhills. Toxaway and Estatoe, resisting Chota overtures, talked of joining the Catawbas.[26] Other Cherokees considered union with their allies the Shawnees north of the Ohio.[27]

The embargo of 1751 and the disaster of the Creek War produced by it undermined Hiwassee-Tellico. The Cherokees had learned that long years of dependence upon the Carolina trading monopoly had rendered them vulnerable in their time of need. If Carolina so willed, their enemies could smash them. Those who had followed Hiwassee-Tellico found their situation

[25] S. C. Council Journals, 1752, pp. 90–91, 119–23, 235.
[26] IBSC, III, 13, 21, 38, 157.
[27] Hanna, *op. cit.*, II, 294–98.

grown desperate. Skiagunsta of Keowee had seen his towns wrecked and his people fleeing to the Overhills for protection. Great Tellico and Hiwassee were themselves in trouble. Great Tellico had suffered bitterly in a late winter attack by the Creeks. Moreover, its subservience to the English had at last failed it; for its Carolina-licensed trader, Robert Goudy, having lost heavily in the spring of 1750 when northern Indians looted the annual pack train taking deerskins to Charlestown, had withdrawn from the town. He sublet its trade to mere pack-horse men who, buying a few horseloads of goods from him at retail, sold them in Great Tellico at higher prices than other Cherokees paid. The Raven of Hiwassee, his towns beset by Creek enemies, now cried for peace. The Hiwassee-Tellico leadership was bankrupt.

CHAPTER THREE

Chota and Fort Prince George

THE PART Chota played in the disaster to Hiwassee-Tellico can only be conjectured. Chota under the Little Carpenter's leadership had brought the northerners into the nation to cause trouble. Though holding its warriors aloof from the Creek war, Chota had resisted the Creek peace terms. Chota alone had sought new avenues of trade during the Carolina embargo. It had held a trader hostage and had refused to join the treaty-making at Charlestown. While aiding the Lower Towns with its northern allies, Chota had permitted the Lower Towns to be crushed and then had sought to augment Overhill strength by their defeated numbers. A ruling clique bent on destroying a rival power could have chosen no more Machiavellian course to achieve its ends.

It must have been with quiet satisfaction that in April, 1752, Old Hop, the Uku of Chota, sent Governor Glen a conciliatory talk with a "great war pipe." Excusing his council's truculence of the year before, he blamed the Shawnees, who, he said, had deceived him. He himself, he said, had always been friendly to the English. However, the Uku's amiability proved short-lived. When, two weeks later, he received Glen's worried apology for the Acorn Whistler's treachery near Charlestown, he replied boldly that Carolina's embargo had violated the treaty of 1730, and that Carolina, in treating only with the Lower Towns to bar Cherokees from entering the English settlements below Long Canes Creek in Carolina, had ignored the highest authority in the nation; therefore it behooved Glen, who had so lately supplied ammunition to the enemy Creeks, to appease the Overhills with presents of guns and ammunition.[1]

Glen's reply to this haughty message is not recorded. He knew that the Overhills encouraged the northerners to enter the nation, thus abetting their war on the Creeks. He also knew that they had not been parties to the treaty of 1751. But apparently he was not yet ready to recognize them as more than mere regional headmen; for he did not see fit to jettison Hiwassee-Tellico, whose fulfillment of the November treaty terms he still awaited, and on whose behalf, albeit slowly, he labored to effect a Creek peace. Not until the next winter when he sent Ludovic Grant, a Carolina agent who lived at Cheoah in the Snowbird Mountains, to Chota, did he indicate recognition of the new Overhill power.

Meanwhile, speeded by the Young Emperor's visit to Virginia in the fall of 1752, the final collapse of the Tellico emperorship occurred. Impatient and disillusioned with Carolina and probably influenced by Enoch Patterson, a free-lance pack-horse man trading from Virginia, Ammonscossittee attempted to recoup the fortunes of his town by seeking that Virginia trade the Little Carpenter had failed to obtain the year before. Early in November, accompanied by his wife and son, the Virginian John Watts as interpreter, and members of the Tellico council, he arrived in Williamsburg bearing the sacred parchment of the 1730 treaty. Lieutenant Governor Dinwiddie entertained him lavishly with a theater party and public fireworks, but the Tellico Emperor was not an effective diplomat.[2]

The Scot listened attentively as the Cherokee presented the familiar case: that Carolina's withholding trade from the Cherokees and supplying the Creek enemy had violated the Treaty of 1730; that Virginia should remedy the infraction by opening a trade. Dinwiddie, mindful of royal orders to woo the Cherokees but hesitant to invade Carolina's sphere, promised unofficially to advise traders to go to the nation. He then took up Carolina's

[1] IBSC, III, 10, 14.
[2] *Virginia Gazette,* Nov. 17, 1752.

charges of the previous autumn against the Little Carpenter. To puff stature into his waning cause Ammonscossittee falsely asserted that Carolina had forgiven the Oconees' murders and that he himself represented the Little Carpenter.[3] Dinwiddie remained unimpressed, but to keep the Indian's good will he gave him lavish presents: fine suits and shirts, a beautiful gown for the Empress, numerous baubles, and some ammunition. Pleased but unsatisfied, the Emperor left Williamsburg still intent upon establishing a trading contact. Journeying to the upper Potomac, he probably visited Cresap's trading house on the Warrior's Path and may have seen Christopher Gist, who two years later sent his son to trade at Chota.[4]

Then homeward-bound he met disaster. Southward-foraging Caughnawagas from the neighborhood of distant Montreal ambushed the Tellico party, killing many and taking several prisoners.[5] As if this were not enough, the defeated Emperor became entangled in domestic difficulties. While he stopped at Enoch Patterson's place, he resented Patterson's too acceptable advances to the Empress. One of Patterson's henchmen beat the jealous Emperor so badly that Watts, who still accompanied him, despaired of his life.[6] When the reconciled couple renewed their journey, their Virginia finery had disappeared, perhaps bargained off for a few drams at a backwoods grog mill but more likely thrown away by the outraged Emperor in resentment of Virginia hospitality.[7]

Returning to Great Tellico in February or March, the Emperor found himself discredited. His mission had not been a success, and a rumor that he had sold the Cherokee northern hunting grounds to Virginians had preceded him. Henceforth

[3] Journals of the Executive Council of Virginia, V, 25–28.

[4] Draper MSS, Preston Papers, QQ, p. 72.

[5] L. K. Koontz, *Robert Dinwiddie: Correspondence Illustrative of His Career*, 273.

[6] Draper MSS, Preston Papers, QQ, p. 72.

[7] B.P.R.O., S.C. B.T., XVII, p. 83.

he was not a factor in Cherokee affairs. Because of his Virginia overture Carolina would not trust him; because of his Virginia fiasco, Chota could ignore him.

Glen finally realized that Hiwassee-Tellico had failed him, that he must, however reluctantly, look to Chota for control over the Cherokees. Chota, eager for recognition, was ready to respond heartily. When Glen sent a request for Overhills to help the embattled Chickasaws, Chota sent four hundred warriors under the Great Warrior Oconostota, who fiercely raided the Choctaw towns along the Tombigbee. Of greater importance was the raid the Little Carpenter made on French convoys upon the Mississippi. He took eight French scalps and thus broke the peace with the French and their northern allies which Chota had maintained since 1745. Save for the Shawnees, who had many relatives among the Cherokees, northern Indians could no longer use the Overhills as a base for raids against the Creeks. Thus what Carolina could not effect through Hiwassee-Tellico, Chota willingly did in return for Carolina recognition.

With Chota thus committed, Glen moved to bring the Creeks and Cherokees together in July of 1753 to confirm the peace he had tentatively obtained the year before. Though actual fighting had ceased, the Creeks had tried to force Glen into renewing his embargo against the Cherokees. They accused Cherokees of killing Carolina constables pursuing a criminal in the Coosa River country between the two nations. When the Cherokees cleared themselves of this charge, Malatchi insisted that, concealed among raiding northerners, they still waged war. Glen, undeceived, threatened Malatchi with the dread embargo if he persisted in fighting. Creek deputies then hurried to Charlestown. But the Cherokees delayed so long in coming that the proud Creeks went home, leaving Glen authority to conclude a peace for them.

Cherokee delay arose from Overhill guile. The presence of the Creeks in Charlestown would interfere with their intended showdown over trade. Then, too, the impatient Lower Towns required disciplining. Skiagunsta of Keowee, eager for the Creek peace, had set off well ahead of the Chotas.[8] But now that Glen could offer it, Chota in Charlestown would ignore the peace as much as possible and press toward a demonstration of its will and authority in other matters. In Chota town house the headmen plotted their course at length. In token of their ascendancy the two former props of the Tellico emperorship, the Raven of Hiwassee and Osteneco of Great Tellico, counciled with them. Now other personalities dominated: Connecorte, or Old Hop, the Uku or Fire King of all the Cherokees; Attakullaculla, or the Little Carpenter, his Right Hand Man; Oconostota, First Warrior of the Overhills and Great Warrior of the Cherokees; Willinawaw, headman of Toquo and cousin of the Little Carpenter; the Smallpox Conjurer, headman of Settico; and Long Jack, headman of Tanase.

Chota's case against Carolina contained several major points: Carolina had long failed to recognize it as the supreme authority in the nation; twice in four years Carolina had suspended the trade; under the Carolina trade monopoly the amount of trade goods and the number of traders had decreased while prices had gone up; Carolina had supplied the Creek enemy with ammunition; and Carolina had been slow to act against Creek aggression. Having demonstrated in the spring what they could and would do at Carolina's request, they now intended to exact a high price from Glen for their favor. The Creek peace they would remove from conference discussion by relegating it to an exchange of messages between Old Hop and Glen, thus clearing the Charlestown meeting for a discussion of the all-important trade.

Glen's eagerness to do business with the new power played into Chota's designs; for, having recognized Chota, he must wait upon it. Never had the prestige of the Lower Towns been so low at Charlestown as it was at the July meeting. Deflated by Glen's unwillingness to confer until the Overhills arrived, the Lower Towns headmen encountered a strong wave of anti-Indian sentiment occasioned by the presence in the Charlestown jail of six

[8] IBSC, III, 226, 264–65, 289, 300, 313.

Shawnees charged with murdering settlers.[9] Nervously they awaited their domineering countrymen. Finally on June 29 the Chotas marched triumphantly down Broad Street under escort of a company of red-coated regulars to meet the Governor in the council house. Skiagunsta and his men filed quietly into the council chamber behind them.

Glen now for the first time faced a power sufficient to force him to meet Indians on their own terms. Though the Chota delegation included compliant Osteneco and the wooable Long Jack, it also included the rugged Smallpox Conjurer of Settico, the blunt field commander Oconostota, and the resourceful diplomat Attakullaculla.

Greatest of these was the Cherokee Second Man, Attakullaculla of Overhill Tomatly, known to the English as the Little Carpenter. He was about fifty, small in stature and slight of build. Courteous in manner, his intense eyes beaming a gracious smile, he concealed a hard power which made him unyielding in the causes he chose to espouse.[10] Cousin to regal Connecorte, he had early been marked for high office and educated by the priestly elders into the traditions and mysteries of his family and nation. As a young man in 1730 he had been one of the six deputies to accompany Alexander Cuming to England to negotiate the great treaty of alliance. He also had been among the French. As a prisoner among the Ottawas for seven years, he had met and talked with French soldiers, traders, and priests and had been before the governor of Canada at Quebec.[11] Since his return to the nation in 1744 or 1745 he had undertaken missions to the Ohio River Shawnees and to the Senecas in western New York. Though believed by Glen to be anti-English, he well knew the importance of the English trade to the Cherokees; but from his knowledge of the Virginia, Pennsylvania, and New York Indian trade he hoped to deliver the Cherokees from the Carolina

[9] *South Carolina Gazette*, Apr. 11, 1753; IBSC, II, 278; B.P.R.O., S.C. B.T., I, K83.

[10] French, *loc. cit.*, III, 93.

[11] S. C. Council Journals (photostats), 1754, p. 52.

monopoly. Wanted by Glen in 1751 as a criminal for leading Senecas into the restless Lower Towns, he now in 1753 faced Glen for the first time, the proud and defiant voice of ascendant Chota. As Right Hand Man to Connecorte, he was the irremovable executive arm, or Prime Minister, of the Fire King whose will he shaped and spoke. Though never king of the nation, as some have believed, he was by position and prestige supreme among Cherokee policy makers. As he confronted the Carolina Governor, he not only spoke with the power of the greatest authority among his people, but he was conscious that he was the only Cherokee living who had been received by the Governor's master, King George II.

The conference formally opened on July 3. Hardly had the Governor's unctuous words setting forth the purpose of the meeting ended when the Little Carpenter rose to demand the release of the imprisoned Shawnees. Not to have done so would have made the Shawnee nation enemies of the Cherokees. Glen, bound by the usages of English justice, could only refuse. He introduced the evidence of settlements Indians to support his case. But the Little Carpenter refused to be impressed. He arrogantly refuted the Indian testimony, and the witnesses quailed before him. Displeased, the Governor sternly informed the Cherokee it was none of his business. But the Little Carpenter refused to be silenced; and, though he could not effect the Shawnee release, he succeeded in placing the Governor on the defensive.[12] When Glen attempted to maneuver the talk into a discussion of the Creek peace, the Little Carpenter boldly demanded that the talk be of the trade. Invoking the Treaty of 1730, he accused Carolina of bad faith in resorting to embargoes. When Glen defended the Carolina course, he threatened to go to England to lay the Cherokee case before the crown. When Glen again reverted to the Creek peace, he told him to take it up with Old Hop and threatened to carry his talk of trade to some other colony. Sorely tried, the Governor flared up and told the Right Hand Man he was a mere unknown with charges against him.

[12] IBSC, II; III, June 28, July 3, 1753, pp. 289, 295–96, 300, 302–306.

But the Little Carpenter would not permit the conference to break up in bad feeling before the Cherokees had achieved their ends. Drawing a pipe from his pouch, he filled it with tobacco, lit it, and had one of his attendants hand it to the Governor. Several moments of silence ensued as the pipe passed from mouth to mouth among the negotiators. Mistaking the move as a concession, Glen again mentioned the Creek peace; but Long Jack of Tanase curtly cut in to say that Chota came neither to seek nor to make peace with the Creeks but to talk of trade.

So the conference discussed the trade. The Little Carpenter chided Carolina on the scarcity of goods and traders and talked of going to Virginia, as, he said, the Cherokees were entitled to do under the Treaty of 1730. Glen vainly defended Carolina, stating that because of high prices for manufactured goods, few traders could afford to operate. To appeal to Virginia, he said, would be fruitless; for Virginia, being also under the crown, must respect Carolina's measures. Unmoved, the Little Carpenter threatened to turn to the French and accused the Carolina traders of charging exorbitant prices, cheating, and abusing Indian customers. Glen, who later said that the behavior of the Cherokees was such as he had never before encountered from any Indians, could not regain the initiative. In the end he promised that the number of traders and the quantity of goods would be increased. He restored the Little Carpenter to favor by issuing him a new commission to replace the one he had lost when he had been taken prisoner by the Ottawas. To each deputy he gave particular presents and to their followers heaps of goods. To amuse and impress Old Hop he sent him a "perspective glass," or stereopticon, with pictures of England and Europe. The meeting was a great triumph for Chota.

Throughout the discussions the Chotas did not once refer to the silent Lower Towns deputies. When finally Skiagunsta voiced his approval of Glen's taking the Creek peace up directly with Old Hop, the hard-pressed Governor could give him little attention. Though toward the end of the conference he signified his willingness to approach the Fire King on the matter, he

45

refused Skiagunsta's request for a fort at Keowee, saying that if peace were made with the Creeks, it would not be needed. The old Lower Towns leader, whom Georgia had once hailed as king of the Cherokees, had lived to see himself humbled by Chota before a Carolina Governor who refused to keep a vital promise. For the moment Chota had the nation in its grasp, itself the channel through which Carolina would treat on Cherokee matters.

Though Glen considered himself wise in Indian affairs, he did not immediately realize that he had delivered himself and Carolina into the proud hard core of the Cherokee nation which knew no subservience. Finally, however, under the Little Carpenter's pounding and from his after-hours conferences with traders who attended the meetings, it dawned upon him that unless he outwitted the Overhills, they would play Virginia against Carolina and become independent in both trade and policy, taking the whole nation with them. Before the deputies left Charlestown, he had determined to keep control of the Lower Towns, nourishing them into autonomy from Chota and dependence upon Carolina.

It was late, for already Dinwiddie sought to employ the Cherokee-English alliance. In May of 1753 he had dispatched a message to the "Emperor, Sachems, and warriors of the great nation of the Cherokees," asking Cherokee aid against a possible French lodgment on the forks of the Ohio.[13] Informed by Dinwiddie of the move, Glen had hurried an answer that Virginia should not concern herself with Cherokee affairs.[14] He had heard the Little Carpenter's threats with misgivings. Privately, Estatoe trader James Beamer had told him that Virginia talk would render the Cherokees "indifferent about Carolina."[15] Other traders testified that a fort at Keowee would halt the Chota drive to pull the Lower Towns from the Carolina orbit.

When on the last day of the conference Glen assured Skiagunsta he would immediately conclude a Creek peace and build

---

[13] Hanna, *op. cit.*, II, 230–31.
[14] B.R.P.O., S.C. B. T., XVII, K83 (encl.)
[15] IBSC, III, 306, 310–13, 320–21.

the promised fort, he reckoned more on tribal dynamics and with English rivals than with the French.[16] Soon after the conference he informed the Creeks that the Cherokees would negotiate; but not until October did Malatchi confirm the peace.[17]

Returned to Chota, the truculent Overhill deputies consulted with Old Hop on the next move in the game of check and countercheck begun at Charlestown. Dinwiddie's message awaited them. Significantly it had found its way into the hands of Old Hop, who henceforth, instead of Ammonscossittee, was to be addressed by the English as "Emperor of the Cherokees." Chota's reply was an enthusiastic promise to send Virginia one thousand warriors whenever Dinwiddie would set a rendezvous.[18] As Glen had feared, Chota was making its own policy. Furthermore, not content that Carolina promises would solve its trade problems, the Overhills sounded out the French at Fort Toulouse.[19] Their messenger, known as French John, lame as Old Hop was lame, a Frenchman captured in a downriver foray and given to the Fire King as a slave, was the chief French agent among the Cherokees. Henceforth he would be at Old Hop's private ear fomenting discontent with the English and holding out the hope of advantages to be had in Illinois, Alabama, and Louisiana.

On October 14, Glen, utilizing money voted by his assembly the previous year, set out with sixty soldiers to build the promised Cherokee fort. After picking up fifty laborers at frontier Ninety-Six, he arrived at Keowee on the twenty-fifth. This first visit of a Carolina governor to the Cherokees should have elicited a greeting from Old Hop and the highest officials of the Lower Towns. But Chota frowned on a Lower Towns fort; Old Skiagunsta was dead; and Wawhatchee, his successor as Head Warrior of the Lower Towns, having been disciplined by Glen in 1748 for his part in the Haig and Brown affair, tended to be

[16] B.R.P.O., S.C. B.T., XVII, K86, K88.
[17] IBSC, III, 344.
[18] Koontz, *op. cit.*, 345.
[19] IBSC, IV, 79; Paris, France, Archives Nationales Colonies, C13 A38, pp. 100–105.

anti-English and skeptical of Glen's intentions. Only the Raven of Hiwassee, mindful of past glories and his long loyalty to Carolina, extended Cherokee courtesies to the Governor. He rode with his son down the Carolina path to meet Glen the day before the English arrived at Keowee. Two days later, the Raven of Toxaway, claiming to be Wawhatchee's deputy, approached the English camp opposite Keowee, accompanied by a hundred warriors who moved toward the Governor in the stately maneuvers of the eagle dance. The Governor, not to be outdone by the Indians, formed his laborers and soldiers in martial array and fired three volleys in salute.

From the conference which ensued came the germ of what was later to be Glen's major stroke of Indian policy. His first business was to purchase the fort site for £500. The transaction covered thousands of acres for cornfields and horse and cattle ranges, and a right of way for sixty miles of road from the Long Canes settlements in Carolina.[20] In making the cession the Raven spoke at length of the westward march of the whites since the Cherokees' first contact with them and then abruptly proposed the cession of all the Cherokee lands in order to put them under the protection of the Governor of Carolina.[21] The idea probably was designed to prevent the Cherokees' being ousted from their lands. Glen embraced the proposition but suggested that the cession would better serve Cherokee ends if made to the crown. He thus stated the concept which two years later in the Treaty of Saluda became a reality and foreshadowed the royal protectorate of all the western Indians established after the French and Indian War. Glen and the Toxaway Raven rode the boundaries of Carolina purchase, and then in a few days the Raven embarked upon a tour of all the towns to advocate his proposed protectorate, which, however, did not immediately find approval.

Glen turned his attention to building Fort Prince George, named for the then Prince of Wales. Constructed by military and Indian labor a hundred yards east of the ford over Keowee River,

[20] B.P.R.O., S.C. B.T., XVII, K88; XVIII, K99.
[21] *South Carolina Historical and Genealogical Magazine, loc. cit.*, 62–63.

it was an insubstantial structure of earth and wc
feet square. At each of its corners a bastion and 1
formed a salient. About the exterior ran a ditch,
and five feet wide at the bottom, its earth tossed u
side forming an embankment five feet high. From (
to embankment top the elevation was ten feet. Alt
logs set vertically in the earth made a palisade six ar
feet high. Within rose storehouses, a guardhouse, and
of log for a small garrison. The gate was on the so
approached by a bridge over the ditch.[22]

Though continually garrisoned over the next thirteen
the fort required constant repairs. Heavy rains gullied br
into the embankments, filling the ditches with dirt. The
timbers of the palisades and buildings quickly rotted. No (
mander ever felt secure in it. Yet when Glen completed the w
in December and marched away leaving a garrison of sixte
men and a sergeant, it looked a brave structure with the Unic
Jack flying above its walls and bastions. The Lower Towns peo
ple, despite the anti-English sentiments of Wawhatchee, flocked
home from the Overhills and Middle Settlements, and rebuilt
Keowee had more people and prestige than ever it had before.[23]

Overhill Chota looked dourly upon the rehabilitated Lower
Towns and the fort which had checked its drive toward national
ascendancy and questioned the value of treating with Carolina.

[22] IBSC, I, 467; V, 153–54.
[23] S. C. Council Journals (photostats), 1755, pp. 574–75.

CHAPTER FOUR

Rivals for the Cherokees

OLD HOP AND THE LITTLE CARPENTER now saw that Glen had frustrated their bid for ascendancy. They embarked upon a course which they must have hoped would, at the least, force the Governor to turn again to them and, at the most, free the Overhills from the Carolina trade monopoly. Covering their designs with friendly messages to Glen, they corresponded with the French at Fort Toulouse and New Orleans and entertained delegations of French Indians at Chota.

In the developing Franco-British crisis in the Ohio Valley the Chota moves appeared to endanger the entire English southern frontier. The alarmed Carolina traders, quick to perceive the menace, strove desperately to counteract it. With liquor and presents they sought to raise up champions in the Chota council and finally succeeded in winning over Long Jack's brother, an influential headman at Tanase, and, perhaps, Osteneco, who had moved from Great Tellico to Tomatly and apparently was now Second Warrior of the Overhills. The council split into pro-English and pro-French factions, the latter headed by Old Hop and the Little Carpenter. For lack of unanimity the council deadlocked; and in an attempt to resolve the dispute the leaders held informal meetings in the houses of Old Hop and the Little Carpenter at Chota and Tomatly.

In January, 1754, the struggle focused directly upon the Little Carpenter, whose loyalties both parties invoked. The arrival in Chota of a party of Detroit River Ottawas with whom the Little

Carpenter had lived as a captive, not unhappily, for seven years, reinforced the French point of view.[1] One of the visitors was the Little Carpenter's former master, for whom the Second Man entertained a deep affection. The Little Carpenter talked of going to Detroit while Old Hop seized the occasion to release a captive Frenchman and send him with a message to Governor Kerlerec at New Orleans stating the Cherokees' desire for a "solid peace."[2] The desperate Carolinians now urged their Cherokee friends to confront the Little Carpenter with his pledge to the English made in 1730 when he appended his mark to the Treaty of London.

So hot did passions burn that one day at Old Hop's house they flared into a brawl among the headmen. The pro-Carolina party leaped upon the Little Carpenter, knocked him down, and beat him so badly that his life was despaired of. Turning upon Old Hop, they fiercely accused him of taking English presents under false pretenses, and the outraged Fire King limped bitterly from the house. Determined to abdicate, he took a bag of the nation's gunpowder and set off downriver alone in a canoe. His horrified family, fearful that the old man meant to take his own life, went after him and finally induced him to return.

The conflict was only resolved when the Little Carpenter, recovered, agreed to support Carolina. Much as he desired and needed independence for policy-making, he could not deny that Cherokee good faith and well being required him to honor his mark on the treaty. His judgment, moreover, appears to have coincided with his decision; for he knew the resources of the English and had seen with his own eyes the trading weaknesses of the French: how in the north they could not compete with English prices and how in the south they could not deliver the Creeks from dependence upon English goods. In the future, held to his word by his pledged faith, he would attempt to wring from the English every advantage for his people the alliance of 1730 offered.

[1] S. C. Council Journals, 1754, pp. 52–53.
[2] Paris, France, Archives Nationales Colonies, C11, A99:290.

As the Little Carpenter went, so at this period went Chota. First fruits of Chota's renewed faith in the English treaty were Oconostota's early spring assault upon the Choctaws and the Little Carpenter's foray with Long Jack's brother against French convoys on the Mississippi. Old Hop, however, to preserve a semblance of independence from Carolina, exercised his kingly prerogative to retain French John in his household.

Chota's commitment to Carolina not only blocked the Fire King's French overtures, but it tended to dampen for a time Overhill interest in Virginia. Ignoring the jealous Governor of Carolina, Dinwiddie late in 1753 sent Abraham Smith directly to Chota with an appeal for the Cherokees to come in force the next spring to help repel the French at the forks of the Ohio.[3] The Chota headmen loftily replied that they could do nothing unless Virginia supplied them with ammunition. Then by one Richard Pearis, a pack-horse man who brought trade goods financed by Christopher Gist, Dinwiddie promised to meet Cherokee demands; but Governor Glen, having learned of the Virginia messages, discouraged Cherokee co-operation. He informed the headmen that the Dinwiddie expedition had fort-building rather than war as its objective, implying that the offensive-defensive aspects of the Treaty of 1730 did not hold in this instance. The Chota headmen received Pearis kindly, took advantage of the generous terms on which he traded, and listened to Dinwiddie's talk; but mindful of Glen's opposition and willing to create a bargaining situation, they demanded that the Virginia Governor produce tangibles. Pearis worked hard to change their minds. He refused to write out their reply to Dinwiddie until they should accompany him to Stalnaker's halfway on the path to the Potomac.[4] There he hoped to find rum and presents. But the headmen would not move. Pearis finally prevailed upon the Little Carpenter to entrust him with a message to Dinwiddie stating that Glen had restrained the Cherokees from going to Virginia. Pearis and Smith, each accompanied by half a dozen

3 IBSC, IV, 7, 24–26, 94.
4 Brock, *op. cit.*, I, 232, 268, 274.

unofficial Cherokees, arrived in Williamsburg too late for the Washington expedition.

Primarily the Virginia failure in the 1754 negotiations with the Cherokees was Dinwiddie's fault. He had insisted on a unilateral approach even after Glen had assured him of help if he would recognize Carolina's paramount interest in the Cherokees and talk to them only through the Carolina authorities. The Virginia overture threatened the Carolina trade monopoly; for Dinwiddie's messengers were men known to be interested in developing a Cherokee trade under Virginia license. When Dinwiddie continued to bypass him, Glen hardened and asked the Cherokees not to move until they heard further from Carolina. Then he wrote Dinwiddie that continued intercolonial rivalry over friendly Indians would make enemies for the English.

But even while Glen and Dinwiddie competed for the Cherokees, Chota found itself forced to reconsider the English alliance; for the early spring downriver warfare of the Cherokees had brought retaliation. In June northern Indians hit the towns on Tuckasiegee and the Little Tennessee. Near panic occurred when a captured Canadian Indian tortured at the fiery stake cried out in his death agony that six hundred French and their Indians would come to avenge him.[5] Old Hop hurried off a runner to demand help from Governor Glen and to blame him for the attack. It was due, he complained, to Glen's having imprisoned the Shawnees the summer before. True Indian, Old Hop was blaming the other fellow for his troubles as he began to pull the nation away from co-operation with the English toward neutrality.

To prevent Cherokee neutrality Glen now launched upon a bold project which was to embroil him further with Dinwiddie. Putting together the long Overhill campaign for an English fort to protect them and the Raven of Toxaway's 1753 suggestion that the Cherokees could become an English protectorate, the Carolina Governor proposed that Old Hop send deputies to Charlestown to cede Cherokee lands to the crown in return for

[5] IBSC, III, 347–48; IV, 16–18, 39, 135.

a fort on the Tennessee. Old Hop replied that "We and all our lands belong to the Great King George over the water"; but he did not sent deputies or mention the fort. Glen gained the impression that the First Man was evading the issue, that perhaps he was toying with the French, and sent him a reminder of the Cherokee position with reference to Carolina. "The Cherokees," he said, "must depend upon this province for goods . . . for years to come."[6] Help, other than ammunition, he did not send; for he had not succeeded in bringing the Cherokees to the desired negotiation.

Already Old Hop had reopened correspondence with Kerlerec. Neutral and anti-English talk ran high in the nation. From the Upper Creeks came their headman, the Gun Merchant, to enjoy forbidden trade with the Carolina Cherokee traders and to talk among the Overhills of neutrality after the Creek fashion. In the Cherokee Lower Towns pro-French Cowetas peddled a story that the English had built Fort Prince George to enslave the Cherokees. Bad feeling toward the traders developed; for when deep snows penned the Indian hunters in their towns, worried traders dunned them for payment of old debts.

Restlessness with the Carolina trade monopoly lay behind renewed Cherokee interest in Virginia. Dinwiddie, now attempting to obtain Cherokee help for Braddock's expedition in the spring of 1755, sent another emissary, Nathaniel Gist, son of Christopher Gist, the Ohio Company's Indian man, to offer a Virginia trade in return for Cherokee auxiliaries. Gist's promise in Chota town house of a "great and constant trade" roused wild enthusiasm. Gist also brought a message from the northern Superintendent of Indian Affairs, Sir William Johnson, that the Six Nations would join the war against the French.[7] Perceiving that Virginia held the key to both the northern Indian threat and the Carolina monopoly, the Chota headmen evinced great interest in the Braddock campaign. Formal commitment, however, awaited the return of several important headmen from their winter hunts.

[6] S. C. Council Journals, Aug. 7, Oct. 18, Nov. 22, 1754.
[7] IBSC, V, 44, 48, 71f.

Meanwhile, Glen was pushing his own program for the Cherokees. He had heard from Dinwiddie that the crown had approved his idea of a Cherokee protectorate and had allotted Carolina £1,000 for an Overhill fort.[8] He also heard that Dinwiddie would seek Cherokee help for the Braddock campaign. Glen's problem was to bring the Cherokees into conference for formal agreements before they went off to Virginia. His idea was a late winter or early spring meeting; so in December he sent Richard Smith, brother of Abraham, the former Virginia messenger, off with a message to Old Hop. But Smith was delayed by the deep snows upcountry and did not arrive at Chota until late in February, after Gist. With the propositions of the two Colonial Governors awaiting decision, the Chota bargaining position with the English had never been better. The headmen would gather in the middle of March to decide on their course.

The interlude was lightened by the drama of Richard Pearis, who, unwanted and unauthorized, now again projected himself into the Cherokee scene where he was to be an important factor for several years to come. Pearis having failed in his 1754 mission, Dinwiddie had refused to see him on his return from the nation. The pack-horse man then relayed the Little Carpenter's pipe and message to Dinwiddie, along with a proposal that he and Nathaniel Gist be licensed to open a trading post for the Cherokees at the Great Island of the Holston. This location being within Virginia, Carolina could not complain against it as an infringement of her monopoly. Dinwiddie, apparently believing that the Gists approved the project, relented toward Pearis and sent him a letter approving the Great Island project. But by then Christopher Gist had seen fit to drop his support of Pearis and had sued him for the money he had lent him. The Great Island project collapsed, and Pearis ceased for the time being to have any connection public or private with Dinwiddie.

Pearis was an adventurer, ambitious for wealth and position. Since he had been dropped by Gist, the large sum Pearis had advanced in credit to the Overhill Cherokees became his own

[8] S. C. Council Journals, 1755, pp. 38–39.

liability and he decided that his future lay with the Cherokees. Though bankrupt, he gathered together a few sacks of trade goods and some kegs of whisky and dispatched them to Chota under the care of a pack-horse man to whom he also entrusted a letter to Old Hop in which he unscrupulously or optimistically announced that he would soon come to the nation as Dinwiddie's agent.

Young Gist appears to have had some idea of what Pearis intended; for when Pearis' man was but three days travel from Chota, a gang of Cherokees set upon him and took from him nothing but the letter to Old Hop. In Chota town house Gist had the letter translated to the Fire King while he mimicked Pearis and ridiculed his pretensions. When a few days later Pearis himself passed Chota on the other side of the river, word got around that he had gone directly to his Indian mistress at Toquo. Old Hop summoned the trader to Chota, where amid raucous Indian laughter the Fire King asked him how long the Governor of Virginia had been corresponding with Cherokee wenches. Pearis turned angrily upon Gist and accused him of treachery. But Old Hop silenced him and, sternly ordering him out of the town house, enjoined him to leave diplomacy alone and confine himself to trade. Nevertheless Pearis eventually achieved more for Virginia among the Overhills than did Nathaniel Gist.

In March, with all the headmen present, Chota under Gist's spell resolved to send warriors to Virginia at once—"Seven warriors out of our seven towns and each of them their gang of men." To placate Glen they composed a message stating that all their lands now belonged to the English and that the English could build forts where they pleased. Deputies would soon go to Charlestown. The way appeared smooth for both Dinwiddie and Glen to achieve their objectives with the Cherokees.

Then abruptly the picture changed. The war parties to Virginia halted in the towns. Gist was sent out of the nation with an evasive message to Dinwiddie, and Chota became silent save for the ominous word "neutrality." It was not Glen's doing. Forty northern Indians—Logstown Shawnees and Mingos—had

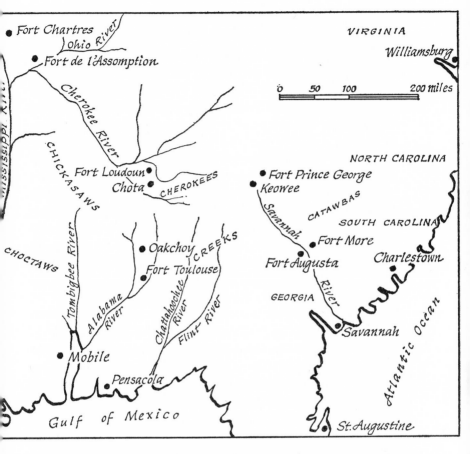

The southern Indian country, 1740–62, showing the approximate locations of various important tribes.

come into Chota town house. When Old Hop, summoned from his winter hothouse, limped to the council house doorway and cried out for his people to put the intruders to death, the Shawnees showed no fear. Runners raced away to the Valley and Middle Settlements with calls for help; but in the sanctuary of the Chota town house, no man could be injured; and shortly Old Hop and the Little Carpenter were closeted with the visitors. Presenting messages from the commander of Fort Duquesne, they told of the strong French position on the Ohio, that Canadian enemies were on the path, and worse, that the Six Nations intended neutrality. The message had truth in it; for even then the Canadian Iroquois were deep in the south; and the Onondagas, refusing to agree with the Mohawks, who alone followed Johnson, had resolved "to stand neuter till they should see who would prevail."[9] Shortly after the French emissaries departed carrying a Cherokee agreement for neutrality in the war on the upper Ohio, terror gripped the nation. On the path which the visitors had followed a Cherokee was killed by hands unknown, and the Lower Towns trembled at the report of French Indians lurking in the neighboring forest. Near Chota itself three Cherokee warriors were killed. With security gone and the Virginia path blocked, Cherokee safety lay in neutrality. Gist would take back to Virginia a false tale that Pearis had used liquor to defeat the Virginia project,[10] and Dinwiddie after Braddock's disaster would wildly blame both Glen and Pearis for the Cherokee failure to support the British expedition.[11] But so close did the frightened mountaineers hug their villages that it was only after several weeks of very earnest talking that Richard Smith could induce the Little Carpenter to go to Charlestown to face Glen.

Late in April at Charlestown, after pleading the inability of the Cherokee leaders to leave the nation in the present crisis,[12] the Little Carpenter persuaded Glen to agree to come up to Sa-

9 IBSC, V, 13, 44–46, 49–51.
10 Robert Orme, *Journal*, 15.
11 Brock, *op. cit.*, II, 77.
12 IBSC, V, 52–53.

luda, halfway to the Cherokees from Charlestown, for the great conference Glen so much desired. Even so the Little Carpenter would not promise that the Overhill fort and the English protectorate should form part of the agenda. Those matters, he said, Glen must discuss with Old Hop in person; the main business of the conference must be the old problems of trade abuses and trade monopoly.[13] The Cherokees would not abandon neutrality until something was done about these matters and concrete measures for their security were undertaken.

Even as the Little Carpenter talked, the English feared that the Cherokees might go over to the French, for Cherokee marauders created disturbances in Georgia. The troublemakers were, however, only a few Lower Townsmen, possibly led by Wawhatchee, who had gone down to Savannah to welcome Captain John Reynolds, the new Georgia Governor, and, as always, to collect presents and to see what could be done about the trade. Reynolds, eschewing difficulties with monopolistic Carolina, had been aloof and given but few presents. In their disgruntlement on their way home the Cherokees had robbed corn bins and threatened a few settlers, until on Reynolds' orders two Georgia rangers disguised as hunters escorted them from the province.[14]

The Saluda conference opened at the end of June. It was a large and colorful meeting. Beneath a hastily constructed arbor of poles and thatch sat Glen and Old Hop. Behind them stood a group of finely attired Carolina gentlemen, five hundred militiamen, Carolina rangers, and smartly uniformed regulars of the Charlestown garrison. Before the two leaders five hundred wildly clad Cherokees sat or squatted on the ground in a great crescent.[15]

Glen's principal object was to bind the Cherokees firmly to the English by making them vassals of the crown and building a fort among the Overhills. But these matters could not be taken up immediately; for the Little Carpenter, conscious that many

---

[13] S. C. Council Journals, 206–207.
[14] Chandler, *op. cit.*, VII, 179–81.
[15] *Maryland Gazette*, Sept. 18, 1755.

of his people opposed strengthening their ties with the English, meant to drive a hard bargain. He made discussion of trade grievances the first order of business. Glen proved very accommodating. He promised to increase the number of traders in the nation. He offered a new and more favorable scale of trade prices; and, on the request of the headmen, he agreed to prohibit the sale of rum by the traders. Apparently the concessions pleased the nativists; for around their council fire at night they decided to cede their lands in return for what they chose to regard as a protective fort to be built near Chota by Carolina.[16] On July 2 the Little Carpenter stood before the assembled throng of Indians and whites and in moving forest oratory gave his formal speech of cession:

> What I am about to speak our father the great King George should hear. We are now brothers with the people of Carolina, one house covers us all. We, our wives, and all our children are the children of the Great King George. He is our King, our head, our father, and we will obey him as such.

Then, leading by the hand a child, he said, "I bring this little child that when he grows up he may remember what is now agreed to, and that he will tell it to the next generation, that so it may be handed down one generation to another." Drawing from his garments a small leather pouch full of earth, which he placed at the Governor's feet, he said he placed it there "as a testimony that they not only delivered their lands but all that belonged to them to be the king's property." Then before the Governor he put down a bow and some arrows and asked that the King send them arms and ammunition, and promised to send war parties against the enemies of King George. Finally, presenting Glen with a string of white wampum in token of his sincerity, he turned to his countrymen and asked if he had spoken their will. "Unanimously and with one voice" they assented in a loud *"Yo-hah."* Then with a request that the Governor "put all that had passed between them in writing, that it might be

16 S. C. Council Journals, 1755, 397–98.

read in their hearing, that the headmen might put their marks to it, and that . . . the governor and those with him might do the same and that it might be sent to their father to keep forever," he sat down. Gratified, the Governor replied that he would send the nation arms and ammunition and would build a fort among the Overhills.

Glen now believed that he had terminated Cherokee neutrality. It was too late to help Braddock, but he had accomplished what he regarded as his greatest achievement: "The adding of near 10,000 people to his majesty's subjects and above 40,000,000 acres to his territories." Not only the land on which the Cherokee towns were seated but "all the lands on each side of the Tennessee River as far as the Mississippi and all from Tennessee to Ohio River," and possibly also the lands between the Ohio and the lakes to which Glen, citing the Treaty of Lancaster of 1744, found a shadowy claim, had become British.[17] Thus the French claim in this area was refuted, and the Cherokee nation had become something akin to a fief of the British crown.

Old Hop and the Little Carpenter, pleased at the Saluda gains in trade and protection, passed from Cherokee town to Cherokee town explaining the transaction and informing their people they no longer had lands of their own.[18] Returned to Chota, they dispatched war parties under Oconostota down the Tennessee against the French Indians of the Illinois-Wabash region.[19]

They did not, however, send warriors to Virginia. Though reports of the Saluda conference do not show that Glen asked them to, they had reasons of their own for not acting. They still hesitated to break their commitment to the Shawnees, and they awaited the "great and constant" trade which Gist had promised them from Virginia. Only tangibles could move the Cherokee headmen to risk Carolina displeasure, and none had yet come from Virginia.

Shortly, however, due to the efforts of none other than Richard

[17] *Maryland Gazette*, Sept. 18, 1755.
[18] *South Carolina Historical and Genealogical Magazine, loc. cit.*, 65.
[19] IBSC, V, 85.

Pearis, the Cherokee mood toward Virginia softened. Late in July, having satisfied Gist and regained Dinwiddie's confidence, Pearis returned to Chota. He bore a message from Dinwiddie, penned before Braddock's disaster, urging the Cherokees to send help to the British general.[20] Greeted coldly at first, for Carolina traders had circulated a rumor that he had come to collect £2,500 owed him by Indians, he endeared himself to the Overhills by publicly burning his accounts and ledgers.[21] The Cherokees could not then ignore his mission. Since, however, they had chosen to limit their commitments, they decided to send Old Hop's adopted son Cappy to Williamsburg to feel Dinwiddie out with a proposition limited primarily to defense of the Virginia frontier against invaders.[22] If Dinwiddie would build a fort on the Great Island of the Holston, they would send warriors to protect the lands and properties deserted by the inhabitants of Virginia's southwestern frontier and go against the Shawnees. Pearis had achieved a major coup in winning the Cherokees to this program. So high did they esteem him that they asked Dinwiddie to use him as Virginia's agent in all future communications to them.[23] But the Cherokee contribution to the Colonial anti-French drive in 1755 was destined to be meager. The sanguine moods of early summer soon gave way to pessimism and uncertainty as Glen was slow to implement his Saluda promises and the French threat moved closer to home. By design or accident that summer French partisans infiltrated the nation. In August the returning Overhill war parties brought news that the French were building Fort de l'Assomption near the mouth of the Tennessee. About a dozen French deserters accompanied them. The Cherokees looked uneasily upon the Frenchmen; then finally, accepting them at their face value, adopted them into families which had lost warriors. However,

[20] Brock, *op. cit.*, II, 76–77.

[21] H. R. McIlwaine, ed., *Journal of the House of Burgesses of Virginia*, 1752–58, pp. 279–81.

[22] *Virginia Gazette*, Sept. 16, 1755; *Maryland Gazette*, Sept. 18, 1755.

[23] Paris, France, Archives Nationales Colonies, C.O. XVI, 453–55.

they took the precaution of sending scouts to watch the French operation at the mouth of the Tennessee lest it prove to be a base for expeditions against them. Shortly a score of Shawnees from above the Ohio appeared at Chota seeking permission to settle among the Overhills. Chota warily consented, warning the newcomers that if they moved away they would be treated as enemies. At the same time anti-English feeling developed in the Out Towns along the Tuckaseigee where deserters from the Virginia forces and free-lance whites hid out. As distrust grew in the nation, and nativists, troubled by the Saluda cession, voiced their discontent, the Little Carpenter sent querulous talks to Glen reminding him of his promises. By October, Old Hop was complaining bitterly of Carolina's failure to improve trade conditions.[24]

Glen, however, was unable to move. The £1,000 that Dinwiddie had sent him for the fort was inadequate, and a recalcitrant assembly refused to grant him further monies to appease the Cherokees. Nor could he improve the trade, for the large Cherokee debt to the traders and the uncertainties of wartime kept Carolina merchants from granting traders badly needed credit.[25] Glen lamely wrote Old Hop that "the ready way to be supplied is to pay for what you get."[26] Though he sweetened the suggestion with gifts for Old Hop, the Little Carpenter, Osteneco, and Oconostota, his and Carolina's prestige continued to fall.

Nevertheless, the Little Carpenter and Old Hop, politically unable to accept Saluda as a failure, continued to support the English alliance. In late October or early November they refused to eat the flesh of an English soldier proffered them by a Shawnee deputation from north of the Ohio. The Shawnees threatened them with a French invasion, but the Overhills determined to take the risk.[27] As soon as the French Indians left,

24 IBSC, V, 82, 85.

25 S. C. Council Journals (photostats), 1755, pp. 505–506.

26 IBSC, V, 83–84.

27 S. C. Council Journals, 1755, p. 557.

130 Overhills, led by Osteneco and the Yellow Bird with Richard Pearis as interpreter, departed for the Virginia frontier where, based on David Robertson's fort on New River, they stood that winter between southwestern Virginia and the Shawnees.[28] Thus the Cherokee headmen finally demonstrated to both Glen and Dinwiddie their sincerity in the English alliance. His people committed, the Little Carpenter with 120 followers went in person to Charlestown to press Glen for action.

The December meeting with Glen was not a happy one. To hold his people to the English alliance, the Little Carpenter had to have positive results, which Glen, oppressed by the knowledge that his parsimonious assembly resented the expense of his Cherokee policy, could not give. When the Little Carpenter painted a grave picture of sentiment in the nation and bluntly questioned Glen's sincerity in the Saluda treaty, the Carolina Governor squirmed with excuses. Hoping for eventual favorable action from his assembly, he held the Indian in town with talk of an impending conference with the Creeks; to keep him happy he lavished attentions upon him, entertained him in his home, and took him to visit churches, forts, and ships. Finally on advice of his council, but without authority from his assembly, he told the Cherokee the fort would be built in April. At the same time he urged that Old Hop surrender French John; and to expedite matters, the Little Carpenter agreed. Perhaps the Second Man hoped to return to the nation with a fort-building party; but, after lingering three weeks and discovering that Glen still could not act, he retracted his promise to deliver French John and left town discontented. He knew his people would be dissatisfied and that implementing his own commitments to the English alliance would be more difficult. To Glen he alleged that his unhappiness arose from the Governor's refusing his regal request for the release of a British sailor held for capital punishment in the brig of an English man-of-war in Charlestown harbor.[29] But the ways of diplomats are devious. The continued presence of

28 Brock, *op. cit.*, II, 296–97.
29 S. C. Council Journals, 1755, pp. 570, 579; 1756, pp. 88–89.

French John in the nation constituted a threat. Glen, gazing at the cold back of the retiring Second Man, hurriedly induced the man-of-war captain to free the prisoner; and shortly, on his own responsibility, dispatched an agent to Chota to survey the fort site. But by the time this news reached the nation, the angry Little Carpenter had turned from Carolina to Virginia to salvage his English commitment. Glen was again confronted with the possibility that Virginia would supplant Carolina in the Overhill trade.

CHAPTER FIVE

The Turn to Virginia

IN DECEMBER, 1755, Osteneco, ambitious for Virginia favor and impatient of defense along the quiet southwestern Virginia frontier, suggested an attack upon the Shawnee town of Scioto on the Ohio. Advised of the proposal by Richard Pearis, Dinwiddie authorized Andrew Lewis to lead 250 Virginians and 100 Cherokees down the Tug Fork of the Big Sandy against the Shawnees. The forces gathered on February 11 at Fort Frederick, and after a week of prayers and daily sermons by Presbyterian ministers and ceremonial dances by the Indians, marched into the Allegheny wilderness.

The Cherokees quickly won commendation. Their Spartan conduct had excited the admiration of the young Virginia officers whose Presbyterian austerity had been distressed by the "cursing, swearing, and confusion" in their own camp. The Cherokees did not reciprocate, for to them the switching of a man for profane swearing seemed undignified.[1] The Indians proved excellent scouts. Though the sight of an occasional fleeting figure by the stream bank ahead and of recently deserted Shawnee hunting camps convinced them that the enemy had detected the English movement, they did not talk of failure or retreat.[2] In heavy rains with the soldiers they forded and reforded the tumbling stream. When game became scarce, Indian as well as white went hungry. The only apparent discontent was

---

[1] Brock, *op. cit.*, II, 294–97, 319–23, 336–37.
[2] Draper MSS, Preston Papers, QQ, pp. 106–107.

that of the soldiers who complained that the Cherokees, expecting a share of what food there was, did not hesitate to stride silently to the carcass of a Virginia slain deer and cut off a portion for their own use.[3]

When the fork deepened, the Indians fashioned dugout canoes for themselves. Lewis' men followed suit but made the fatal mistake of piling the sacks of ammunition and flour which they had borne on their backs into but one or two of their boats. Ineptly handled in the wild river, the Virginia supply-laden canoes soon swamped. Guns, ammunition and the meager food supply were lost. With this accident the expedition disintegrated, and the soldiers began to straggle for home in small groups. Osteneco then advised Lewis to turn back. Though he himself was ready to go on with the officers, his warriors, he said, would be discouraged by the soldiers' defection.[4] It was not a Cherokee failure. Mindful of this, and that during their stay on the Virginia frontier the Cherokees had received no rewards, Dinwiddie invited Osteneco to Williamsburg, where on April 26 he received him with the unguents of diplomacy and flattery. Osteneco rode down Duke of Gloucester Street in the Governor's coach and four between long files of the local militia standing at present arms.[5] Thenceforth Osteneco was to believe himself the proprietor of Cherokee relations with Virginia.

The presence of the former Tacite of Great Tellico in Williamsburg dramatized the newly made Treaty of Broad River which Dinwiddie was about to ask his burgesses to implement. Contracted in the wilderness of North Carolina with the Catawbas and Cherokees, the treaty represented Dinwiddie's disillusionment with pack-horse and trader diplomacy and his determination to treat with the Cherokees on a serious level. Late in 1755 he had decided that "gentlemen of standing" should carry a "handsome present" to the reluctant red men and con-

---

[3] *Virginia Historical Register and Literary Notebook*, Vol. IV, No. 3 (July, 1751), 143–47.

[4] Draper MSS, Preston Papers, QQ, pp. 119–21.

[5] *Maryland Gazette*, May 6, 1756.

clude "a permanent league" with them.[6] He had appointed William Byrd and Edmund Randolph commissioners, and dispatched Abraham Smith to Old Hop with an invitation for the Cherokee headmen to meet his commissioners on March 5 at the junction of Pacolet and Broad rivers where the old Lower Towns path to the Catawbas crossed.[7]

Delayed by high waters, Smith did not reach Lower Towns Keowee until February 5. There he found the Little Carpenter homebound from Charlestown, disturbed by his ill success with Glen. The Second Man quickly decided that Cherokee opportunity lay with the Virginians on Pacolet River,[8] where on March 13 the Overhill deputies for whom he had sent joined him. Though unaccompanied by Old Hop, who deigned to leave the nation only to meet a man he considered of equal rank, the deputies were the heart of the Chota council: Standing Turkey or Connetarke, within three years to succeed Old Hop as Fire King, the Great Warrior Oconostota, and Willinawaw, Prince of Toquo and the Little Carpenter's cousin, and others of lesser note. Few Lower Towns and Middle Settlements leaders came, for Chota did not want them. As usual a large crowd of attendants— women, boys, and young men—had been brought along to bear witness to the words and partake of the presents.

Formal discussions opened on March 14 with the Virginia commissioners reading Dinwiddie's message to a great crescent of Indians seated on the ground against a backdrop of white-blooming shadbush and pale blue mountain ranges. Asserting the Virginia Governor's friendship and cautioning them against allowing the French to build a fort in their country, it countered the Shawnee report of Six Nations neutrality with the news that the Mohawks had fought for the English in the great September victory over the French on Lake George in upper New York colony. It proclaimed support for the new treaty from the great King George with whom the Cherokees had made the Treaty

[6] *A Treaty Held with the Catawba and Cherokee Indians*, v.

[7] Brock, *op. cit.*, II, 267–68.

[8] S. C. Council Journals, 1756, p. 182.

of 1730. There would be presents of powder and lead and great quantities of goods to be distributed before the Indians went home. All this the Cherokees greeted with a loud, approving "*Yo-hah.*"

Byrd and Randolph then developed the British case against the French. With strings of wampum they emphasized each point. The French had tricked the Shawnees and Delawares into deserting the English and attacking the Virginia frontier. The French desired not only the English lands but those of the Indians also. The fate of the Natchez in 1729, the assaults upon the Chickasaws, the repeated attempts to disrupt the Six Nations all demonstrated this. The Cherokees should therefore join the English in resisting the French, and the English would provide their warriors with arms, ammunition, provisions, and clothing. They concluded their bold message with an invitation for the Cherokees to seal the alliance by sending two boys to William and Mary College at the expense of the mission societies of Virginia. They were at pains to refute the rumor snaking through the Cherokee camp that the Virginians had already given most of the presents to the Catawbas.

The next day the Little Carpenter, who had from memory repeated to his people the interpreter's full rendition of the talks, gave the Cherokee reply which had been worked out about their council fire at night. It was a direct bid for Virginia entry into the Cherokee trade. Asserting that the Cherokees might go over to the French because Glen had "forfeited his word" by failing to build the promised fort, he asked that Dinwiddie meet Old Hop at Stalnaker's far out on the Virginia frontier to talk of trade. Ominously he pointed out that the Overhills suffered from high prices, a scarcity of goods, and unreliable smooth-bore muskets which were no match for the long-range, accurate rifles which the French supplied to their Indians. He concluded by spreading before the Virginians a deerskin, forceful reminder of the importance of trade.[9]

On the third day, the commissioners formally promised Vir-

9 *A Treaty Held with the Catawba and Cherokee Indians,* xiii–xvi.

ginia aid in building the Overhill fort. Informally, for it does not appear in the treaty, they probably agreed to enter the trade, and they must have led the Cherokees to believe that Dinwiddie would meet Old Hop.[10] In return they asked that two hundred Cherokees go immediately to the Virginia frontier.

On the fourth and final day of the conference, after the Little Carpenter had talked, the headmen set their marks to the treaty while a harassed secretary laboriously supplied spellings for their wild names. By the terms of the formal instrument the Cherokees agreed to fight the French, to report any French attempts to induce them to break away from their treaty, and to prevent the French from building a fort among them. In return for Virginia assistance in building the Overhill fort, the Cherokees agreed to send four hundred warriors to Virginia whom Virginia would supply with clothes, arms, and ammunition. Both sides would punish violators of the treaty.

The Broad River treaty was a major diplomatic triumph for the Little Carpenter. He had obtained Virginia's promise to build the fort which Glen had failed to provide and which he had determined should be the seal of the protectorate. He had also obtained, as it appears from subsequent acts of the Virginia assembly, a Virginia promise to break the Carolina trade monopoly, a promise to be ratified in a meeting of Old Hop and Dinwiddie. These benefits would dampen the smouldering nativist criticism of the Little Carpenter's Saluda treaty with Glen.

The day Osteneco rode in state through Williamsburg, Dinwiddie presented the Treaty of Broad River to his burgesses. They immediately underwrote the construction of the fort with up to £2,000 of Virginia paper.[11] On April 24, Dinwiddie ordered Andrew Lewis to proceed with sixty men to the Cherokee country to work on the fort. Lewis was to help Carolina; but if Carolina failed, he was to construct the fort on his own responsibility. Thus in two weeks' time Dinwiddie set in motion something

10 IBSC, V, 162–63.
11 *A Treaty Held with the Catawba and Cherokee Indians,* xix–xxiii.

Glen had been unable to do in a year. South Carolina's position with the Cherokees was now in peril.

Meanwhile, prodded by Washington's pleas for Indian help on a harassed frontier, Dinwiddie pressed Osteneco's warriors to go to the Virginia borders.[12] They agreed to do it, but not until they had treated the entranced populace of Williamsburg to a four-day spectacle of dances, ceremonial pipes, and orations while they cemented their ancient league with the Nottoways visiting from southeastern Virginia. Then all save Osteneco, who decided to accompany Andrew Lewis to the nation, set off for Winchester.[13] At Augusta from the Virginia stores they picked up a few presents and met a party of the Big Sandy Cherokees, already returning from a success on Washington's front. They had defeated a French patrol and had taken the scalp of its commander.[14]

All, however, was not harmony. Some of the participants in the Big Sandy failure, not having received rewards for their services, had traveled homeward exacting compensation from the countryside. During early May they had foraged southward along the path through North Carolina and to the Lower Towns, stealing horses and saddles, picking up a runaway indentured white woman who from private spites advised the Indians whom to plunder. Behind them they left knots of angry settlers, bitterly swearing to repel "force with force."[15] The King of the Catawbas finally caught them, took away their prizes, and haled them before Justice Hensley at Salisbury for a reprimand. The foray sowed seeds of later trouble. While settlers along the route future parties of Lower Townsmen would follow to Virginia were in a vengeful mood, the disgruntled marauders took home a festering sense of the Englishman's iniquity. For their six months' hardship on Virginia's behalf they had nothing to show.

---

[12] Koontz, *op. cit.*, 955–56.
[13] Brock, *op. cit.*, II, 445–46.
[14] Koontz, *op. cit.*, 955–56.
[15] W. L. Saunders, ed., *The Colonial Records of North Carolina*, V, 604–605.

It was otherwise with Osteneco as he marched with Lewis down the Warriors' Path toward Chota. Once an English favorite in the days of Hiwassee-Tellico's ascendancy, he now strove to rival the Little Carpenter in English esteem and in influence at Chota. Learning of the misbehavior of his countrymen in North Carolina, he reassured Lewis of Cherokee friendship;[16] and, as the party neared Chota, he struck out ahead to stir Old Hop to a proper welcome for the benefits he was bringing from Virginia.

Osteneco's arrival at Chota was timely. Every day that English promises went unfulfilled the undercurrent of bad talk which circulated through the rumor-fed towns gained strength. With Braddock's defeat, Carolina's delay, and the failure of the Big Sandy expedition English prestige had plummeted. In the Little Carpenter's absence, French intrigue at Chota had grown. The Cherokees had refused to yield up to the English the Frenchmen among them. The gang of Ohio Shawnees settled near Chota sang French praises, and in midwinter another Shawnee deputation had proffered Old Hop barbecued English flesh.[17] Though Old Hop had reprimanded them, they had gone off to Great Tellico to play upon the old sores there. Great Tellico, deserted by the pro-English Osteneco, and peripheral in national affairs since the ascendance of Chota, became a center of pro-French feeling.[18]

In the Lower Towns talks were bad. Pinched by the failure of the 1755 corn crop, the Lower Townsmen became moody. Refugees from the war-struck Virginia frontier had begun to occupy the Long Cane's lands which Glen insisted had been ceded by the Keowee Treaty of 1753.[19] Outraged by reports that a settler had horsewhipped one of their countrymen, the Lower Towns had a grievance which bootlegging Georgia traders harped upon in order to discredit their legitimate Carolina rivals.[20]

---

[16] Journals of the Executive Council of Virginia, June 12, 1756.

[17] S. C. Council Journals (photostats), 1756, pp. 557–58.

[18] IBSC, VI, 34–35.

[19] S. C. Council Journals, 1756, pp. 352–53.

[20] IBSC, V, 118–19.

Nativist sentiment was strong. Many Cherokees never went near the English settlements, and few Cherokees, particularly headmen, deigned to learn English.[21] Large numbers resented the Little Carpenter's inviting the English to build another fort among them.[22] Despite their dependence upon the trade they did not want many whites living in their midst. Creek propaganda—some of it French in origin, some of it nativist, and some of it resentment that their old enemies should now have English protection—seeped into the nation.[23] It opposed the new fort and disseminated the French-inspired story that the English intended to kill all the Cherokee men and enslave their women and children.

Despite all this, the surface of Cherokee life appeared unruffled. Officially the Cherokees were allies of the English and enemies of the French. War parties went down the Tennessee to operate against the French on the Mississippi. While the Overhills had deputies at Broad River, the Middle Settlements, inveterate against the Shawnees, sent a strong party to raid on the upper Ohio. The long lines of traders' pack horses bearing bundles of deerskins from the winter's trade crawled over the mountain paths toward Charlestown.

As undercurrents of anti-English sentiment built up, Old Hop listened to the counsels of French John who, through the northern relatives of the local Shawnees, communicated with Detroit and Governor Vaudreuil of Canada. Even though Glen's agent, John Pearson, came into Chota and with Old Hop's help selected a site for the fort, Carolina's prestige did not improve. Moreover, the slow implementation of the Broad River treaty caused the skeptical to assert that four years of negotiation with Virginia had brought nothing, that the English had already proved their inability to fulfill promises. Hence it was that early in June a message originating in Chota informed the French commander of Alabama's Fort Toulouse that the Cherokees desired to

---

[21] William Richardson, "Report," Dec. 25, 1758.
[22] S. C. Council House Journals, 1756, p. 246.
[23] S. C. Council Journals, 1756, pp. 309–10.

treat.[24] If English promises were not soon turned into tangibles, dissident forces among the Cherokees might force a *rapprochement* with the French.

Into this moody setting one bright June day, Major Lewis led his Virginians. Almost simultaneously with Osteneco's announcement of the near approach of Lewis, a runner came from the Lower Towns bearing news that a South Carolina force had reached Fort Prince George. Nervous though the nativists might be that two English forces had arrived at the outposts of the nation, the Little Carpenter's diplomacy had triumphed. The Shawnee gang which had frequented Chota all winter and spring started up like a guilty thing and fled southward to Chartier's Shawnee settlement among the Creeks. On June 26, Old Hop put on the face of welcome and, accompanied by his councilors and seven hundred warriors, went up the Virginia path to give Major Lewis a ceremonial greeting.[25]

[24] IBSC, V, 132–33, 147–48, 230–31.
[25] Koontz, *op. cit.*, 1030.

CHAPTER SIX

Doubts and Hesitations

IN JANUARY, 1756, after the Little Carpenter had departed, Glen seriously attempted to fulfill his promises to the Overhills. Obtaining £2,000 from his assembly on the understanding that the crown would refund it, he dispatched John Pearson to Chota to select a fort site and to arrange a corn supply for the workmen.[1] But in June, while leading a force of provincials and regulars to build the fort, he learned that his successor, William Henry Lyttelton, had arrived in Charlestown and desired the Cherokee expedition halted.[2] Lyttelton, ordered by the crown to obtain from the assembly an unconditional grant for the fort, had no choice but to suspend Glen's march until the assembly complied.[3] Glen sent Captain Raymond Demere of the Independent Company ahead with his regulars to Fort Prince George to await further orders. Then, taking with him the Indian presents purchased on his own credit, he returned to Charlestown. Lyttelton hurried information to Old Hop that the expedition would soon be renewed.[4]

Arriving at Fort Prince George on June 19, Demere found Keowee restless. Glen's advance had caused Creek visitors to spread a rumor that the Governor's wagons contained iron for manacles with which to enslave the Cherokee women and chil-

[1] S. C. Council Journals, 1756, pp. 68–72, 147.
[2] IBSC, V, 134.
[3] Lyttelton to Loudoun, Aug. 25, 1756, Loudoun Papers.
[4] S. C. Council Journals, 1756, p. 273.

dren. The alarmed Keowee headmen had suggested to Chota that the time had come to kill all the English in the nation.

Nevertheless, on the morning of June 20 four smiling Lower Towns headmen, led by Wawhatchee, came to the fort to welcome Captain Demere and to deprecate the bad talks of which the English had already heard. Naturally they expected presents. Wawhatchee, seeking to demonstrate that he rather than Old Hop and the Little Carpenter could do something for his people, asked Demere to separate the Keowee presents from those for Chota so that he and not the Overhills could distribute them. The presents, however, had gone back with Glen. The Conasatchee warrior swallowed his disappointment and prepared an elaborate demonstration of good will for the English, which Demere on the twenty-first paraded his troops outside the fort to receive. In a little time the Cherokees appeared:

> . . . in regular procession, a numerous train dressed in their best apparel which with their faces were painted all over. They had large belts of wampum around their necks and plates of silver hanging to their breasts and round their arms; the first that appeared was a large body of young men in regular order moving in a slow solid pace singing and displaying in the air eagles' tails and rattle boxes. On each wing was a young man playing on a flute of their own make. Next to those singing were the chief men and head councillors attended by a person beating a drum of their own make in the rear. In the midst of them a person bore a large bow [*sic*] of a sycamore tree exalted in the air and another a white flag tied to a stick.[5]

The Captain responded to this demonstration by maneuvering his troops in "all the honors due to a king." As the Indians marched into the fort, the four swivel guns on the bastions fired salutes. Immensely pleased, the headmen made formal speeches of welcome. As they left, the guns again sounded. The next evening the women of Keowee performed the welcome dance in the fields beside the fort. The Captain sent out "a small refreshment." The following day, "notwithstanding provisions were so

[5] IBSC, V, 132–33, 139–41.

scarce with them as had ever been known," the women reciprocated with a "great number of cakes of bread of their own make and green peas and squash."

Hunger played a part in the show of enthusiasm for the Carolina forces. So great was the scarcity of corn that many Indians had traded their store clothes to settlers and to other Indians for food. Apprised of this, Demere sent barrels of rice and other provisions to Keowee. He repeated the gesture so often that by September his own men were reduced to short rations. Indian poachers had cut his herd of one hundred beef cattle to seventy-five and had left behind in the woods heaps of bones and ashes. The Overhills were hungry also, and they consumed the corn Pearson had reserved for the delayed Carolina fort builders.

Despite the amenities of welcome, within two weeks the Lower Towns became restive. Demere's failure to bring presents worried them. Creeks who had been in the towns when the troops arrived had hastily departed. With the tribesmen's faces darkening about him, the Captain saw Fort Prince George as a disintegrating ruin, its earthen ramparts washed into the ditches with each rain; and he set his men to work widening and deepening the ditches and repairing the breaches in the wooden palisades.

Chota also fretted. The delay of the Carolina fort builders at Fort Prince George was unaccountable; and the Virginians were a disappointment. The headmen told Lewis they would send no warriors to Virginia until the promised fort was built; so Lewis finally began the work on his own responsibility.[6] The site allotted him, however, was not that chosen by Pearson but one five miles away across the river from Chota. It was Chota's intention to have two forts: one Virginian and the other Carolinian. Apparently their objective was to break the Carolina trade monopoly with the Virginia fort as a base for a Virginia trade. But again Chota diplomacy met a setback, for Lewis had orders not to garrison the fort.[7] Therefore when Toquo trader Sam

---

[6] *Ibid.*, V, 144–45, 149–52, 170–72, 193, 200, 219.

[7] Koontz, *op. cit.*, 1030–37.

Benn arrived with an invitation from Lyttelton to Old Hop, asking the First Man to come to Charlestown, Chota balked. It would send neither warriors to Virginia nor the Fire King and his deputies to Charlestown. Instead it sent the Little Carpenter to Fort Prince George with a message chiding Demere for his slowness and needling him with the statement that "The Virginia people promised us a fort the other day and are now building it." Lewis at Chota, however, could not look upon his mission as a success. When he continued to press for four hundred warriors, Chota truculently demanded ammunition which he feared to spare.

Then Great Tellico became troublesome. Benn, having failed to raise a deputation at Chota, stopped on his return at the dissident town hoping to find support there. Tellico had decided to act upon its own to remedy the failure of its trade. Ammonscossittee, still called "the Young Emperor" by the English; Kenoteta, a headman and son of the Smallpox Conjurer of Settico; and Old Caesar of Chatuga, ancient pillar of the defunct Hiwassee-Tellico alignment went with Benn to Charlestown. En route they stopped at Fort Prince George where Demere quieted their alarm over the manacle rumor by explaining that the iron he brought was shaped for wheelbarrows and other construction tools.

While Demere talked with the stuttering Ammonscossittee, news came that the Little Carpenter had arrived at Keowee, and the Tellico aspirant hastily took his departure only to meet the Little Carpenter on his way to the fort. The Second Man stalked coldly by the discredited sycophant, the symbol of decayed Tellico grandeur, to enter the post where flags flew and troops stood in stiff ranks to greet the ascendant Chota diplomat.

The Little Carpenter welcomed Demere to the nation, then plunged haughtily into Chota's demands upon Carolina. He had come to escort the Carolinians over the hills. Contrary to the Saluda agreements, the trade continued bad: goods were insufficient and prices high; Chota trader John Elliott particularly offended, and the Governor should revoke his license. He restated the old Overhill hope and threat that if Carolina failed to meet their trade needs, they would go elsewhere. Vigorously maintaining Chota's supremacy over the nation, he asserted that he and Old Hop were the "rulers and commanders-in-chief of all the towns in the Cherokee nation."[8] Ammonscossittee, he said, lacked authority; nor should any Lower Townsmen be allowed to go to Charlestown without specific authority from Chota.

Demere was impressed, and promised that on July 23 his advance guard under Sergeant Gibbs would be ready to go to the Overhills. Gratified, and keenly conscious of what he believed to be Virginia perfidy, the Little Carpenter intimated that he would direct Chota's war effort into channels less threatening to Carolina's trade monopoly by leading a war party down the Tennessee against the French. He then went over to Keowee to await the departure of the advance party, which he intended personally to lead into Chota in vindication of his pro-English policies.

Soon, however, he found himself in a difficult situation. One day while he visited the fort Dinwiddie's courier on his way to Chota came in with an urgent plea that the Cherokees honor the Little Carpenter's Broad River promise of four hundred warriors.[9] Demere turned on the Little Carpenter and accused him of playing Virginia's game against Carolina. Fearful of losing his hold on Carolina, the Cherokee baldly denied that he had ever asked Dinwiddie for a fort. Technically he was correct. He had only asked that Virginia assist in building the Overhill forts. He became officially anti-Dinwiddie. When Glen read him Dinwiddie's protest over the Cherokee April and May depredations in Virginia and North Carolina, he said, "If the Governor complains against the few men that were in Virginia, pray what ought he to expect from the great number he wants?" He made it clear that he now felt under no obligation to send anyone to Virginia; for, said he, Dinwiddie had failed to keep a promise

8 IBSC, V, 151–52, 154–58.
9 Brock, *op. cit.*, 445–46.

to meet him in conference on the Holston River. He, therefore, was ready to serve Carolina.

The Little Carpenter's diplomacy was in a bad way. He had been caught playing in rival camps and had been unable to obtain full satisfaction from either. One morning he came to the fort to demand that the advance start immediately with him for the Overhills. When Demere objected that the men were not yet ready, the Little Carpenter bitterly accused him of bad faith and finally induced him to move up the date for departure. The Indian's private dismay at the complexities which confronted him must have been great; for that evening he indulged in a drunken orgy at Keowee and the next day, accompanied by two tippling companions, he came into the fort for more liquor. As he sat drinking with Demere, he became violent and threatened the Captain's life with a bottle. Demere ordered him to leave, and his friends staggered with him to Keowee where the headmen scratched him from head to foot with a snake-tooth comb until his "blood run good," and he sobered up. The following day the chastened diplomat went to Demere and apologized: "There was three of us," he said, "You was the first; I was the second, and rum was the third."

On the twenty-fourth, escorted by Sergeant Gibbes and eighteen soldiers, the Little Carpenter set out for Chota. Demere rode part way with him; and, belatedly remembering Lyttelton's orders to co-operate with Lewis, advised the Cherokee to help Virginia with as many warriors as possible. The captain was not favorably impressed by what he had seen of the Little Carpenter; for he wrote Lyttelton at this time that the Second Man had "a brutish temper" and a "bad disposition," that he was deceitful and selfish, being "convinced by long experience that he cannot do better for himself than to remain in friendship with the English."[10] Certainly the Little Carpenter had not shown to advantage in this first encounter. He probably had even been a bit overweening in his expectations of personal presents for favoring Carolina over Virginia. Demere had yet to see the Little Carpenter's power and statesmanship in action.

[10] IBSC, V, 162–64, 169–70.

While the Little Carpenter had led his face-saving force of Carolinians over the hills, events moved in Charlestown to make the Carolina Overhill fort a reality. Lyttelton had received Ammonscossittee; but, learning that he was a Cherokee of fallen prestige and on no official mission, he had politely wined and dined him and sent him back to Great Tellico with a few presents and no message.[11] His orders from home were to co-operate with Dinwiddie, so he sent a message to the Little Carpenter asking him to provide warriors for Virginia. Then he ordered Captain John Stuart to proceed with 150 regulars and provincials to Fort Prince George where Demere would take command and lead them over the mountains to build a fort on the Little Tennessee.[12]

During the Little Carpenter's absence at Fort Prince George, Chota considered Dinwiddie's May 13 message, which the Little Carpenter had heard from Demere. The council concocted a grudging reply in which they alleged that because of enemy pressure and their fear that the Shawnees would induce the Creeks to attack them, they could not send more than one hundred men "the next moon." In return Dinwiddie should supply one hundred Virginians to garrison the fort and commence the trade soon. Carolina, they said, promised much and delivered nothing.[13] Sergeant Gibbes's coming with the Little Carpenter did not alter Chota's mind, for Gibbes lacked authority to start building.

Chota had little actual intention of putting warriors in Virginia that summer. Like Carolina, Virginia had essentially failed to meet the Overhill trade and security demands. Sentiment favorable to the French mounted among the Indians, just as French pressure increased. In June the commander of Fort Toulouse advised Chota that he had referred earlier Cherokee peace talks to Governor Kerlerec at New Orleans.[14] Soon afterward Shawnee runners brought a bid for an alliance from Governor Vaudreuil of Canada.[15] Both the northern and southern Shawnees,

11 S. C. Council Journals, 1756, pp. 320–24.
12 Lyttelton to Loudoun, Aug. 25, 1756, Loudoun Papers.
13 Koontz, *op. cit.*, 1027–29.
14 IBSC, V, 186.
15 O'Callaghan, *op. cit.*, X, 592.

undisturbed by Osteneco's bloodless participation in the Big Sandy expedition of the previous winter and the spring actions of a few Cherokees with Washington, refrained from major hostilities against the Cherokees. Instead they fed blandishments and threats into the nation by whatever means possible. Numbers of southern Shawnees had appeared at Great Tellico while others held friendly meetings in the woods with Cherokee hunters. Late in July or early in August the King of Nequassee's son, captured by northern Shawnees from a Middle Settlements war party, came into Chota arrayed in fancy French garments with the tale that Shawnees had beaten him, dressed him up, and then released him. He bore a message asking the Cherokees why they "went so naked" when the French could supply them with "large presents of clothes," and informing them that it was the English intention "to destroy them and make slaves of their women and children"; that unless the Cherokees immediately joined the Shawnees, the Shawnees would dispatch a large body of warriors against the Cherokee nation.

When Demere learned of the Shawnees in the Overhill towns and heard that two hundred Shawnees on the Holston River blocked Andrew Lewis' return to Virginia, he feared the worst. He hurried several pack-horse loads of ammunition to Lewis and orders for Sergeant Gibbes to join forces with the Virginians should trouble break out.

The general situation was beginning to threaten Old Hop's and the Little Carpenter's control of policy. Finally the two men sent Demere a demand that Carolina immediately fulfill its promises lest they "be laughed at by their young men" and lose their hold on their people.[16]

Early in August the Virginia fort was completed. It stood across the Little Tennessee from Chota on the west bank of Four Mile Creek. A simple structure, 105 feet square, its earthen wall was "as thick," said Old Hop, "as from my elbow to the ends of my fingers on the other hand extended." A log palisade seven feet high rose from the top of earthen banks, giving the structure

16 IBSC, V, 186, 188–89.

Attakullaculla, at the far right, and six other Cherokees who accompanied Sir Alexander Cuming to England in 1730.

From a drawing by Dennison

Reconstruction of Fort Prince George

an overall height of sixteen feet from the bottom of the ditch to the top of the palisade.[17] Inside were houses for the nonexistent garrison, into which Cherokee families moved when the Virginians left.

But with the fort built, Lewis found the headmen indecisive and evasive, reluctant to honor their July promise of one hundred warriors. Lewis saw them as "like the devil's pig, they will neither lead nor drive." Ordering his workmen off for Virginia via Fort Prince George to avoid the Shawnee threat, he and Pearis stayed on at Chota with twenty men to escort whatever Indians they could prevail upon the headmen to send with them. But, obviously, strong forces at Chota worked in opposition, not the least being the Little Carpenter's awareness of Old Hop's disposition to look into Vaudreuil's overture and his own disappointment with both Carolina and Virginia. Finally on August 15 the wavering headmen asked the Virginians to remain until after the green-corn feast on August 26, when they said they would go north with them.

While the Overhills shifted from one position to another, new unrest stirred in the Lower Towns. Ammonscossittee, returning discontented from Charlestown, stopped at Keowee with four kegs of rum which the Keowees consumed in a big debauch. Visiting Catawbas reported to Demere that drunken Keowees declared their intention of killing all the white people. The Keowees had heard from one of their headmen, Tistoe, who had been at Chota, the report of the Nequassee King's son that the English intended to enslave them. Now giving apparent reality to the threat, Captain Stuart was on the road to the nation with a sizable reinforcement for the soldiers already at Fort Prince George. In mid-August the Oakfuskee Captain, an official Creek deputy, had come into Estatoe, fifteen miles from Fort Prince George, to express Creek disapproval of the English building a fort among the Overhills. Presumably he poked at every sore of discontent he could detect.

About this time, too, Demere learned of depredations com-

17 Koontz, *op. cit.*, 1030–37.

mitted on white settlers by Middle Settlements Indians. The Prince of Joree's young men had brought horses, a rifled gun, and some women's apparel into their town, probably looted from settlers on the south Catawba and Broad rivers. Demere sent a firm message to the Prince demanding that the booty be delivered up at once and that the Prince give his people a strong talk on the subject.

The summer of 1756 had been bad for the English cause among the Cherokees; and Demere must have experienced great relief when on the twenty-fourth of September he saw riding up the path from Charlestown a party of horsemen in scarlet and blue uniforms. They were Captain Stuart and the officers of the reinforcements come to build the Carolina Overhill fort, fifteen months after the Treaty of Saluda.[18]

[18] IBSC, V, 175–76, 189–91, 196, 201.

CHAPTER SEVEN

The Conspiracy of Tellico

THE MOOD OF THE OVERHILLS in September, 1756, was black. Undercurrents of dark doubts eddied to the surface as the French-inspired story that the English came to enslave their women and children snaked through the nation. Chota runners, sent ostensibly to welcome Stuart and Demere, stopped first at Keowee to inquire how the English behaved toward the Cherokee women. A Seneca deputy had stalked into Chota presumably to offer the Cherokees the alternatives of joining the French or of maintaining neutrality after the fashion of the Onondaga council in New York colony.[1] Tentatively favorable answers to the overtures of Kerlerec in Louisiana and Vaudreuil in Canada had been prepared.[2] When on September 2, Andrew Lewis went into Chota town house with a final plea for aid to Virginia, a grim and hostile council refused to give him satisfaction.[3] Even the Little Carpenter, harassed by nativist distrust, French pressures, Carolina failures, and apparent Virginia perfidy, uttered harsh words against the English and demanded that the Virginian go to Fort Prince George and tell Stuart and Demere to leave the nation. Only Lewis' stern talk, reminding them of their trade dependence, brought them grudgingly to agree to welcome the Carolinians. Even so the Major and his men left Chota fearing an attack before they reached Fort Prince George.

[1] IBSC, V, 222, 230.
[2] S. C. Council Journals, 1756, p. 386; O'Callaghan, *op. cit.*, X, 592.
[3] Saunders, *op. cit.*, V, 612–14.

However, at Keowee a far different disposition prevailed. Bad talk which had flared in mid-August had died down. The presence of two hundred English soldiers was a damper, but even more important was Lyttelton's acceptance of Wawhatchee's bid for recognition as a power independent of Chota. Lyttelton had invited the Lower Towns' First Warrior to Charlestown. To discredit Chota and to build confidence in themselves, the Lower Towns headmen reported the Overhill bad talk to Demere. When arrogant Creek emissaries, bearing anti-English talk, loitered on the outskirts of Keowee, the Keowees asked Demere to make a demonstration of Cherokee-English solidarity.[4] Demere paraded his red-coated troops to Tomatly Old Fields where they marched around the startled Creeks and fired volleys answered by the swivel guns of the brave fort across the river. The delighted Keowees told Demere that if the Overhills became hostile, the Lower Towns would divide the nation. When in the quiet hours of the night in Keowee town house the undaunted Creeks proffered assistance in destroying the English troops, the Cherokees refused.[5] In the anti-English mood of Chota, the Lower Towns saw an opportunity to slip from under Overhill dominance.

Already the Lower Towns had responded to the Virginia appeal. Twenty of their men under the leadership of Estatoe warrior Seroweh had left with Richard Pearis to fight the French on the Monongahela.[6] That only ten more joined Lewis was occasioned in part by the opposition of Estatoe trader Beamer, who objected to losing his customers in the hunting season, and in part by the intentions of many to go with Wawhatchee to Charlestown.[7] They were not, however, the four hundred warriors Attakullaculla had promised Byrd and Randolph in the spring. Young Colonel Washington, riding through the autumn color in southwestern Virginia to greet the long-awaited Cherokee aux-

---

4 IBSC, V, 225.

5 Koontz, *op. cit.*, 1107–1109.

6 S. C. Council Journals, 1756, pp. 384–85.

7 IBSC, V, 215; VI, 31–32. Brock, *op. cit.*, II, 555.

iliaries, was dismayed when he met Lewis and his little band coming up the path.[8]

As Lewis trekked back to Virginia, Wawhatchee with Tistoe, headman of Keowee, and two hundred Lower Towns folk went joyfully to Charlestown where Lyttelton treated them to the greatest martial welcome Cherokees had ever received. The uniformed Charlestown militia regiment lined Broad Street. The Carolina horse paraded, and formations of red-coated regulars volleyed salutes. Answering the French threat in the nation, Lyttelton demonstrated the might which supported the wilderness garrisons. Wawhatchee had come to town to be wooed and won, and he did not hesitate to point up his accessibility by tales of Chota correspondence with the French and of Creek bad talks. When Lyttelton complained that Cherokee marauders annoyed the Long Canes settlers, the Conasatchee warrior promised to restrain his young men, and when asked to send warriors to Virginia, he said he had already done so. Pleased, Lyttelton assented to his every demand. When the warrior complained that three meals a day were insufficient to appease the irregular appetites of Indians, he made food available at all times.[9] A demand for weapons and a horse he likewise fulfilled. And not yet attuned to the trading interests' pressure, he heaped sufficient presents on the red men to supply two or three traders' stores for a year: white linen shirts; blankets; scissors; needles; buttons by the gross; yard upon yard of duffels; calico, linen plains, and gartering; pounds of vermilion face paint; brass wire for earrings—paraphernalia enough to dress scores of Indian dandies and their women in handsome style. Wawhatchee had demonstrated to his henchmen that he was a good provider and that following him to the English could be immediately profitable. While Charlestown felt more secure, it was a disaster for Chota and in the long run for the Cherokees; for Wawhatchee neither respected the English nor had that fundamental devotion to policy which characterized the more astute Overhill leadership.

[8] J. C. Fitzpatrick, ed., *The Writings of George Washington*, I, 477.
[9] S. C. Council Journals, 1756, pp. 373–74, 382–83, 385–86.

While Wawhatchee luxuriated in his Charlestown success, Demere marched toward the gloomy Overhills. On the morning of September 21 with 180 men he forded Keowee River, passed the tawny autumn cornfields of the village, and followed the rocky path over Tomassee Mountain to Stecoe Old Fields. By-passing the Middle Settlements, he marched by the shortest route to the wide flatlands of the Valley. On the twenty-seventh by swift-flowing Hiwassee River he met the Old Raven of Hiwassee in the last conference that staunch friend of the English was to have with an agent of the Great King. For a generation in times of trouble the Carolina traders and authorities had relied on him, and he had never failed them. Now he listened quietly while Demere reported that Pennsylvania Shawnees had deserted the French and had made a treaty with Sir William Johnson. Then in awareness that both the Ohio and southern Shawnees schemed at Chota in the French interest, he reported the hostile talk of the Overhills, the undercurrents of bad feeling in the Lower Towns, and that an important delegation had left Great Tellico for Fort Toulouse. Even so, he perhaps did not know the full extent of French John's intrigue with Old Hop and that an Overhill mission had gone to Detroit. Yet he was a Cherokee and apprehensive that the English should be building another fort in the nation. But that prospect was not to trouble him for long. In three months he was dead.

On the twenty-ninth the redcoats marched by Great Tellico. No welcoming delegation came from that sullen and silent town, rumored to be seeking a French fort and perhaps fearful that punishment was at hand. Only when the soldiers encamped three miles beyond did the once regal Ammonscossittee and his wife, who, working in their fields, had looked up in surprise to see the military and their train of pack horses filing past, appear bearing a gift of squashes. With them came the Tellico headmen. Demere, chiding them for their pro-French activity, accepted their invitation to stay over a day to listen to the talks they would give. The next morning, while his cooks prepared a sumptuous repast, the Captain listened to the Tellicoes repudiate hostile

88

intentions and profess hatred of the Shawnees. But the details of Shawnee perfidy and Tellico good will Demere never heard; for the conference ended abruptly with a message from the Little Carpenter denouncing the Tellicoes as evil and unauthorized to treat. It ordered the Tellicoes to break off their talks and come to Tomatly with Demere where they would hear the Little Carpenter and Old Hop speak for them. Leaving his guests to eat their dinner without their hosts, Demere put his men into immediate movement.

Up the path four miles the Little Carpenter approached on horseback with a great number of headmen and warriors who came to greet the long-awaited Carolinians. On nearing Tomatly, Demere ordered his swivel guns fired in salute. Cherokees hoisted the English colors to the top of the town house, and the Captain commanded his men to attention. According to Demere:

> Old Hop in the midst of two hundred warriors was at a little distance all painted and dressed in their best. He sent two warriors to me who desired me to alight from my horse. They supporting me under each arm carrying me to Old Hop. We embraced each other lovingly and many compliments passed one to another.[10]

There was no hint here of deep intrigue and bitter doubt, only the Oriental urbanity of the Fire King extending his people's courtesies to an ally who came at the head of a force not to be trifled with.

On October 2 formal talks took place in Chota town house. Demere spoke eloquently to allay Indian fears and suspicions. His men, he said, had no hostile intent and their delay had been due merely to a change of governors. The English force, though the largest ever seen in the Cherokee towns, was the smallest possible for the task. It came not in treachery as the French and Shawnees alleged, but to give the Overhill women and children the protection Chota had asked. The Cherokees should not trust the French; for, as they all knew, the French could not supply their needs. Only the English could do that. The Overhills must

[10] IBSC, V, 239, 241, 248.

not allow the French to build a fort at Great Tellico; for French and English would destroy each other's trade, and the Cherokees would be left without goods of any kind. He was authorized by the Great King, their father, to renew the ancient friendship and to protect them from the greedy French who desired their lands. Wishing to capitalize upon the fears of those Cherokees who distrusted the Shawnees, he made no mention of Johnson's treaty with the Susquehanna Shawnees.

Old Hop, conferring briefly with the other headmen, decided to strike immediately for bargaining supremacy. The Carolinians, he said, should build not one but two forts that there might be three forts, one Virginian and two Carolinian, all within gunshot sound of each other. Possibly in this preposterous request the headman was merely softening the soldier up; for, failing to evoke a favorable response, he next chided Demere for not having brought the presents required when coming on a peace mission. Touching the central problem, he pointed out the naked condition of his countrymen and asked that Carolina maintain trading posts at her forts to supply the Indians when the traders could not. Apparently if he was unable to induce Virginia or the French to provide the means of cracking the Carolina traders' monopoly, he would use the Carolina government for that purpose. In conclusion he asked that Demere give a bag of powder and a bag of bullets to each Overhill town.

The Fire King's demands forced Demere's hand. He gave the desired ammunition from his slender resources. Then to appease the dissident Tellicoes, the Fire King graciously presented them with two bags of the powder, remarking as he did so that the French had never treated them as well. The meeting broke up with the Indians in a joyful mood, even the Tellicoes proclaiming it a great occasion. But Demere went back to his camp to ponder what might be brewing in the wilderness around him.

It soon developed that harmony between the English and the Overhills would be more easily kept than harmony among the English. Demere and his engineer, William de Brahm, disagreed violently over the fort site Pearson had selected. De Brahm chose another a mile away which, according to Demere, was a dismal place at a fork in the river. Only the intervention of Old Hop and the Little Carpenter, who decided for the Pearson site, terminated the dispute. The two British officials were to be at loggerheads for the next three months.

The presence of Demere's force and its immediate settling down to work represented a triumph for the Little Carpenter. The bad mood in which he had confronted Lewis early in the month evaporated. He turned his back on Virginia and planned a war party to ambush French bateaux on the Mississippi. It was his device to block a French *rapprochement*. Before he left he assured Demere that no French fort would be built in the nation. He was confident of his hold on the Chota council, for he said that if on his warpath he met any of the Tellico emissaries to the French he would kill them. Demere began to perceive something of the Little Carpenter's stature. "He is," he wrote Lyttelton, "a very great man in this nation and what he says is law." Certainly the great majority of the Overhills now accepted his policy as an accomplished fact and quietly went off on their winter hunts, indicating that they, too, believed the French negotiation a false move. Old Hop was left alone to face the uncertain events his connivance with French John might cause.

The English camp proved an irresistible attraction for those Cherokees who remained at home. Off-duty soldiers were always willing to barter, and Cherokee women did a thriving business trading pumpkins, melons, and other delicacies for ribbons, buttons, and whatever else the soldiers would offer. Old Hop ordered each town to send a canoeload of corn as a present to the officers, a welcome gift in a camp where supplies brought over the mountains dwindled rapidly.

Much to Demere's relief, Chota trader John Elliott hauled over the rough trail the cannon the expedition had left at Fort Prince George. At the fort site De Brahm, having located part of the works on a rocky rise, was blasting out a moat. Men cut logs for an extensive palisade, while around the busy scene stood a guard detail of watchful soldiers.

With the work progressing rapidly, Demere set about getting better acquainted with Old Hop. The First Man blandly admitted his correspondence with the French but insisted that he had no intention of injuring either Carolina or Virginia.[11] He was angry at trader Elliott's practices and firm in his demand that the English pay for the planting lands about the fort. Despite the English power that overawed his people he did not accept subservience to the foreigner, and Demere was to spend an anxious autumn with repercussions of the Chota French overture welling about him. He worked unceasingly to win friends among the Overhills whom he could use as agents of the English will, and many succumbed to presents, liquor, and the prestige of English confidence.

On September 23, after French John, with Old Hop's knowledge, had dispatched a Cherokee mission to Detroit, twenty or thirty Cherokees left Great Tellico for the Upper Creeks.[12] They were led by the Mankiller of Tellico. Though represented to the English as intending to thwart the French efforts among the Creeks, they were accompanied by French John and several Shawnees. It was common knowledge that they marched for Fort Toulouse. Shortly one of their number, Kenoteta, the son of the Smallpox Conjurer of Settico, returned with an alarming report. He had heard Shawnees boasting in the night that they and the Creeks and the French would attack the new English fort. Disturbing though the story was, Chota insisted that the mission went only to the Creeks and would return on October 20. But soon the Little Carpenter returned from downriver, saying that the omens were bad. By October 29, the mission unreported, he was telling Demere that he feared an attack. Then he, himself, scouted down the Creek path.

Watching the situation narrowly, Demere plied Old Hop with hospitality and soon learned that he, too, feared the mission had encountered trouble. Talkative, the First Man complained of English weakness, hinted of Shawnee treachery, and babbled of

11 *Ibid.*, V, 243, 249, 251–53.
12 O'Callaghan, *op. cit.*, X, 592.

92

far-flung negotiations with the Iroquois, the Ohio Shawnees, the French, and the Creeks. He feared that at any moment these combustibles might explode. He had not been alone in these matters, he said, for the Little Carpenter had been party to everything.

November 1 passed without news of the Tellicoes. Demere watched impatiently as De Brahm toiled at setting up the endless lines of palisades at the rocky fort site. By then, however, Old Hop and the Little Carpenter had regained their composure and tried to convince Demere that Chota had withdrawn from the French negotiation. They said that if the French attacked, the Overhills would support the English, and Demere soon became confident that the mission was an enterprise of Tellico alone. He even thought his position strong enough to permit him to insist on satisfaction for the murder of one Thompson, trader Elliott's assistant, who had quarreled with a Cherokee girl in Elliott's store and had been savagely assaulted by her friends. Osteneco, who, now that the Virginia project had failed, courted Carolina, warned that the murderer was Old Hop's relative; and Demere, suddenly aware of the meaning of blood ties among the Cherokees, stayed his hand.

Early in November, Demere learned that some of the Mankiller's party had gone to New Orleans. Old Hop professed ignorance. Probing, Demere gained information that the Mankiller had induced the French to establish a trading settlement at Hiwassee Old Fields, only a few miles from Great Tellico, and that the Tellicoes would winter hunt toward the Creeks to meet the returning New Orleans delegation.

Old Hop began to understand the realities which accepting English protection required of him and his people. Under Demere's pressure he became morose. He said that in the spring he had a foreboding that something bad would happen, that now he was improperly informed of what the Tellicoes did among the French. Sending his wife to Tellico to pick up the gossip, he learned that Lantagnac, a former Carolina trader of French extraction, and one Brown, the mixed-blood son of a Creek trader, would handle the French trade. To Captain Stuart he talked bitterly of Shawnee deceit and insisted that the Mankiller had exceeded his authority. When Demere asked him to seize Lantagnac, the old man promised to deliver to the English all Frenchmen who came near.[13]

Demere thought that if he could wipe out Tellico, he could stop the French negotiation, but the project collapsed when the Captain learned that the Tellicoes had relatives in all the other towns who were bound to avenge them. He was relieved when the Old Warrior of Tomatly reported that few Tellicoes liked the French, and he was content to believe that the great French conspiracy involved merely a handful of malcontents.[14]

But on December 7 the Mankiller himself arrived in Chota. To allay suspicion Old Hop invited the English officers to hear his report. Demere, knowing there would also be private talks, asked Osteneco to keep him informed. The Mankiller, introduced by Old Hop as his personal messenger to the Creeks, presented a peace talk from the Gun Merchant, now officially a friend of the English, who sent the Cherokee Fire King "a prick of tobacco" and a belt of white wampum. Old Hop then blandly dismissed his English guests. Osteneco remained. The Mankiller now communicated a talk to Old Hop from the commander of Fort Toulouse and a Creek proposal for a Cherokee-Creek-Choctaw alliance against the Chickasaws. The Creeks, he said, were strongly anti-English. Amazed and disquieted, Osteneco bitterly accused Old Hop of making policy without consulting his council. Old Hop quickly changed the subject, and Osteneco left him in disgust. Osteneco suspected that the Fire King had become somewhat tortuously involved in an intrigue which might backfire.

Demere's probings into what he considered a deep-seated anti-English conspiracy, headed by the Little Carpenter and Old Hop, revealed the Mankiller's intention to return to the French, and that the French would join the Creeks and come up the river to

---

[13] IBSC, V, 87, 252, 259–60, 263–66, 269–72, 275–76, 279.
[14] R. Demere, Journal, Nov. 25, 1756, Loudoun Papers.

attack the English. But Nancy Butler, a mixed-blood employed by Demere to buy corn for the garrison, told him that the Old War Woman of Chota had heard Old Hop mutter, "Who would have thought that it would come to this; must we then throw away our white men at last?"[15] Apparently the Fire King, having turned to the French to counter the English trade monopoly, was fearful that the Mankiller would bring down a holocaust. But there was no doubt that under the Fire King's policy the nation was dividing into pro-French and pro-English camps and that, having countenanced French John's machinations, Old Hop had been forced to throw his protective mantle over the pro-French party even though that group threatened disaster to his and the Little Carpenter's objectives. His position with the English had been weakened, and he had deep cause for worry.

Meanwhile, full of foreboding, Osteneco informed Demere of the transactions in Old Hop's house after the Captain had been dismissed. Self-righteously he declared that the French would soon appear and that all the Overhills except himself would join their cause. He urged the Captain to send at once to Virginia and Carolina for reinforcements.[16]

In the mounting tension the English force threatened to disintegrate. Since November 1, Demere and De Brahm, his engineer, had hardly been on speaking terms. Frightened at the possibility of attack, De Brahm had gone to live with Indian friends at Tomatly, the Little Carpenter's and Osteneco's town, where he thought he would be safe. Determined not to linger in the nation, he thought to speed the work by telling Demere's provincials that when the fort was completed, they could go home with him. Since the troops were needed for the garrison, Demere's council of war agreed that De Brahm had exceeded his authority. The Captain then paraded the provincials, read them the articles of war, and informed them they could only be discharged on order of the Governor. Captain Postell of the provincials, determined to go to Charlestown to urge the case

15 IBSC, V, 296–98, 303.
16 Letter of Judd's Friend, Dec. 13, 1756, Loudoun Papers.

of his men, said that orders or not, he would leave when De Brahm gave the cue.

On December 15 the return of the Little Carpenter from a brief hunting trip clarified the situation. Where Old Hop had fumbled, the Little Carpenter acted with decision to assert the official pro-English position of the Chota council. Accused by Demere of complicity in the French negotiation, he faced the commander with dignity and replied:

> I am not a boy but the headman of this nation. I give talks to the Governor of Chota [Old Hop] and not he to me. My mind has always been straight. I always think one way and now I take you by the hand and you hear what I have to say. If I do not perform it, when I come back make me a liar.[17]

With these bold words he left.

When on the sixteenth Old Hop came into Fort Loudoun where the Little Carpenter already had talked to Demere, his Right Hand Man sternly accused him of corresponding with the French. Old Hop answered evasively and scoffed at Carolina. Thereupon the Little Carpenter asked that they be closeted together for a while. Left to themselves, the two men engaged in heated discussion for an hour or more but finally agreed that in nine days the Little Carpenter, accompanied by Osteneco, should start for Charlestown to assure Lyttelton of Cherokee allegiance and to press for improvements in the trade. Whatever Old Hop had expected from the French negotiation, he did not intend that it should destroy the English alliance.

Naturally the French had hoped that the plotting of French John and the Shawnees with the susceptible Tellicoes would break the alliance, as appears from the stories of the Fort Toulouse and Detroit missions. In September the Mankiller of Tellico, who had designs of his own, had led the Cherokee deputies directly to Peter Chartier's Shawnee town among the Abeikas in north central Alabama and at Chartier's had given the Shaw-

17 IBSC, V, 303, 308–10.

nees a painted tomahawk he had carried from Tellico. "When the Shawnees saw it they were pleased for they knew what it was, vizt.: to go to war against the English." Escorted by some of Chartier's Shawnees, the Cherokees went on to consult with the Upper Creeks. But for the opposition of two of their number, the principal Upper Creek headmen, fearful of English retaliation for the murder of two whites on the Ogeechee and primed with French propaganda, would have taken up the hatchet then and there. At the Tukabatchis other Creeks, hearing the pro-French talk, were only restrained from war by old Brisket, reputedly one hundred and forty years old. The retired king rose from his couch and, sticking his hair full of turkey buzzard feathers, came into the council and delivered a talk so strong that it frightened all thought of war out of the belligerents.

The Shawnees then escorted the Tellicoes to Fort Toulouse where the Shawnees delivered the painted hatchet the Mankiller had given to them. The French commander "cried for joy," for the Shawnees told him the Cherokees were ready to turn against the English. But the Shawnees had been somewhat precipitate; the majority of the Tellico delegation was more conservative than the Mankiller. They had come to sound out the French for a trade and to urge them to visit the nation. The Frenchman strove to commit them to belligerence. "For many years," he said, "[the Cherokees] had been upon the wrong path," and he was sorry to see them go astray. "The Carolina people had conjurers among them that would send up different kinds of sickness . . . from which proceeds the decrease of their people . . . . With several hundred English in their towns their condition is now worse . . . . [The English] would abuse their warriors and debauch their women . . . . They brought huge loads of handcuffs and irons for their feet."

Having run the gamut of atrocity stories, the Frenchman pulled a paper from his pocket and hinted that his spies had informed him of English designs. Even the Catawbas, he said, worried that so many Englishmen should be near Chota, "and they were listening to hear [the English] guns fired and then they would conclude their brothers in Chota dead."[18] Then he urged the deputies to go to New Orleans to make a treaty with Kerlerec. After a feast and the presentation of a matchcoat, a shirt and a gun, powder and ball, to each of the deputies, the Frenchman spoke again. He promised to dispatch an officer to study Cherokee trade needs and to show the Indians how the English imposed on them. As soon as the deputies returned from New Orleans, he would meet them in the woods with a great supply of low-priced goods to be handled by Antoine Lantagnac, currently a French agent among the Cherokees.[19]

The Mankiller optimistically agreed to send one hundred pack horses to transport the goods and deputized five of his party to go to New Orleans. He then returned toward Chartier's town by way of the Oakchoys. There he may have heard rumors that Creeks had gone against Carolina and Georgia, or soon would go, and discussed with the Gun Merchant the late developments in Creek-Chickasaw relations.[20]

The brave Chickasaws, staunch friends of the English, were, that autumn, in a fair way to have themselves exterminated. All summer they had annoyed the communications of the intriguing Tellicoes, Shawnees, and Creeks. In August or September they were suspected of having attacked a French and Shawnee party going to the Cherokees. In October, believing that the Cherokees had killed three of their people, they sent a war party against their old allies. Fortunately the commander of a Chickasaw-bound Carolina pack train dissuaded them. Firmly resisting the French line, the Chickasaws threatened war on all who succumbed to it. They warned the pro-French Creeks, who promptly accepted the challenge and killed three Chickasaws.[21] Rumor ran through the forests that the Cherokees would join the Creeks in wiping out the Chickasaws.[22]

---

[18] *Ibid.*, V, 285, 346.
[19] Paris, France, Archives Nationales Colonies, A.C. C13 39:37; IBSC, V, 277.
[20] IBSC, V, 300.
[21] Old Warrior of Tomatly, Nov. 25, 1756, Loudoun Papers.
[22] IBSC, V, 300.

Oconostota's commission from Kerlerec, governor of Louisiana, 1761.

Courtesy of Glen Drayton Grimke

James Glen

The Mankiller had been but a few days upon the path to Chartier's when he was recalled to Fort Toulouse to confer with a Choctaw delegation which had arrived too late to join in a French-projected conference with the Creeks, Cherokees, and Shawnees.[23] The largest body of French Indian allies, the Choctaws urged the Cherokees to join a coalition which would send the three greatest southern Indian nations against Carolina. The French believed that such an alliance if properly employed could destroy the southern English colonies; but the Mankiller of Tellico was a weak reed upon which to lean for such an enterprise. He lacked the power to commit his nation.

With Choctaw blandishments ringing in his ears, the Mankiller returned to Chartier's town to await the report of the New Orleans delegation. There the Shawnees prevailed upon him to wear next his heart a war belt of their make.[24] They gave him a war hatchet and won his promise to strike the English, and he sent runners to Great Tellico advising his people to meet him in the woods for the fall hunt. Finally, after waiting a month between Tellico and the Abeikas, the Mankiller returned to the nation without either the hundred horseloads of French goods he had expected or news of the New Orleans negotiation.

The New Orleans party, escorted down the Alabama River by Lantagnac and several Shawnees, consisted of Willinawaw of Toquo's son; the Warrior of Tellico, Ammonscossittee's brother-in-law; and a young woman proficient in Shawnee. At Mobile they were joyously received into the brick-walled fort and entertained after the French fashion for a few days. Then they departed by ship for the Louisiana capital, Lantagnac hastening ahead to apprise Kerlerec of their coming.

On November 15 in New Orleans, Kerlerec and an impressive array of uniformed officials received the Cherokees at Government House. A great heap of presents charmed the Indian eyes. Kerlerec's speech of greeting followed the usual French line: the English professing friendship lured Cherokees to their deaths

23 Old Warrior of Tomatly, Nov. 25, 1756, Loudoun Papers.
24 S. C. Council Journals, 1757, p. 44.

in Charlestown where the Carolina Governor mixed poison in their drink. He alluded, of course, to the frequent deadly illnesses which fell upon the Indians as they returned from visits to the Carolina capital. Laboring this theme in detailed and melodramatic variation, Kerlerec roared to a climax and thrust a war hatchet toward the Shawnees. Those bellwethers each in turn grasped it and shouted hatred of the English. Kerlerec then rapidly passed it to each Cherokee. Then he referred to the Cherokees who had in former years died of disease upon the Carolina path and exhorted the deputies to vengeance.

But the Cherokees were responsible men and bargainers. Willinawaw's son confronted Kerlerec with the all-important question: Should the Cherokees drive the English away, from whence would come the goods they needed? Kerlerec assured them of a French supply; but when a French officer proposed war on the Chickasaws, Willinawaw's son refused.[25] For several days the talks continued, while the Cherokees, so desperately did isolated Louisiana seek allies, were the heroes of the town. When they appeared in the streets, crowds formed and people invited them into their homes to give them presents. At last the discussions reached a point at which Kerlerec thought he could trust the deputies with a treaty negotiation. On November 26 he presented a parchment listing twelve articles. Should Chota accept it, the Cherokee nation was to release all French prisoners, send negotiators to Canada, make war upon the Chickasaws, eject the English, destroy English forts, and send war parties against the English frontiers. The French would establish a trade and, after the Cherokees had driven out the English, would supply them with arms and ammunition. When the deputies demanded an immediate supply of ammunition, Kerlerec demurred. They should have nothing until he had definite assurances they had made war upon the English "and . . . had made some coup d'etat of note upon them." The Indians made the Governor promise that immediately upon the return of their deputies from Canada in July, 1757, he would open up a trade.[26] That left the French-

25 IBSC, V, 272, 295–96; VI, 86–88.

100

man but seven months to inform the home government and receive from them a supply of trade goods, a precarious margin in view of the British command of the sea.

After a few more days in New Orleans, the deputies set out on the long trip home via Mobile, Fort Toulouse, and Chartier's home. Oppressed by the need of tangibles to show their pragmatic countrymen, they repeatedly demanded of Lantagnac how soon presents and ammunition would be sent. Lantagnac always replied that those articles would only become available after Cherokees had brought English scalps to the Alabama fort.[27] The deputies did not reach Great Tellico until late in March.

Meanwhile, perhaps accompanied by the Seneca Great Elk who was much in and out of the nation, the mission sent with French John's letter to Detroit had conferred with Du May, commander of that post.[28] As had the New Orleans deputies, they warily probed into trade possibilities, suggesting that they represented Chota. Alliance, they said, could only be had when the French definitely opened a trade in the nation. The French, of course, could not produce the trade. By January, Great Elk had returned to the Overhills.

[26] James Sullivan, A. C. Flick, A. W. Lauber, et al., eds., *The Papers of Sir William Johnson*, IX, 569–73.

[27] IBSC, VI, 86.

[28] O'Callaghan, *op. cit.*, X, 592.

CHAPTER EIGHT

A Winter Lull

WINTER NORMALLY BROUGHT peace and quiet to the Cherokee villages. The old holed up in their close ovenlike hothouses while most of the able-bodied dispersed into the forests to live upon the deer. But the winter of 1756–57 was an exception. Uneasiness over what portended from their French missions kept hostile Tellicoes and cautious river townsmen close to home. The Mankiller of Tellico stalked the neighborhood of Chota giving bad talks. Old Hop worried. Demere's informant, half-blood Nancy Butler, said the Mankiller had returned from his mission not only to report to Old Hop but to prove his fidelity to the French by taking an English scalp. Old Hop's wife, fondling the English beads Nancy had given her, spoke her and her husband's distrust of the Tellico warrior and burst into tears as she recounted the evil intended against the English if the Mankiller prevailed.

In late December, as Demere and Stuart contemplated their precarious situation, they mounted cannon on the half-built walls of the fort. With the provincials restive and mutinous, they flogged a sergeant with two hundred lashes for saying he would leave when De Brahm discharged him.[1] The frightened De Brahm surreptitiously departed one night accompanied by provincial Captain Postell to plead his and the provincials' case in Charlestown.

At this juncture John Allen brought Chota fresh overtures

[1] IBSC, V, 310–11.

from Dinwiddie. The Virginia Governor had at last decided to try bargaining a garrison in Lewis' fort for four hundred Cherokee warriors.[2] As bait he sent arms and ammunition to Augusta County and outfitted one of the Indians who had ventured north with Pearis in the best raiment Virginia could offer.[3] Allen, accompanied by the handsomely attired Cherokee, had orders to contact Osteneco and induce him to fulfill his Williamsburg promises. Dinwiddie prodded Lyttelton to co-operate by sending him Lewis' report of Chota's hostility and the Carolina traders' obstruction.[4] Washington urged the Catawbas to use their influence on the Cherokees.[5] But Dinwiddie's message had made no mention of the all-important trade.

Chota remained cold. It answered that its men were now needed to protect the Carolina garrison; that most of them were busy with their winter hunts; that the Little Carpenter had business in Charlestown; that later, perhaps, Virginia's needs might be considered. So spoke "Connecughte" (Old Hop), "Aculla-culla" (the Little Carpenter), Willinawaw (the Prince of Toquo), Osteneco (Judd's Friend), The Old Bark (Osteneco's brother), and "two more old men." Oconostota and Long Jack's brother of Tanase were absent, probably hunting. Osteneco, as an official link with Virginia, added his own exoneration of Old Hop, blaming Tellico and the Shawnees for the summer trouble. But in a private message to his Virginia friend John McNeil, he hinted that Carolina obstructed, and that Old Hop was a double-dealer. The Fire King's talk, he said, was like a smoke that went up crookedly.

Plainly the Carolina trading interest, aided by the sympathetic Stuart and Demere, who apparently had private understanding with Charlestown merchants, and by the Little Carpenter's perhaps by now not disinterested determination to hold his people to the English alliance, had scored against intercolonial needs.

[2] Brock, *op. cit.*, II, 292–93, 517.

[3] S. M. Hamilton, *Letters to Washington*, I, 379–80.

[4] Brock, *op. cit.*, II, 556.

[5] Fitzpatrick, *op. cit.*, I, 486–87.

Allen was left to make a private effort, glinting Virginia presents about among the laity, none of whom responded.

With the Virginia business disposed of, the Little Carpenter, accompanied by the dubious Osteneco, attendants, and Captain Stuart, departed on December 27 for Charlestown.

Old Hop and his councilors now had the problem of circumventing the intransigent Mankiller; for despite Chota's coolness toward him, he had not abandoned the French cause. On Christmas Day, Old Caesar of Chatuga told Demere that the French were expected in Tellico any day with a host of Choctaws, Shawnees, and maybe Creeks whom the Mankiller proclaimed already at war with the English. On January 2, Old Caesar came again to the English camp, escorting Kelly and Leaper, two Tellico pack-horse traders. Warned that the Mankiller sought English scalps, they had taken refuge in Old Caesar's house. It was rumored that Tellicoes had attacked trader Dougherty at Hiwassee, that the Seneca Great Elk had waylaid the Chota-Tellico path to take an English scalp.

Demere moved his troops into the unfinished fort, which he named Fort Loudoun in honor of the current British commander in North America, increased the guard, and sent a warning to Dougherty that white men should avoid the Tellico path. He then tried winning the Mankiller with kindness. At first the Tellico headman refused Demere's invitation to the fort, saying frankly that his thoughts were bad. The Captain persisted. Shortly, Old Hop sent word that in the Settico town house the Mankiller had proposed killing all the traders, and that even then he was approaching with 30 men in a bad mood to make mischief at the Fort. Old Hop himself was hurrying over with 120 warriors to deal with the situation.

But Demere had no need of Old Hop's aid. The Mankiller came alone, "painted all black," and "looking cross and illnatured." The Captain greeted him cordially and promised that, if he came into friendship with the English, all would be forgotten. Ostracized in the river towns, the Indian found the white man's friendliness soothing. "I know," he said, "I was hated and

104

disliked by everyone in the nation which has made me so uneasy I did not know what to do with myself. I was a lost man but now I begin to have another way of thinking by the good talk I have heard."

When the Mankiller assured Demere that his young men, who were near, bore no arms, Demere invited them into the fort for dinner. Old Hop and his 120 gunmen came also. After dinner talks took place before the crowd. The Mankiller insisted that he had not gone to the French without authorization, that Old Hop had approved. Sketching a portrait of himself as an injured innocent, he even cleared his friends, the Shawnees. Intense silence greeted the Mankiller's statement. Not even Old Hop protested. The next move was Demere's, and the Captain simply invited the distressed Indian to stay the night. That evening Demere felt he made progress. When the Mankiller complained that the English gave presents to all the Overhill towns but Tellico, Demere offered to send presents to Tellico if Tellico would drop its French correspondence and the Mankiller would tell the truth about his autumn activities. The Mankiller responded with copious confirmation of what Demere had picked up bit by bit. He even promised to surrender to the English the French traders when they arrived. Penitent, he took Kelly and Leaper, only a week before refugees from doom at his hands, under his protection.

Demere's adept handling of the Mankiller relieved the Chotas. The Captain soon put them further at ease by refusing Old Hop's suggestion that he punish Tellico by denying them trade. Indeed, he defended the intransigent town and declared that punishment would only cause the Tellicoes to prey on traders carrying goods to the other Overhills. The Tellicoes, he said, should be treated as a father treats a child distant from him and in danger: as he loved the child, he was bound to help him. Very much moved by this approach, the headmen said it was the attitude they wanted him to have.

Privately distrusting the Mankiller, Demere dared not leave the Tellicoes to the bad man's manipulation. He deputized Lieutenant Wall to go to the rebellious town with a gift of goods purchased from trader Leaper and inform the Tellicoes of his good will.

Wall's appearance at Tellico was a great occasion. Arriving on January 10, he was the Mankiller's guest at an elegant dinner. The next morning he gave Demere's talk in the crowded town house where the Tellicoes listened intently to its conventional and homely phrases. A sentimental people, the Tellicoes were swayed by Wall's reminder of their long association with the English. Practical opportunists, they mellowed at the sight of the presents heaped before the speaker. The Mankiller, holding the white beads of peace and sincerity, replied eloquently avowing a change in his people's dispositions. Once "the very breath which came out of his people's hearts had been infected." Now, he said, their hearts were good. Denied presents, his people had doubted the English; but now that Demere noticed them, "they saw their error in going to the French. They would now be friends of the English and go to the fort to give Captain Demere a long talk."

While the Tellicoes went about in a glow of good will, Wall visited Old Caesar of Chatuga to take soundings. The old man was skeptical. He said that the French failure to send important tangibles had altered the Tellico mood; but that if the French sent a handsome present, he did not know how the Tellicoes would behave.

In the dim light of Tellico town house that evening the Mankiller entertained the Lieutenant with a dance. According to Wall:

As soon as it was dark, a drum beat in the town house and I received a message from the Mankiller to come immediately. As soon as I came there, he told me that he never danced except upon some extraordinary occasion; but as his thoughts were good and his heart was light, he would give a talk at the head of his warriors and young men. He then went out of the town house and returned in half an hour. Before he entered the town house, he gave several whoops which were answered by a number of different voices and seconded by a sort of yelling howl by every Indian in the town house.

106

The drum was immediately beat and the Mankiller came in almost quite naked and painted in streaks of white all over his face and body. He was followed by fifty-seven of his warriors and young men and they were all painted in the same manner which is among the Indians a token of peace and fellowship. They continued to dance in their usual manner round a large fire about an hour and then were joined in the dance by every man in the town house and continued dancing three hours without interruption. They then ceased and the masquerade came in which I cannot possibly give you a description of; after that was over the Mankiller ordered all the young women to dance. They danced for some time and were joined by all the women in the town house.[6]

Colorful though the entertainment was, Wall nearly suffocated in the smoke, heat, and deafening noise. At two o'clock in the morning he tried to leave, but his effort only brought on a flood of oratory. Not until an hour or more later could he get away. The ecstatic Tellicoes danced the night through.

In the morning the Mankiller told Wall that he would kill Lantagnac if the Frenchman came with presents. But the Lieutenant had seen and heard enough to report to Demere that lack of trade goods was the fundamental reason for dissatisfaction in Tellico and Chatuga.

Demere's success with the Mankiller, having eased the possibility that Tellico unrest would become outright rebellion, won the Captain a great tribute from Old Hop. Invited to Chota for a ceremonial talk, as he passed Toquo, 150 warriors standing on a hill fired a salute. At Chota over 400 warriors were assembled to take him by the hand. In the town house Old Hop exhorted them to friendship with the English, who like themselves were "children of King George." Denouncing Peter Chartier, he warned against French propaganda; and, denying that he had approved the Mankiller's going to the French, he embraced Demere amidst the noisy acclamations of the crowd. What Old Hop probably meant by this was that he had not authorized the Mankiller's outspoken belligerence.

[6] IBSC, V, 311–14, 321, 346–47, 349–50, 353, 362–65.

Instructed by Lyttleton, Demere now strove to commit hesitant Chota to a major war effort against the French. On January 29 in Old Hop's home, holding a great war belt made for the occasion, he gave the English talk "straight and cold." He reminded them that Fort Loudoun had been built at Chota's request. Recounting the bad talk that he had heard ever since he had entered the nation, he demanded that the Cherokees prove themselves by taking the offensive. "I want some French scalps," he cried. A reward of £30 awaited every bloody trophy. Presenting Old Hop with a belt, he demanded an answer. Old Hop was cordial but not electric as he urged his people to take up the hatchet. The scalp bounty, he intimated, was too small. Oconostota responded that his men would soon go to war. However, formal council would be required to make his promise official, and Old Hop asked and received a keg of rum to facilitate deliberations.

The Tellico Mankiller also had tasted Demere's rum and had found it good. Returned from Old Hop's, Demere read a message from the bad man of Tellico requesting rum and paint. He wished to prepare himself to give a good talk to his people as a preliminary to his going out to catch Lantagnac.

The Valley too felt the English war fever. Hiwassee trader Cornelius Dougherty planned to wreck the French negotiation by plunging the Cherokees into war with the Creeks. He escorted the dead Raven's son, Moytoy, and the Black Dog of Nottely to Fort Loudoun to hear Demere's talk. In their absence, four Creeks of the band called Stinking Linguas, assisted by the Pigeon, the Raven's second son, went into Dougherty's store and kicked Dougherty's Negro assistant around. They then swaggered about Hiwassee boasting of their friendship to the French. When Moytoy returned from Fort Loudoun, heavily laden with Demere's gifts, he gave his brother a severe switching and called in the valley headmen to hear him urge war against the French.

As January ended, the only weakness in Demere's position appeared to be the fort itself. De Brahm had left the work sprawling and incomplete. Referred to by the Indians as "the fort to put horses, cows, and pigs in," it did resemble a settler's rambling, picketed farmyard and cowpen. It extended for two hundred yards along the southern bank of the Little Tennessee. De Brahm's plan had called for a log wall almost half a mile in circumference which, Demere complained, would require near four hundred defenders. Fortunately, the engineer had decamped; and Demere reduced the size of the work. Completing its hilltop citadel, he built barracks and so, finally, pulled his troops up out of the winter mud.[7]

While Demere promoted the English line among the Overhills, Lyttleton bore down on the Little Carpenter in Charlestown. Aware of the Overhills' French negotiation, he pointed out that the English navy would prevent supplies from reaching the French. In the terms of the Treaty of 1730, he demanded that the Cherokees send two hundred warriors to Virginia. Scalp bounties, he said, would make hunting the Frenchmen more profitable than hunting the deer. He offered £1,000 apiece for Lantagnac and French John alive. He also protested Wawhatchee's failure to halt depredations against the Long Canes settlers and the murder of Elliott's helper.

The Little Carpenter refused to accept the onus of the French negotiation. He blamed Great Tellico and asserted his intention of going to war against the French; but he wanted an English supply of weapons for Cherokee war parties, and he wanted trade conditions improved. Contrary to the Saluda agreement, prices were high and quality poor. Chota trader Elliott, with whom the Little Carpenter had a personal feud, refused credit to hunters and should be removed. On aid to Virginia, however, he was unenthusiastic. Warriors should go there, but decisions as to the number awaited his return from Charlestown. He preferred action in the direction of the Alabama and the Mississippi rather than toward the forks of the Ohio. Indeed he hinted that Demere and Stuart had so prevailed upon him that he would act in Carolina's interest. Such being the case, it is reasonable to suppose that he expected Carolina's reward.

[7] *Ibid.*, V, 356, 367–70, 372–74.

But Lyttelton, intent upon co-operation with Dinwiddie, asked the Little Carpenter to go directly home and aid Demere if necessary; otherwise, he was to urge the Overhills to go to Virginia. The Right Hand Man countered by asking the Governor to obtain from Dinwiddie a garrison for the Chota fort; but Lyttelton chose to ignore what was from the military point of view a wasteful enterprise.

Rebuffed, the Little Carpenter turned to matters of more moment to his people. He obtained agreements that the English would outfit Cherokee war parties and that families which lost a provider in the English service should receive a share of presents distributed to returning warriors. He then promised to curb the Lower Towns young men who annoyed the Long Canes settlers for invading their hunting grounds. Lyttelton responded with a promise to rebuke the traders for their high prices and false weights, and to put Elliott on probation of Old Hop and the Little Carpenter.

The Right Hand Man then sought to obtain from Lyttelton recognition of Chota's ascendancy in the nation. He discredited both Ammonscossittee, the Governor's first Cherokee visitor, and Wawhatchee, who, he said, was capable of "pulling and hauling white people." Lyttelton assented to bringing Tellico to terms under Chota authority by agreeing that they should have English presents only through the Little Carpenter.

On one of the conference days, the Cherokee lifted his eyes from business long enough to question the English society about him. Conveying the good wishes of the Cherokee women to the Governor, he observed to his excellency that it was customary for the Cherokees to admit women to their councils. There probably were official Cherokee women present among those who sat in the chamber as spectators, for official business appears not to have been done without them. Since the white man as well as the red was born of woman, continued the Little Carpenter, did not the white man admit women to their councils? Nonplused, the Governor mulled the question over for two or three days before he lamely came up with the answer that "the white

110

men do place confidence in their women and share their councils with them when they know their hearts are good."

The conference almost terminated in bad feeling when the Little Carpenter did not attend the appointed last day and came two hours late the next day. Piqued because the presents failed to meet his expectations, he may have intended discourtesy; when Lyttelton haughtily rebuked him, he disparaged the gifts. However, good sense prevailed. Lyttelton read aloud for all to hear the letter written at the Little Carpenter's request, rebuking the cheating traders. The Cherokee then accepted an English pipe for Old Hop, dignifiedly thanked the Governor for his hospitality, and withdrew with his following.[8]

Chota meanwhile showed no disposition to hurry warriors into the field. On February 5, Old Hop summoned Demere to hear the formal reply to his war talk on January 29. The First Man began with a list of grievances: the English had failed to pay for the extra corn lands they had taken over near the fort; the traders had failed to adhere to the price scale set at Saluda; trader Elliott had been defrauding them. Demere, hoping for the best, called in Elliott who admitted guilt on prices and that he had mixed lead in the vermilion he sold to increase its weight. The Indians had suffered bad cases of skin poisoning. Demere reprimanded him and promised to report him to the Governor.

Old Hop then called in Bullet Head to give Chota's reply to the war talk. It was brief. "Where," said Bullet Head, "is the war?" He had looked about and seen no bloodshed. Where, too, were the goods to outfit war parties? The Overhills were not yet ready to go to war. Demere returned to Fort Loudoun convinced that someone had tampered with his Indian allies. He suspected trader Elliott and the Virginian John Watts, who might have talked of a major trade from Virginia.

While Overhill hesitancy may have been caused by the English failure to supply presents and equipment, and their own determination to barter for improvements in the trade, it may also have arisen from their own estimate of their situation. The

[8] S. C. Council Journals, Feb. 1, Feb. 2, Feb. 9, Feb. 12, Feb. 17, 1757.

Tellico matter had not yet been fully resolved. The New Orleans mission had not yet returned. Should it bring Frenchmen and a French trade, there would be trouble. Moreover, the deputies on the mission were in a sense hostages for Cherokee good behavior toward the French. Until they had marched clear of the possibility of French retaliation, warlike action against the French was not feasible.

Early in February a runner brought the news to Great Tellico that the New Orleans deputies were already at Chartier's. The deputies had no Frenchmen with them, but few goods, and they reported no great armies of Frenchmen and their Indians approaching. With this turn of events came a disposition for action. On February 14 forty warriors from Chilhowee and Telassie set out for Virginia under Youghtanno. The next day Oconostota said he would go to the Middle Settlements to encourage their warriors to go to Virginia. In the Lower Towns bad talks, heard when there was yet possibility of division on the French issue, ceased. Many Indians visited Fort Prince George to profess friendship for the English.[9] The Swallow Warrior and Tacite, the Mankiller of Estatoe, readied one hundred men for the north.

Though Oconostota held back the main body of Overhills until the Little Carpenter should return, Lower Towns warriors who had gone north in the autumn under the Second Yellow Bird had by March 1 taken prisoners and scalps near Fort Duquesne.[10] Dinwiddie feted this party in Williamsburg. Late-winter blows by Cherokees and other southern Indians bred uneasiness among French Ohio River Indians and caused them to move up the Allegheny toward the Senecas.[11]

The Overhills' hesitation to flood out to war soon had its justification. In March the Mankiller of Tellico, having masqueraded all winter as Demere's friend, triumphantly announced Kerlerec's talk and treaty in Chota town house. To dramatize

[9] IBSC, V, 375–77, 381–82; VI, 1.
[10] Journals of the Executive Council of Virginia, Mar. 18, 1757.
[11] Sullivan, etc., *op. cit.*, IX, 739–40.

the news he stalked about the river towns naked except for a tattered and dirty blanket which he proclaimed to represent English treatment of his people. Outraged, his father, the Smallpox Conjurer of Settico, ordered him to leave town. The other Overhills laughed at him. Rebuffed by his countrymen he tried blackmailing Demere for £100 in presents; but Demere sent him packing. When Demere learned that the New Orleans mission had marched into Tellico with a white or French flag which they hoisted above Tellico town house, he determined to march on the unruly town and destroy it. But Tanase trader Sam Benn dissuaded him by telling him that it was customary for the Cherokees to put up a white flag when they had important news of peace. Moreover, he pointed out that the Tellicoes alone could do nothing and that their neighbors, the Chatugas, planned to take a party of Tellicoes, Chatugas, and Valley warriors southward to "spoil the French talk by making the path dark and bloody." Soon came word that Moytoy of Hiwassee and his partner, the Black Dog, had already gone southward to war.

On April 1, Old Hop sent for Demere to come to Chota to hear the French talk. The First Man gave the Captain a fair summary of what had occurred on the mission but failed to mention the French treaty. That and whatever else he had omitted Demere learned by bribing the Cherokee young woman who had accompanied the mission. What Old Hop had hoped for from the meeting was to use the French bid to spur the English into giving more presents and correcting abuses in the trade. The French treaty, however tantalizing privately, had fallen upon official deaf ears. Its promises were contingent upon anti-English action which Chota was in no position to sanction. No deputies were sent to Canada.

Pushing the French overtures into the background, Old Hop turned to a serious domestic concern: Elliott's continuing misbehavior.[12] The shrewd and unscrupulous little man was bent on salvaging his large stock of rum, which Demere in compliance with the Saluda agreement had sequestered in the late

[12] IBSC, VI, 8–10, 21–22.

113

summer at Fort Prince George. During the winter Elliott had supplied Fort Loudoun with corn, which had been transported by Indians hired with promises of rum which he did not have. He told his help that Captain Demere had his rum and that they must see him about it. Old Hop, accompanied by Oconostota, who also had a claim on Elliott's rum in a horse trade, listened while Demere patiently and humorlessly invoked the Saluda prohibition on providing the Indians with rum. Unwilling to be bilked of their pay, the Indians forced Demere to summon Elliott to the fort to vouch for their claims and then give them orders for their liquor on Ensign Boggs, now commanding Fort Prince George. Elliott's prestige among the Overhills rose appreciably from its December low.

In mid-April the Little Carpenter returned, and the warriors who had lingered at home began to move. Despite Lyttelton's request that he remain among the Overhills to encourage warriors to go to Virginia, the Little Carpenter set off down the Tennessee to waylay French bateaux on the Ohio and the Mississippi.[13] Shortly Oconostota followed him with the main force of Overhills. Even the Mankiller of Tellico, under the Little Carpenter's discipline, changed his tune and went out against the Twightwees.[14] Only secondary parties under Osteneco, who had a promise to keep, and Youghtanno's Chilhowee and Telassie men went to Virginia. The empty Virginia fort and Virginia's failure to provide a trade spoke too eloquently to the Little Carpenter of failure. The bulk of the Cherokees appearing in Virginia in 1757 were Lower Towns warriors, who under Wawhatchee's headstrong leadership pursued their own course. They may not have been unwilling to reply to Chota's harsh slights by upsetting the Overhills' bargaining position.

13 *South Carolina Gazette*, June 9, 1757.
14 IBSC, VI, 43.

CHAPTER NINE

"They Acted Like Freebooters"

IN THE SPRING AND SUMMER OF 1757, 250 or more Cherokees were among the 400 Indians who defended the Virginia frontier.[1] They came in seven or eight bands numbering from 13 to 60 warriors. The largest group was Wawhatchee's Lower Townsmen which included the band of Swallow Warrior from Estatoe. From the Overhills came Youghtanno's band, followed in June by Osteneco's. There were few from the Middle Settlements. The bands usually subdivided into war parties of 13 or 14 Indians, which, joined with an equal number of soldiers under a lieutenant, composed a forest patrol. Most operated from Fort Cumberland far out on the Virginia-Maryland frontier. They patrolled the south branch of the Potomac or out the north branch and over the mountains into the neighborhood of Fort Duquesne.

Their presence in Virginia was not an unmixed blessing. Early in April, Dinwiddie received an anguished letter from Clement Reed, justice of the peace in Lunenburg County. He had found 128 angry Cherokees unexpectedly encamped upon his place. Led by Wawhatchee, and accompanied by Richard Smith as interpreter and Pearis as guide, they behaved barbarically and terrified the justice and his family into living almost as slaves for the duration of the Indian stay. The justice dared not refuse their demand that he write an insolent letter for them to Dinwiddie. He, however, tossed in an account of his own trials:

[1] Koontz, *op. cit.*, 1353.

He [Wawhatchee] further ordered me not to fail to inform you that the presents wrote for he expected would be sent up to Winchester soon, and he made me promise that they should, and seeing that I have promised it and the appearance of the Indians at my house . . . equipped for war when I had only five white men and ten negroes at home and unprepared would have made Alexander the Great have promised it . . . . For, sir, the evening before they had their grand council, they tomahawked, ripped up the bowels, and scalped a fellow in the yard. . . . they gave me leave to bury him after which myself and the whole family behaved with the greatest order and decorum towards them, granted them all they asked and yielded to every demand . . . . However by our passive obedience and non-resistance after their eating and destroying 1000 lb. of pork and bread and meat in proportion in about thirty hours they were persuaded to march toward Bedford Court House for their presents. But in their way, following the practice and lewd example of their leader, two of them ravished a girl of about 12 or 13 years old, they met on the road five or six miles from my house and tore her in a manner too indecent to mention and visited every plantation within three or four miles of the road plundering the plantations and frightening the inhabitants . . . in short, sir, they acted like freebooters in an enemy country and on our court day in the morning . . . . crowds of people came to my house and solicited me to do something . . . . they appeared enraged and ready to take up arms . . . . At Lunenburg Court House they [the Indians] mutinied and they were for returning. Smith prevailed upon them to stay there until I could be sent for. I went and pacified them. I prevailed on them to consent to go to Winchester to Colonel Washington . . . . they should have their presents, they should be provided for according to treaty, should be well used.[2]

The cause of the Cherokee insolence at Reed's was the Justice's failure to provide the presents they had expected. The main store of Virginia Indian presents lay at Bedford Court House, convenient to the Overhills' route to the Potomac. The Lower Townsmen had traveled a more easterly route. There was nothing for them at Lunenburg. Disappointed, Wawhatchee, following the usual Cherokee pattern in such instances, appears

2 Amherst Papers, Apr. 5, 1757, B.P.R.O., W.O. 34/35.

to have given his following free license. The Indian they murdered on Justice Reed's lawn was a Chickasaw who had rebuked them for their excesses.[3]

Reed blamed Pearis for the trouble.[4] The Virginia council had employed Pearis to meet approaching bands of Cherokees and to guide them in an orderly fashion to Winchester. But at Justice Reed's Pearis, absorbed in the charms of a young Catawba woman, was indifferent to Cherokee excesses. Very likely he felt very much as the Cherokees did.

On receipt of Reed's letter, Dinwiddie sent the Justice orders to raise the county militia and "in a mild method" to round up the Indians and send them down to Williamsburg.[5] But by the time the order reached Reed, the Indians were well advanced toward Winchester by way of Bedford. Though at Bedford they had received "a considerable present," at Winchester they expected more.[6] Captain Mercer, Washington's deputy, had nothing. Angry, Wawhatchee refused the wampum Mercer held out at the end of his talk and stalked away, leaving Swallow Warrior to bully the Captain and to threaten Cherokee desertion to the French. The distraught Mercer, risking everything upon his own word, urged them again to take the wampum and promised that he would have presents when they returned from war. Swallow quieted and said that he personally did not want anything but that his men had followed him because he had promised presents, and he was angry that the Governor had made a liar of him amongst his own men.

Wawhatchee strode about Winchester demanding that Dinwiddie himself come to the frontier to appease him. Mercer, almost frantic with fear that the whole Cherokee nation would go over to the French, lifting English scalps on the way, wrote Washington who was at Winchester, urging him to send presents immediately. But presents were not to be had.[7] Everything

[3] Pennsylvania *Archives*, Ser. 1, III, 175–76.
[4] Journals of the Executive Council of Virginia, Mar. 18, 1757.
[5] Brock, *op. cit.*, II, 613.
[6] Pennsylvania *Archives*, Ser. 1, III, 175–76.
[7] Amherst Papers, Apr. 24, Apr. 26, 1757, B.P.R.O., W. O. 34/47.

at Bedford had been given out; and Sir William Johnson had bought for the use of his northern department the Ohio Company's entire supply of Indian goods stored at Cresap's farther west on that frontier. Confronted with Mercer's pleas, the Virginia council relayed them to the burgesses which had been complaining of the expense of Indian presents. The council also appealed to the newly appointed Superintendent of Indian Affairs for the Southern District, Edmund Atkin, to travel to Winchester.[8]

Cherokees continued to arrive at the frontier base. But, despite their disappointment, they did not intend to give up the war. Leaving Mercer to make good his promises, they separated into two main parties to go against the French. Eighty gunmen, led by Swallow Warrior, with Richard Smith as interpreter, accompanied Major Lewis up the Potomac to Fort Cumberland. The others, including Youghtanno's Overhills from Chilhowee and Telassie, followed Wawhatchee and Pearis farther north, ostensibly to track enemy marauders.

It was Wawhatchee's party which initiated the new superintendent of southern Indians into the complexities of his office. On April 29, having been successful in an action in the Pennsylvania hills, Wawhatchee's men arrived at Fort Frederick in Maryland where Captain Beale gave them a hearty welcome. Maryland, too, needed Indian allies. Wawhatchee, Pearis, and Beale soon reached an understanding. The Cherokee leader composed a letter to Governor Sharpe indicating a willingness to serve Maryland and an expectation of presents for what they had already done.[9] Without waiting for Sharpe's reply, Pearis, the Cherokees, and some Maryland troops under the command of Lieutenant Shelby left Fort Frederick to go toward the forks of the Ohio. Virginia's auxiliaries had for the time being become Maryland's.

The mixed force conducted a successful operation. Two weeks out and well over "Allegheny Mountain," they picked up

8 Journals of the Executive Council of Virginia, May 3, May 7, 1757.
9 Pennsylvania *Archives*, Ser. 1, III, 143–44.

an enemy track and followed it for two days. On the morning of May 13 near Reastown their scouts sighted fifteen or sixteen Delawares and Shawnees squatted about their breakfast fire. Swiftly the soldiers and Cherokees disposed themselves for the attack. At a given signal the provincials fired and the Cherokees raced in. Four enemies fell and the others ran into the laurels pursued by Cherokees who dragged down two of them. Shelby leaped upon a wounded warrior, the notorious "Beaver's Son," struggling to rise. As the white man fought to fasten thongs upon the Indian's hands, the Delaware, crying "Kill away, kill away," died.[10] It was the kind of attack Indians liked: surprise and victory with scalps and prisoners but no loss to themselves.

At Annapolis Sharpe, receiving Wawhatchee's talk, asked his assembly to appropriate at once for Indian presents. But the assembly, having already posted a £50 scalp bounty, debated long before it voted the Governor £150 for Wawhatchee's party. On news of the mixed patrol's success, Sharpe added the bounty for four scalps to the assembly's grant, spent £300 on presents, and sent them in wagons under his secretary to Fort Frederick. He commissioned Pearis captain in one of the newly authorized Maryland emergency regiments. Confronted later by Atkin, Sharpe maintained that he had no intention of detaching Pearis and his Indians from the Virginia service but wished to reward with a temporary appointment a man for whom a parsimonious assembly would make no provision.[11]

Wawhatchee's party, returning from its success, stopped briefly at Fort Lyttelton in Pennsylvania where they learned that Armstrong, the Pennsylvania Indian agent, conferred at Lancaster with the Mohawks and other friendly Indians. Pearis sent the agent word of Wawhatchee's success on Pennsylvania soil and talks from Wawhatchee and Youghtanno inviting him to meet them at Fort Frederick in Maryland.[12] The Pennsyl-

[10] *Maryland Gazette*, May 19, 1757.

[11] Horatio Sharpe, *Correspondence of Governor Sharpe*, I, 551; II, 8, 17–18.

[12] Pennsylvania *Archives*, Ser. 1, VII, 528–29.

vanians, hungry for Indian auxiliaries to shield their long frontier, hastened with presents to meet the Cherokees.

On May 18 at Fort Frederick the Cherokees, awaiting Maryland's offerings, opened a conference with the Pennsylvanians. Armstrong apologized for having brought so few presents: three rifles, four ruffled holland shirts, and a little wampum. He had come in haste to meet them. If they would come to Pennsylvania, he would give them more. Wawhatchee became very amiable. The next day he replied with pious thankfulness that he and his men had been able to protect Pennsylvania from an impending blow. He must first go to Winchester, then to Pennsylvania.[13]

On the twentieth the Maryland reward arrived. The Cherokees, as was their custom, shared the gift with all, soldiers and Indians, who had been in the Allegheny fight. But they refused to surrender the scalps for which Maryland had paid them a bounty.[14] On the twenty-second as Sharpe's empty-handed envoy rode back to Annapolis, the Indians set out with their gifts and scalps for Winchester, entranced with the dream of Virginia's bounty to be followed by Pennsylvania's largess.

Disappointment awaited them at Winchester. Captain Mercer had gone. A tall, sandy-haired Virginian, Colonel Washington, had taken over and had orders to leave Indian affairs to Edmund Atkin.[15] Mr. Atkin, however, had not yet reached Winchester, and Washington told the indignant Cherokees that he lacked the power to give them anything. Promptly the twenty-five-year-old Colonel was in hot water. "They are the most insolent, the most avaricious, the most dissatisfied wretches I ever had to deal with," he informed Dinwiddie. "If anything should detain Mr. Atkin's arrival . . . all the rhetoric I can master is not likely to detain them more than two or three days."[16]

His Majesty's Superintendent of Indian Affairs for the Southern District was then at Williamsburg devising a more system-

---

13 *Minutes of the Provincial Council of Pennsylvania*, VII, 353–55.
14 Sharpe, *op. cit.*, II, 7–8.
15 Brock, *op. cit.*, II, 619.
16 Fitzpatrick, *op. cit.*, II, 36–37.

atic approach to Indian problems. Though repeatedly urged by Dinwiddie to hurry to Winchester where an immediate crisis existed, Atkin proceeded deliberately and meticulously about the program he had planned. With Dinwiddie he worked out a system of escorts, passports, and supply depots for Indians, designed to prevent repetition of the April disorders.[17] He did not arrive at Winchester with the promised presents until June 3.

Before the Superintendent could unpack his saddlebags, Wawhatchee burst into his quarters and demanded to hear what he had come to say. Wawhatchee's bluster derived partly from fear that Atkin had come to punish him. Atkin had been a member of the South Carolina council which had threatened Wawhatchee with punishment in connection with the Haig and Brown affair a decade before. Ignoring the impatient Cherokee, Atkin went firmly about the business of unpacking and placing his gear. Finally he quietly told the headman he would give his talk when he was ready and not before. Wawhatchee, shouting that he would take his people home at once, flung from the room, slamming the door as he left.

But the door-slamming, it developed, had been but figurative. That evening Youghtanno visited Atkin, laughed at Wawhatchee's anger, and hinted that matters could be mended. Atkin was conciliatory, and the next morning a quieted and dignified Wawhatchee accompanied by Youghtanno came to the Superintendent. With composure he listened to the terms of the new dispensation. In the future the southern Indians should heed only those talks given by the Superintendent or sent under his seal; they should obey no orders except those the Superintendent sent; and there should be no presents except as the Superintendent approved them. Wawhatchee gravely uttered his approval. Indeed, according to the superintendent's report, the Indian seemed highly pleased—perhaps because the old unpleasant Haig and Brown matter did not come up. That afternoon in public conference with the Cherokees he repeated his morning's talk to Wawhatchee. In addition he emphasized that

[17] Journals of the Executive Council of Virginia, May 24, 1757.

they must make no arrangements with any government without his approval. The talk ended, Wawhatchee again expressed his approval.

There remained the matter of Pearis' conscienceless carrying of Virginia's dear-bought allies into Maryland and Pennsylvania and, incidentally, into the jurisdiction of George Croghan and Sir William Johnson. This constituted not only a menace to Virginia's frontier defense but an invitation for the northern officials to trespass upon the authority of the newly created southern superintendency. Moreover, Dinwiddie, suspecting that Pearis used the Cherokees to further his own interests, had decided to drop him from the Virginia service, and had chosen Atkin to deliver the news. When Pearis informed Atkin of the Cherokee engagement to go to Pennsylvania, Atkin told him he had acted without authority; for he had been discharged from the Virginia service before the date of his conference with Colonel Armstrong at Fort Frederick. Having thus informed Pearis of his discharge, the Superintendent enjoined him to keep the matter secret from the Cherokees.

The dismissal of Pearis was no service to Virginia. Whatever his faults, he understood Cherokees; and the Cherokees liked him and respected him. Without his management Wawhatchee might never have reached Winchester in the first place and might even have prevented all other Cherokees from going to Virginia. His shopping for presents in Maryland and Pennsylvania arose from the need, in the face of Virginia failure, to make Wawhatchee happy.

With Pearis cashiered and a ban put upon their Pennsylvania trip, the Indians' behavior altered. When Atkin assembled them to receive the presents Dinwiddie had sent, Wawhatchee was unhappy. The goods, "by no means contemptible," according to Atkin, were to be shared with the absent Swallow Warrior's party. Disdainfully glancing at the heaped presents, Wawhatchee grunted that they were not worth dividing; Swallow Warrior could have them all. As he moodily walked away, the worried Atkin hastened after him and told him he could take them all if his conscience would permit. Whereupon Wawhatchee, whose conscience was not tender, turned back, and took all the presents, "without remorse."

Oblivious to the Indian's contempt, the Superintendent then developed the subject of the Pennsylvania visit by reading an invitation from Croghan. The Cherokees listened coldly to Atkin's promise that if they would go to war, he would send to Croghan to learn what sort of reward could be had. Wawhatchee, perceiving that Atkin wished to prevent present-collecting on the scale to which he aspired, disdainfully left Croghan's wampum dangling in the Superintendent's hand. Nevertheless, the conference broke up with intimations that the Indians might be more tractable the next day.

The morrow came, but no Indians waited upon His Majesty's Superintendent. Youghtanno, after an all-night debauch, had early in the morning reeled off toward the nation, followed by thirteen of his men. Though Wawhatchee remained in Winchester, rumor said that thirty-five of his band had left in the night to collect on their own Croghan's Pennsylvania present. When Atkin heard the news, he dispatched a messenger by another route to forbid Croghan's giving the present; and the crestfallen Indians slunk back into Winchester to join their headman in preparations to go home.

No longer in the Virginia service, Pearis received Atkin's permission to take up his new duties in Maryland. Then, having promised not to leave Winchester until Richard Smith returned from Fort Cumberland to act as interpreter, he walked out on the Superintendent. For a few days Atkin was unable to communicate with his Cherokee charges.

When finally a penitent Wawhatchee came to Atkin to take formal leave, he repudiated Pearis, blaming his own conduct upon his benefactor, who, he said, had claimed sole authority over the Cherokees. Already prejudiced against the adventurer, the Superintendent believed the headman's statements, assuming that Wawhatchee's denunciation of Pearis represented a heartfelt conversion. On June 15 in a farewell conference held

123

out of doors before all his warriors, Wawhatchee asserted his undying loyalty to the English, promised to send out fresh war parties when he returned home, and ceremonially bowed out of the Superintendent's presence.[18] When late in the month his band left, Virginia lost sixty-two much-needed auxiliaries.

Zealous to assert his supremacy in his first encounter with his new Indian charges, Atkin had brought an arrogant and avaricious Indian to heel, but at the cost of the services he was appointed to obtain.

While Wawhatchee wrestled with Atkin in Winchester, Swallow Warrior's band defended Virginia's western frontier. It worked in two groups: one under Andrew Lewis on the South Branch, the other operating from Fort Cumberland into the forests toward Fort Duquesne. The former went out about May 19 with Richard Smith as interpreter. Consisting of fifty soldiers and fifty Indians, it surprised enemies marching toward Virginia and took five scalps and nineteen prisoners. On June 10 the party returned to Winchester.

Swallow Warrior's Cherokees, in two parties of fifteen each, operated sometimes on their own and sometimes with the Virginians. Near the end of May the Swallow Warrior and Lieutenant Baker with fifteen Indians and five whites scouted from Fort Cumberland toward the forks of the Ohio. On June 5 in the forest near the head of Turtle Creek about twenty miles from Fort Duquesne, as the Cherokees followed an enemy track toward Pennsylvania, their foremost warrior saw a ten-man French patrol coming down the path. The Indians ducked below the bushes to await the near approach of the enemy. The patrol advanced to within fifty paces before its leader saw the motionless Indians and called out a challenge. Volleyed rifle fire roared the answer. Four Frenchmen fell; but the others stood their ground, shooting desperately. Not waiting to reload, the Cherokees threw down their guns and rushed in with knives and tomahawks. In the French fire the two foremost Indians fell, Swallow Warrior in the act of leaping upon a fallen enemy to take a

[18] Pennsylvania *Archives*, Ser. 1, III, 175–81, 197–200.

scalp, and his son following close upon him. The Indian on-slaught swept by them, and the Frenchmen broke and ran. Two were seized before the Indians realized they had lost their leader. In a rage they tomahawked one of the captives and a wounded Frenchman struggling to rise. Then hastily concealing the Swallow Warrior's body, they scalped the dead Frenchmen; and, with one of their number carrying the Swallow Warrior's wounded son on his back, they hurried their lone prisoner back to Fort Cumberland.[19] He was Ensign Belestre, later instrumental in fomenting hatred of the English in Lower Towns Estatoe.

The second party, Lieutenant Spotswood commanding, had bad luck. Scouting almost to Fort Duquesne, on June 8 its Chero-kees sighted what they believed to be tracks of a major assault against the settlements. They reported by runner to Fort Cum-berland that several hundred of the enemy with cannons and wagons approached.[20] Tremors of apprehension reached even the tidewater; but the alarm proved false. A day or two later Cherokees took a scalp within one hundred yards of Fort Du-quesne. With these episodes Spotswood's party disappeared in the dark of the Allegheny forests. Weeks later two Cherokees came into Pennsylvania's Fort Lyttelton with the grim report that Spotswood, hard pressed, had ordered his party to disband, each man to look out for himself.[21] He was never heard from again.

The party once headed by Swallow Warrior was incorporated into the band with Andrew Lewis under the leadership of Swal-low Warrior's nephew, Seroweh, the Mankiller of Estatoe.[22] Since their arrival in Virginia they had lost thirty warriors, some by illness and wounds, but fifteen by death. It was a near dis-aster as Indians reckoned loss. With Youghtanno and Wawhat-chee gone home, the Estatoe party and possibly one other from Keowee were the only Cherokees on the Virginia frontier.

[19] *Maryland Gazette*, June 16, July 14, 1757.
[20] Hamilton, *op. cit.*, II, 91.
[21] Pennsylvania *Archives*, Ser. 1, III, 189.
[22] Fitzpatrick, *op. cit.*, II, 51.

Shortly after the Mankiller of Estatoe came to Winchester, George Croghan brought in the Pennsylvania gift for Wawhatchee's party. Atkin decided that it was excessive and gave the lingering Wawhatchee but a part. The remainder he turned over to the Mankiller of Estatoe for accompanying Croghan to Pennsylvania to help Colonel Stanwix.

Led by Croghan and accompanied by Richard Smith to keep an eye on Johnson's deputy for Atkin, the party reached Carlisle on June 29. Now on Pennsylvania soil Croghan took advantage of Atkin, who had forbidden Johnson's deputy to speak to the Cherokees. Convincing himself that the northern and southern Indian districts were geographical rather than tribal units, Croghan decided that Cherokees in Pennsylvania were outside the southern Superintendent's jurisdiction.[23] He approached the Mankiller with presents and the promise that if he remained in Pennsylvania there would be further reward. The Cherokees agreed to stay twenty days.

The Cherokee sojourn in Pennsylvania ended inauspiciously. On July 21 a Cherokee runner arrived from the south with such disturbing news that Colonel Stanwix had difficulty holding the Indians to receive their presents.[24] All fifty-five Cherokees surged from the fort down the road toward Winchester.

Winchester had been very quiet after Croghan left for Carlisle with the Estatoes. Late in June, Osteneco passed through on his way to the frontier after having delivered a message in Williamsburg from Old Hop and the Little Carpenter. Then in July what appears to have been a backdoor deputation of Overhills, accompanied by Mingo warriors, bound for upper New York to confer with the neutral Onondaga council, arrived. Atkin, at the moment without a skilled linguister, gained the impression that enemy spies were in his midst and threw the deputies into Winchester jail.[25] Horrified, convalescent Cherokees lingering at the base dispatched a runner to Chota and sent for

[23] Pennsylvania *Archives*, Ser. 1, III, 186–89, 197; Ser. 1, VII, 630–31.

[24] Hamilton, *op. cit.*, II, 131.

[25] IBSC, VI, 82–83.

help to the nearest war party, the Mankiller's Estatoes at Carlisle. The Estatoes, boiling into Winchester, effected a jail delivery before young Washington could convince them that a mistake had been made. Only after the deputies' wounded pride had been assuaged with presents did the Estatoe Mankiller send a runner to counteract the story already proceeding toward the nation.[26]

Meanwhile, Sir William Johnson had taken steps to thwart the adverse effects of Cherokee correspondence with Onondaga. Through the Mohawk Little Abraham, who visited with Croghan at Lancaster, he persuaded the Mankiller of Estatoe to send deputies to Johnson Hall to talk with the Mohawks. There over the scalp of a dead enemy the deputies proclaimed friendship for the English and cemented the alliance by joining Johnson's brief August excursion to Fort Edward to oppose Montcalm's invading army.[27] Finally, accompanied by the famous Mohawk Silver Heels, they carried a Mohawk belt back to the nation.[28]

By August 1 most of the Lower Townsmen had gone home from Virginia. Thereafter small Overhill bands provided the Virginians with scouts. As if by prearrangement a rotation of parties occurred. In mid-August Osteneco's party returned to Winchester after nearly two months on the South Branch.[29] A smaller group took its place. A month later another band consisting of twenty warriors and one woman joined Major Lewis and appears to have fought the quarter-hour battle on George's Creek eight miles from Fort Cumberland in which a French officer was killed and scalped and his orders carried to the fort. The victors, thinking they had done enough, set out for home to show the scalp they had taken. In November, thirty Chotas—led by Cappy and Sour Hominy—on their way to Winchester encountered three enemy Indians and took two scalps.[30]

War parties returning to the nation with scalps were received

[26] Fitzpatrick, *op. cit.*, II, 114–15.
[27] Sullivan, etc., *op. cit.*, IX, 763, 806, 809.
[28] IBSC, VI, 119–20.
[29] Atkin to Connetarky [*sic*], Aug. 6, 1757, Loudoun Papers.
[30] Fitzpatrick, *op. cit.*, II, 141, 150.

at the forts with presents and the firing of the cannon. One coming into Fort Prince George was induced by Wawhatchee to demand double the scalp bounty. Though Lachlan McIntosh, then in command, wailed to Demere that Wawhatchee was "one of the greatest villains unhanged," he paid the price. As for the Indians, the bounty was their only bonus, and they had no pensions.

It is remarkable that there was not more friction between the Colonials and the Cherokees. The system of guides, passports, and supply planned by Atkin failed. Hiring guides proved difficult. The Cherokees preferred travel through the heart of Virginia to Williamsburg rather than along the frontier paths to Winchester. The inhabitants "were greatly disquieted, being often robbed and otherways ill-treated." But the Indians also suffered. Wrote Atkin, "Many of the inhabitants living on this rout [*sic*] purchase from the said Indians with spirituous liquors (the cause of the most disorders) and much undervalue the presents given to them, and often make use of indiscreet speeches and behavior toward them prejudicial to the service." Atkin optimistically hoped that future serious trouble could be avoided if the Cherokees were "guided to Fort Cumberland along the line of the frontier forts west of the Blue Ridge."[31] The language barrier also caused trouble. Atkin himself was something of a problem. Conscientious and systematic, he was new to his job and lacked that fluency and flexibility which caused Indians to feel that Sir William Johnson was one of them. Where Johnson was a prodigal, Atkin, limited to what the parsimonious southern assemblies would grant him for presents, pinched pennies, and lacked the suavity to cause Indians to forget that what he gave was much less than what they expected. Though his eliminating of scalp bounties in favor of larger rewards for all Indians was statesmanlike, he angered the Indians by doing away with the familiar and expected. Finally, he had not yet learned to delegate authority. When he was not on the scene, no one had power to act with the Indians. Exasperated, Washington wrote Dinwiddie:

The sincere disposition the Cherokees have betrayed to espouse our cause has been demonstrated . . . . But in the stead of meeting with that great encouragement which . . . that brave people . . . merit, several of them after having undergone the rudest toils and fatigues . . . destitute of all conveniences and almost necessities of life, and . . . in that situation went to war, and in the way behaved nobly . . . and when they returned here with an enemy's scalp . . . they must have gone home without any reward or thanks, or even provisions to support them on the march, justly fired with the highest resentment for their maltreatment, had not I and my officers strained a point and procured them some things of which they were in absolute want. [32]

Virginia failed to recognize that the Cherokees were mercenaries. Though high policy made them allies, their headmen had the duty of requiring the English to reward their services. The mischief lay in the term "presents," a holdover from the peacetime practice of giving annual presents to allied tribes and distributing gifts at Indian conferences. Actually, in wartime presents constituted an Indian's pay. The Cherokees not only expected their employers to outfit them but knew that they must take home from the Englishman's war what they otherwise might have made from hunting. When they fought for glory and excitement only, they could not stay long in the field. They must return home in time to hunt to pay their debts to the traders and buy "necessaries" for their families.

Virginia and Atkin handled the matter of presents badly. Though Cherokee threats to go over to the French were bluster, failure to meet their expectations could have serious consequences. The Cherokees, like mercenaries in other times and lands, would collect forcibly from the citizens the pay their employers failed to give them. When vulnerable Virginia, having promised much, failed to keep its promises, friction between traveling bands of Cherokees and the Virginia settlers became inevitable.

[31] Atkin to C. Gist, Nov. 16, 1757, Loudoun Papers.
[32] Fitzpatrick, *op. cit.*, II, 156–59.

CHAPTER TEN

Tellico Reconciled

IN MAY, 1757, with Lower Townsmen fighting Virginia's battles in the north and the Little Carpenter attacking the French on the Mississippi, Demere wrote contentedly to Lyttelton, "The whole nation is inveterate against the French."[1] But he was mistaken. Tellico smarted under Lyttelton's refusal of presents or a trade until a Tellico had taken a French scalp. Tellico visits to the pro-French Creeks and to Chartier's town in northern Alabama, where French John lingered, increased. In the Little Carpenter's absence, Old Hop, uneasy over Carolina's failure to broaden the trade, was eager for peace to the southward, and still reached undercover feelers toward the French. His embassies to the Creeks conferred with the Mortar and talked with the commander of Fort Toulouse.

Creeks, glad to discredit their ancient enemies, kept Charlestown informed of Cherokee discontent. Some reported Overhill uneasiness at the presence of so many English among them and Cherokee talk of a rising against the traders to be followed by an assault with northern Indians upon Fort Loudoun. Most Creeks approved such talk; for Fort Loudoun deterred Creek aggression, and a conflict between Cherokees and English would be grist to the Creek mill.

In early June, Demere discovered that he had been too optimistic. Lame Arm, the First Man of Tellico, informed him that several of Chartier's Shawnees had come into Tellico to recruit

[1] IBSC, VI, 43.

raiders against the Virginia frontier. Lame Arm could only warn the Shawnees to leave, for drastic action would endanger the Tellicoes then visiting Chartier's town. The Shawnees lingered insolently to peddle tempting stories of great quantities of French goods available at the mouth of Hiwassee River.

Demere now determined so to smear Tellico with Shawnee blood as to force a break. He sought first to move Chota to act. He called in Old Hop, Standing Turkey, and the Smallpox Conjurer, and demanded that in the name of the English alliance, they kill the Shawnees. The headmen demurred. The Shawnees would retaliate on innocent Cherokees among them. They did not mention the risk to two official Cherokee missions then at the Creeks, about whom Demere knew nothing. However, after Demere had wined and dined them, and entertained them all night at the fort, they consented to English action, provided no Cherokees were hurt. Demere sent an agent to warn Old Caesar of Chatuga and to scout the house where the Shawnees stayed.

Late on June 7, thirty-three soldiers, commanded by Lieutenant Adamson and guided by Old Hop's son Cappy, set out for Tellico. Timing their arrival for the dark of night, Cappy brought the party into the woods a mile and a half from Tellico where the path could be easily ambushed. Through Demere's agent they kept in touch with the Shawnee movements. Early in the morning the agent informed Adamson that the enemy would leave between eleven and twelve and that their departure would be signaled by a gunshot. When the Black Dog of Chatuga "accidentally" discovered the ambush, Adamson sent him with a handful of beads to keep Tellicoes from accompanying his intended victims. Soon a gun sounded, and seven Shawnees strode down the path. Wary, for they could not have been oblivious to the treachery about them, they were well spread out. The English fired. Four Shawnees fell. The survivors fled. Pursuit proved impossible; for not-so-innocent Tellico hunters, "appearing suddenly everywhere," caused confusion. The Tellicoes, of course, hoped that the Shawnee survivors would not accuse them of complicity. Cappy took the scalps and plunder from the dead and returned with Adamson's party to Fort Loudoun where he was richly rewarded.

Quick to capitalize upon the episode, the next day a large number of Tellico headmen and warriors came to Demere. Soberly they told the Captain "that before the Savannahs had been killed they had had a free path to walk in, clean and neat without any danger, but now that [Demere] had set the white people in it and whooped and hallooed in it, they had made it dirty and all bloody and dangerous for them."[2] In short, they now needed protection. They desired a trader and ammunition. Demere, urging them to war on all Shawnees, gave a bag of ammunition for Tellico and Chatuga. He promised to speak for them to Lyttelton, and the Tellicoes left in high spirits.

But their visit had another angle. Having stated their case without Old Hop's permission, they did not visit him. The next day the Fire King and his councilors sent the Tellicoes a command to meet them at the fort. High words ensued. After recriminations had died down, the Tellicoes left, and the Chotas confronted Demere with the complaint that they too were bloodied and needed to be made clean. Demere understood them, and gave each a matchcoat and a white shirt; for fresh clothes symbolized "cleanness."[3]

Shortly the Mankiller of Tellico returned from war bearing a scalp and a tale of Ottawas defeated on the Ohio. Delighted, Demere paid the hero a four-scalp bounty, and the Mankiller solemnly approved the liquidation of the Shawnees in his absence. However, it soon developed that the scalp was that of a friendly Chickasaw who, accompanying his party, had been secretly disposed of by the Mankiller. Though the incident tickled Cherokee risibilities, Demere failed to appreciate the jest.

The rout of the Shawnees from Great Tellico by which Demere hoped to silence the French party in the nation proved but an episode in the unceasing contest for Cherokee partisanship. Though Old Hop's envoys at the Oakchoys labeled the Tellico winter overtures as unauthorized, they listened to French talk

2 *Ibid.*, VI, 38, 48, 51–52, 57, 61, 108.   3 *Ibid.*, VI, 50, 55–56.

at Fort Toulouse. Feted, given ceremonial tobacco to carry to Chota, they returned accompanied by two Creek deputies from the pro-French Coweta town laden with French and Spanish talk. Protocol required that they be heard in Chota town house. On July 17 the headmen of many towns heard the most violent anti-English demonstration in a year. After the Cherokee deputies had protested that the English assault upon the Shawnees had endangered their lives while upon official business, they presented the French tobacco. The Creek deputies then voiced the everlasting friendship of Creek for Cherokee, and delivered Spanish tobacco to Old Hop with warnings against the Carolinians. Old Hop responded with a tirade against the English conduct of the trade.[4]

The English alliance once again seemed endangered. Since the Saluda promises there had been a steady deterioration in the trade, for high wartime prices and goods scarcities had discouraged the promised additional traders from entering the nation. The financial position of the remaining active traders had weakened with the mounting Indian debt due to the Cherokee practice of outfitting themselves and their families on credit and then going to war instead of hunting. In the minds of most of the warriors, fighting for the English justified failure to pay debts. Others frequently sold their hunting take to itinerants in the woods instead of to the licensed traders to whom they owed money. Traders could not pay their own creditors in Charlestown and were forced to replenish their stocks at a markup from Goudy at Ninety-Six and from Rae and Barksdale at Augusta.[5] Goods became fewer and more high priced than ever.

The absent Little Carpenter's prestige suffered materially, not only from these circumstances but from the machinations of Chota trader John Elliott with whom he had quarreled. Six young men for whose credit he had vouched to Elliott had bartered their winter's take to an itinerant.[6] The angry trader had

[4] R. Demere to Lyttelton, June 26, July 11, July 20, 1757, Lyttleton Papers.
[5] J. Stuart to Lyttelton, July 11, 1757, *ibid.*
[6] P. Demere to Lyttelton, Aug. 30, 1757, *ibid.*

berated the Little Carpenter, and the vengeful Second Man, complaining of false weights and measures, had induced Lyttelton to suspend his license. After the Little Carpenter had gone to war down the Tennessee, Elliott had begun a campaign among the goods-less, pro-French elements at Chota to blame Overhill trade difficulties on the Right Hand Man. He further schemed to promote Osteneco's rivalry with the Little Carpenter by inducing Chota to commission the Second warrior to carry a trade appeal to Virginia.[7] Elliott accompanied him to obtain Virginia trade goods.

The Little Carpenter returned and, informed of the bad talk and Elliott's intrigue, struck hard. He sent Oconostota to seize the absent Elliott's steelyards and measuring sticks and take them to Demere who, not disinterested, found the scales registered two pounds underweight and the measuring sticks several inches short. Chota was angry.

Elliott, however, was a fighter. Returned from Virginia, his pack horses empty, for wartime Virginia used all its scant Indian goods to reward fighters on its frontiers, the trader brought Old Hop, the Slave Catcher of Chota, and Oconostota together over a keg of rum and violently accused the Little Carpenter of fostering policies which caused goods shortages. The Chotas, facing the hard facts of the trader's vacant shelves and his lack of ammunition for their fall and winter hunts, began to rage at the Right Hand Man and Demere. The Creek emissaries laughed and taunted the Overhills, and their French line began to gain ground.[8]

The Little Carpenter, facing defeat, hurried to Demere and Stuart and convinced them that Elliott must be restored to favor. Elliott's departure for Charlestown with Demere's approval and a letter to Lyttelton stating that the English alliance depended upon restoring his license and increasing the flow of goods to the nation eased Overhill tension.[9]

---

[7] J. Stuart to Lyttelton, May 29, 1757, *ibid*.
[8] R. Demere to Lyttelton, July 11, July 20, July 23, 1757, *ibid*.
[9] J. Stuart to Lyttelton, July 23, 1757, *ibid*.

The Little Carpenter's position was bolstered barely in time to meet a new French threat. On July 27, French John, having heard that Chota listened favorably to the Creeks, returned to Chota town house accompanied by two Cherokee stalwarts of the French intrigue, Savannah Tom and the Thigh. He brought French gifts (baubles and ribbons); a story that the Great King, George II, had died; a report that the once neutral Gun Merchant of the Oakchoys had joined the French; and a letter from the commander of Mobile.

A crisis ensued. The report of King George's death might convince the Cherokees that the English alliance had also died and turn them to Kerlerec's treaty. Had the great Creek exponent of neutrality become anti-English, the time might be ripe for an anti-English rising of the southern tribes. The Mobile letter held promise of an adequate French trade. Strong voices spoke for a favorable reply. But the Little Carpenter and Oconostota stood firm for the English alliance, disparaging the French capacity for trade. The Little Carpenter talked French John down and raised the specter of hostile French designs in building Fort de l'Assomption and sending scouts up the Tennessee. His enemies said that he had surrendered his people to the English so that the English no longer needed to provide traders; but when he retorted that trade had fallen off because the English distrusted the Cherokees, no one could answer him.

Despite the Little Carpenter's efforts, French John's influence continued to be felt. Finally the Second Man declined to attend meetings to discuss correspondence with the French. His refusal amounted to a veto, and Old Hop hung his head as one rebuked. The French intrigue lost its momentum.

Demere now attempted to dispose of French John. When Old Hop truculently defended his slave and his French correspondence, the Captain, knowing he should not be guilty of having a member of the Fire King's household killed, offered the Little Carpenter, Oconostota, Standing Turkey, and Willinawaw several hundred dollars worth of goods to deliver the Frenchman at Fort Loudoun.

135

But the issues were delicate, involving the family rights of the First Man and a considerable division of sentiment. The wily headmen took another course. On August 2 in Chota town house they blandly debated whether French John should be killed or surrendered to Demere. In the midst of their debate, they were informed that the Frenchman and his companion had fled. To the Little Carpenter and Oconostota, Old Hop vehemently denied complicity in the escape; but, interestingly, no pursuit was attempted, and the fugitives came to rest at Great Tellico.

Demere, learning the news, quickly conspired with the Tellico Mankiller to take the scalps of the fugitives. The Mankiller, obviously insincere, merely sought a present; for Chota's disturbance over trade conditions that summer was mild compared with Tellico's. The Tellicoes were disillusioned with Raymond Demere, and were ready tinder to French John's spark. They flared up dangerously the next day.

Near Great Tellico, Captain Paul Demere, leading a detachment to relieve his brother at Fort Loudoun, was threatened by a crowd of angry Cherokees. They pressed so closely upon the marching column that the Captain ordered the rear to hold them off. Twenty-five armed Indians, painted black and gesturing menacingly, came out of the crowd to demand rum. But a clash did not occur.

That night in Great Tellico the English scalp which Kerlerec had demanded was taken. A pregnant Englishwoman traveling to join her husband at Fort Loudoun had straggled from the convoy and come into Chatuga hours after the troops had passed. Hearing of her presence, the Tellicoes sent the Thigh's wife after her; and in Tellico, Savannah Tom struck her down, ripped open her belly and flung out the babe, and scalped her.

Raymond Demere wanted immediate satisfaction from the hostile town. He sent for the Little Carpenter to accompany a detachment with his demands upon the Tellicoes. But the Little Carpenter knew well that the Great Tellico murder proceeded from a minority effort to precipitate the nation into the French camp, and he set about nullifying the blow. He kept the detachment waiting a full day while he talked around among the headmen using the ominous situation to beat out resistance to his leadership. Finally he brought Old Hop and all the river towns headmen to the fort to pledge allegiance to the English and to announce that immediately after the green-corn dance they would go against the French. The Tellico outrage, he said, should be treated as the act of individuals rather than as that of the town. But the Thigh and Savannah Tom had already fled Tellico with French John and could not be delivered immediately, thus delaying the animosity certain to be aroused should they be seized and killed by the English. Demere was induced merely to indicate displeasure by sending all the towns but Tellico a gift of rum. Then Old Hop ordered the head warrior of Tellico to appear before Demere for a terrifying tongue-lashing. The Little Carpenter had once again shielded his people and demonstrated the power of his influence with the English.

Nevertheless, the scalping had so unnerved the Fort Loudoun garrison that for weeks no Englishman dared go near Tellico. Soldiers refused to renew expired enlistments. They dreaded night sentry duty; for dark figures, presumed to be Tellicoes ready to take English scalps, prowled under the walls. All longed to be out of that fiendish country.

In mid-August with his brother firmly in command of the fort, Raymond Demere, for whose scalp certain Cherokees lusted, was guided by the Little Carpenter out of the Overhills. They followed the newly favored Twenty-Four Mountains route which avoided dangerous Tellico, passing through the Snowbird and Nantahala Mountains to Cowee. Somewhere on the difficult path Demere met the vindictive Elliott returning from Charlestown, swearing that now he once again had his license, he would withdraw from the Overhill trade. Knowing that such a move would strengthen the anti-English faction, the Captain persuaded him to continue at Chota.

Recalled to Chota by report of a Virginia message arrived there, the Little Carpenter set about nullifying Osteneco's efforts to obtain a Virginia trade. The message was Atkin's apology for the Winchester arrest of Chota's Iroquois-bound deputies.[10] The headmen, ignoring Atkin and the idea of a central British authority over the southern Indians, sent protests to Dinwiddie. Chiding him for the arrests, and warning him against future incidents of the kind, they reminded him that his failure in the trade and garrison matters had prevented many Overhills from going to Virginia. To Osteneco they sent a runner asking his return and stating that an enemy had killed his brother and that the French threatened the Overhills.[11]

There was no French threat to the nation that summer, except for faraway Fort de l'Assomption near the mouth of the Tennessee. To prevent the pro-French faction's achieving a French peace, the Little Carpenter's strategy was to lead war parties against the Choctaws and the French-allied Twightwees in the Illinois-Wabash country. Before making his autumn downriver raid, the Little Carpenter acclimated Paul Demere to Cherokee patterns. In September he and Old Hop invited the new commander to sit with them at the outdoor green-corn feast. Then he had him witness ceremonial honors to a Catawba headman whom Osteneco had brought home, a public demonstration of friendship frequently necessary in a wilderness where everyone knew his neighbor to be no better than himself. The Little Carpenter also brought the suspect Tellico headmen to Fort Loudoun to hear the new Captain's stern injunctions and to surrender a new offering of beads the French had sent.

On September 24, with Oconostota and threescore warriors, the Little Carpenter took leave of Paul Demere. As the Indians paddled their half-dozen long dugouts toward mid-stream, from the picketed ramparts of Fort Loudoun cannons belched flame and smoke, their thunder echoing through the valley, and painted warriors shouted a wild reply.[12] Not until January, 1758, did

10 IBSC, VI, 61–62, 64, 68, 70–75, 80–81.

11 Old Hop, Little Carpenter, etc., to Dinwiddie, Aug. 23, 1757, Loudoun Papers.

12 P. Demere to Lyttelton, Oct. 11, 1757, Lyttelton Papers.

the Little Carpenter see the fort again. In his absence important changes occurred.

The Overhills now displayed more interest in the northern war. Fort Loudoun was no longer a center of opposition to Virginia. Lyttelton, working in the spirit of intercolonial co-operation, had withdrawn the trader-allied Raymond Demere from the fort and had substituted his brother Paul with orders to encourage Overhills to go north. Acting on Raymond Demere's advice, in October he filled Fort Loudoun with trade goods, salt, guns, and ammunition with which to supply many Overhill ordinary needs, outfit war parties, and reward those who returned from the fighting. Those who brought back scalps, even though they had received Virginia's bounty, were to receive added largess. Old Hop relented somewhat, and as evidence of the new dispensation, his son Cappy with the warrior Sour Hominy led out a Virginia-bound party and others soon followed.[13] Virginia, however, was never to become a main theater of Overhill operations. Dinwiddie's failure in the garrison and trade matters still rankled.

The greatest change occurred at Great Tellico. Any easing of the trade situation there would go far to altering unfriendly attitudes. But the South Carolina council, angry over the August scalping, had refused concessions and warned that if the town received Shawnees again it would be treated as enemy.[14] It remained for a private trader's initiative to resolve the situation. In the fall of 1757, Cornelius Dougherty, the greatly respected Hiwassee trader, risked personal ruin and possible imprisonment by invading the town for which the absentee Goudy held license and opening a trade. Tellico, happy, quieted.

The immediate repercussions of the move threatened more disaster for the English. Goudy, learning of Dougherty's act, hastened to Hiwassee with two constables and seized the Hiwassee trader's goods, horses, and Negro slaves and took them down to Ninety-Six. No white man was regarded more highly

13 IBSC, VI, 108, 113.
14 S. C. Council Journals, Aug. 27, 1757.

than the Valley people regarded Dougherty. For thirty years he had been their trader, adviser, and friend. When alarms had frightened all other traders from the nation he had moved freely among the Indians counseling patience and moderation. On this occasion, having violated Carolina law in order "to keep the Indians in peace and to clear the path to the fort," he was embittered. He now had debtors in Great Tellico besides those in the Valley. He had lost his Hiwassee goods, was in debt to Charlestown merchants, and a judgment stood against him. He was not alone in his plight. The Valley people, seeing Dougherty's goods moving off with Goudy, found their winter necessaries gone and their trader left with empty shelves. They did not need Dougherty's bitterness to tell them they would suffer.

Shortly they made trouble. Tanase trader Sam Benn, passing through the Valley with a caravan of goods, was set upon near Nottely by a horde of angry Cherokees demanding rum. Benn, adhering to the law, refused. The outraged Indians pelted him with sticks and stones. When one bold red man reached to pull Benn from his horse, the trader shot him, and the assailants momentarily drew back. Benn's Negro slave, safe in the immunity Cherokees granted Negroes, shouted to Benn to leave his pack train and run, that he would care for the goods. Badly bruised, Benn rode for his life. The Indians instantly calmed and, rounding up the caravan, ordered the slave to camp with it in a designated spot until they gave him permission to leave. They then drove off a horse loaded with goods.

When Old Hop heard of the Nottelies' misbehavior, he was calm in his new-found confidence in the English. He told Benn he had done right in killing the offender, that the Nottelies had behaved badly, and that as soon as his warriors came in from hunting, he would send for the goods and demand satisfaction for damage and losses. The Fire King then sent physic to the Warrior of the Long Savannah, whose brother Benn had killed, with orders to cleanse himself of bad thoughts. The Warrior obeyed.

Before the Chotas returned from their hunts, Tellico had

140

acted to prove its good will. Headman Lame Arm of the formerly hostile town sent to Nottely with Tellico warriors, obtained the Nottely headman's promise of satisfaction, and led the pack train intact to Tanase. He was so heartily welcomed with presents by Paul Demere that he ordered his men to treat the English well and took the hatchet Demere held out to him. Proceeding directly to Chota town house, he informed the assembled headmen that he had ended his quarrel with the English and had taken the English hatchet against the French. He then threw Demere's hatchet to the floor and demanded that each of the headmen prove his sincerity by picking it up. The response was immediate and affirmative.[15] Thus ended the conspiracy of Great Tellico, and the schism occasioned by the Little Carpenter's pro-English policy appeared closed. Had there been statesmanship in Charlestown which recognized that the key to Cherokee good will lay in abundant trade, neither would have occurred.

[15] IBSC, VI, 106–107, 109–12, 123.

CHAPTER ELEVEN

Disaster in Virginia

DESPITE THE DIFFICULTIES encountered in Virginia the year before, in 1758 the Cherokees had a strong disposition to join the Forbes campaign against Fort Duquesne. This was due primarily to Governor Lyttelton of South Carolina who appears to have ordered the commanders of the English forts in the Cherokee nation to spare no effort to encourage the Indians to go north. At Fort Prince George, Ensign Lachlan McIntosh held frequent councils with Lower Towns headmen, kept Keowee supplied with rum, and held constant open house. At Fort Loudoun, Paul Demere lavished presents on returning war parties and roused Overhill enthusiasm for the northern war. Old Hop, freed from the intrigue of French John and the pressure of the absent Little Carpenter, dropped his opposition to Virginia.[1] In February several score Overhills marched toward the Potomac, one of them bearing a message to Dinwiddie weakly reminding him of unfulfilled promises.[2] Wawhatchee, recovered from his discontent, led two or three hundred Lower Townsmen to join Forbes. Indeed, Colonel William Byrd's belated mission to recruit Cherokees for service with the British had been rendered unnecessary.

However, an ominous event had occurred in the south which sowed the seeds of major trouble. In December on Edisto River well within South Carolina, four Estatoe tribesmen had been

[1] IBSC, VI, 13.
[2] Atkin to Loudoun, Mar. 25, 1758, Loudoun Papers.

killed and scalped.[3] Lyttelton, apprehensive, blamed enemy Indians and sent Keowee white beads of peace.[4] But rumor in Estatoe attributed the murders to Carolinians; for the atrocity had been committed far from the reach of enemy Indians, and the hunters' deerskins had been stolen. That the episode did not occasion an immediate clash may have been caused by the fact that the victims were Natchez Indians which Estatoe had adopted. Even so, the situation called for reprisals. Furtively, Virginia-bound Estatoes killed two isolated white hunters in North Carolina and cut their scalps into four on which they intended to collect the Virginia scalp bounty. The vengeance frightened some of the Estatoes, who turned back and dissuaded other war parties from setting out. On March 2 the Keowee council returned Lyttelton's white beads with a string of their own black beads, grimly confronting the Carolina Governor with the issue as one of peace or war. Probably unaware that Estatoes had already taken vengeance in North Carolina, the Keowees promised to refrain from hostile action until the governor could complete his investigation; but they hinted that if the English settlers at Long Canes continued to encroach upon their hunting grounds, there would be difficulty.

Though portending trouble, the Edisto murders but briefly interrupted the northward flow of warriors; for McIntosh assured Keowee that Lyttelton would give full satisfaction. It was also apparent to the Indians that if they struck in Carolina, they would jeopardize the lives of their countrymen who were already in Virginia.

Meanwhile at Chota the English had been so successful in winning their way that the absent Little Carpenter's influence was weakened, and the English had begun to perceive that they could get along without him. Having taken prisoners and scalps under the walls of Fort de l'Assomption on the Ohio and visited the Chickasaws to prevent the threatened breach arising from Cherokee murders of a few Chickasaws, the Little Carpenter

[3] IBSC, VI, 99.
[4] S. C. Council Journals, Dec. 14, 1757.

returned to the nation in January to find that his fences needed mending. He determined to take his triumphs directly to Charlestown to remind Lyttelton of the services he had rendered the English and Carolina.[5] In March, after he had dispatched Willinawaw down the Tennessee to keep up the war on the Ohio, he set out with Oconostota and a host of retainers for Charlestown. At Joree in the Middle Settlements he hushed anti-English talk generated by the Edisto murders and by James May's unwillingness to see his Indian customers leave off hunting and go to Virginia. At Keowee he frowned on the black beads sent to Lyttelton and quieted bad talk.[6]

But the Little Carpenter was to find that in Charlestown times had changed. Lyttelton had accepted the ascendancy of Superintendent Atkin in Indian Affairs and regarded his own role as but secondary. The Superintendent had commissioned Colonel William Byrd of Virginia to treat with the Cherokees for auxiliaries. The Carolina trading interest had ceased opposing Cherokee participation in the Virginia campaigns; for the Carolina assembly had voted £20,000 to underwrite rewards to Cherokees returning from service in Virginia, the goods to be purchased from the traders and their suppliers.[7] This statesmanlike measure relieved the credit difficulties of important traders and mitigated the hardships Cherokee families experienced when their men were too long at war to do much hunting. Though the policy appears to have grown from his proposals of the year before, the Little Carpenter himself was not wanted in Charlestown. Colonel Byrd, going tardily up the path to commence his mission in the nation, met the Second Man on his way down and attempted to convince him that he would be much more useful to the English if he returned to the nation or went to Virginia; but the Indian would not be convinced. However, to show Byrd his good will he promised to go to Virginia on his return and detached sixty

---

[5] IBSC, V, 129–30; VI, 114–15, 123–28, 131–32, 144.

[6] S. C. Council Journals, Apr. 11, 1758.

[7] Amherst Papers, Mar. 21, 1758, B.P.R.O., W.O. 34/35.

of his warriors to accompany the colonel to Keowee. Then he continued his way to the colony's capital.

On April 10, uninvited and unwanted, he entered Charlestown. Diplomatically concealing his thoughts, the Governor received the Cherokee with all the honors due a visiting potentate. While cannons thundered and kilted regulars lined the streets, a red-coated column escorted the proud and painted headman to the council house. He deserved well of the English, and to remind them of it, he bore a pole from which dangled the scalps of two Frenchmen he had killed on his Mississippi raid.

Eager to speed his return, Lyttelton greeted him with a show of warmth and proceeded immediately to inquire his business. Conscious that he confronted a bargaining vacuum, the Little Carpenter could only speak for himself and his personal services. Not altogether disingenuous, he spoke of the return of Great Tellico to friendship and presented White beads from Keowee to wipe away the memory of the black beads that town had sent earlier. He stressed the importance of his services against Fort de l'Assomption, which he pictured as a threat to Fort Loudoun, and he promised to expose French agents who came to the nation. Then, as usual, he made demands. They were minor; ammunition for the Overhills, a remedy for trader Elliott's continued unregeneracy, silver arm bands for each of his men.

Lyttelton, unwilling to be troubled further by Cherokee affairs, said he had already sent sizable amounts of ammunition to the forts for Cherokee use. Petty trade complaints should be made only to the commanders of the forts, and all other Cherokee troubles should be taken to the Superintendent of Indian Affairs, Edmund Atkin. Finally, however, when faced with the problem of obtaining Attakullaculla's French prisoners, he promised to remove the incorrigible Elliott and to give the Indian the ammunition he desired. The Little Carpenter then attempted to exchange the Frenchmen for two Negro slaves to take their places as helpers for his wife. But Carolina law forbade the giving or selling of slaves to the Indians. Nor could his

145

request for silver arm bands be met; there weren't enough silver-smiths in Charlestown to do the job. He had to be content with a wagonload of ammunition and a heap of sundry presents, a bare sufficiency to indicate English good will. Lyttelton honored him with a review of the Charlestown militia and the regular garrison; and he returned to the nation apparently ready to go to the Virginia wars.

In the nation the Byrd mission was proving fruitless. Arriving at Keowee on April 7, Colonel Byrd found no great conclave of warriors awaiting him. His aid, Colonel Howarth, went conscientiously from town to town presenting the British case. At Chota, Old Hop said that all his men intending for war that year had already gone—as indeed they had. At Great Tellico the town was celebrating a mass drunk brought on by an itinerant peddler who had become senseless on his own wares. At Hiwassee the headmen, perhaps reflecting a past carelessness with back-woods horseflesh, perversely said that Virginia was too danger-ous, for they always had trouble with the settlers. Then the Mankiller of Great Tellico, his banishment apparently figurative, appeared and promised sixty warriors in return for cloth with which to bind up his conjuring instruments. Howarth provided it, but the Mankiller, true to form, failed to keep his promise. At Joree no one would go, alleging lack of authority from Old Hop. Joree trader James May had spoken ominously of death awaiting Cherokees in Virginia. Even the sixty Overhills assigned to Byrd by the Little Carpenter had impatiently gone home.[8] When on May 1st, Byrd set out to join Forbes in Pennsylvania, but fifty-nine Cherokees, mostly Estatoes, accompanied him.[9] The fact of the matter was that already nearly four hundred Cherokees had gone north from the Overhills, the Middle Settle-ments, and the Lower Towns. It was near the maximum number of warriors the Cherokees ever committed to one theater of action. Their dependence upon spring hunts, the demands of home defense in wartime, and their unwillingness to risk too

[8] S. C. Council Journals, Apr. 10–12, 1758.
[9] Amherst Papers, May 14, 1758, B.P.R.O., W.O. 34/35.

146

much in one quarter probably prevented further commitment.

Certainly the ominous note of Cherokee-Virginia hostility struck here and there in the nation had not been in evidence in the north in the winter months. Throughout the winter devoted Cherokees accompanied by volunteers from the Virginia provincial regiment attempted fruitlessly to spy on Fort Duquesne. One party was caught in deep snows and forced to hole up near the fort for ten days. Finally discovered and attacked by enemy Indians, they fled through the winter woods to Fort Cumberland.

The continual disappointments affected even the stoic Indians. Round O's group from Stecoe working out of Fort Frederick with Richard Pearis blamed the partisan Captain for their failures and went to Annapolis in mid-March to complain to Governor Sharpe. Honored guests, they were lodged in a house on the main street and pampered and visited, wined and dined.[10] In the Statehouse they conferred with the Governor and his council in the grand manner with calumet, talks, beads, and presents, and the assembly voted substantial sums for additional presents.[11] Gratified, the Indians entertained the townsmen with ceremonial dances and after three weeks of the white man's fare returned to outpost duty at Fort Frederick with Pearis' high standing in Maryland unaffected.[12] They carried with them the impression that Forbes's ponderous expedition would soon be moving.[13]

The presence of Cherokees on the Virginia-Pennsylvania frontier complicated the English effort through Teedyuscung, headman of the eastern Delawares, now at peace, to detach the Ohio Shawnees and Delawares from the French. In the previous autumn Teedyuscung had sent a belt to Keowee with the deputies returning from the six Nations. But he feared that the Cherokees might attack deputies of the French Indians on their way to negotiate with the English; and the English, fearful that the southern Indians might withdraw from the war if they heard

[10] Sullivan, etc., *op. cit.*, II, 784–85.
[11] Sharpe, *op. cit.*, II, 163.
[12] *Maryland Gazette*, Apr. 6, 1758.
[13] Sharpe, *op. cit.*, II, 185–86.

of these overtures, kept the negotiations secret. However, the chance of a clash was remote; for already the Lower Towns with Chota's approval had sent Teedyuscung a favorable reply.[14]

Toward the end of March, the early tide of Cherokees began to register in Virginia. With the arrival of 150 Lower Townsmen at Winchester the number of Cherokees on that front reached 250, with 200 more on the way. The Overhills journeyed along the Warrior's Path from Chota to the Great Island of the Holston and thence to the Shenandoah Valley. Through the spring woods of budding oak and poplar they came in parties of 10 to 40 men each. The Lower Townsmen in larger force followed the Catawba path through Salisbury, North Carolina, and across the Yadkin to the Moravian log and stone village of Bethabara. At Bethabara, which they designated "the Dutch Fort where they are good people and much bread,"[15] they usually lingered several days, camping in the pastures, watching the settlers at mill and forge, and never tiring of the chapel bell which summoned to morning and evening worship. Leaving Bethabara, they crossed Dan River into Virginia, reaching the Warrior's Path just before it entered the Shenandoah Valley. Near the junction stood the hospitable home of Andrew Lewis. At Winchester, Atkin's deputy, Christopher Gist, outfitted them from Virginia stores at royal expense. They then dispersed, some to Fort Cumberland and the forts on the South Branch, others to Fort Frederick, and to Forbes' advanced posts at Shippensburg and Carlisle.

Though hearts still burned, the intercolonial rivalry for Indian auxiliaries had officially ceased. Washington might grumble that Cherokees went to Pennsylvania rather than to the Virginia frontier, and Governor Sharpe could rejoice in Indians based on Fort Frederick; but the Indians belonged to one force, that under Forbes. Gone, too, was the dispute between Johnson's deputies and Atkin's. All Indians regardless of nation when north of the Potomac were Johnson's; when south, Atkin's.[16]

14 Sullivan, etc., *op. cit.*, II, 842–51.
15 A. L. Fries, ed., *Records of the Moravians in North Carolina*, I, 194.
16 A. P. Jones, *Writings of General John Forbes*, 138.

Both principals being far away, their deputies, Gist for Atkin, Trent and Croghan for Johnson, handled matters amicably. The only defect was the usual shortage of goods and presents which crown and colony too slowly remedied.[17]

As the snows dissolved in the Alleghenies, Cherokees and Catawbas probed toward Fort Duquesne and kept it under almost constant surveillance. Some of Wawhatchee's men scouted as far north as Venango on the Upper Allegheny and Presque Isle on Lake Erie.[18] From the pen of George Washington comes an account of one party's adventure:

> The first of last month [April] Lt. Gist [Christopher's son] with 6 soldiers and thirty Indians left the south branch of the Potomac River; and after a tedious march occasioned by deep snows . . . they got upon the waters of Monongahela, where Mr. Gist . . . got lamed and was rendered incapable of marching. . . . the white men and some Indians stayed with him, and the remainder of the Indians divided into three small parties . . . . Ucahula and two others went down the Monongahela in a bark canoe, and landed on the north side not far from Fort Duquesne . . . . They lay concealed two days to make discoveries and, if possible, get a prisoner; but no favorable opportunity offering . . . they attacked a canoe in which two Frenchmen were fishing; both of whom they killed and scalped in sight of some other Frenchmen also fishing . . . . He saw a party on the other side of the river, which he supposed to be newly come, because there were several canoes near them and they seemed to be putting up bark huts . . . . When he had got . . . fifteen miles this side of Fort Duquesne he came upon a large encampment and tracks steering toward Virginia . . . . Lt. Gist came upon a track of another large party . . . . These parties have since fallen upon the back inhabitants of Augusta County . . . . I have . . . engaged Ucahula with a small party of brisk men, to go immediately to Fort Duquesne to try to get a prisoner.[19]

Late in April manifestations of Cherokee discontent appeared. The "Raven" party—probably of Estatoe—arrived in Win-

[17] Sullivan, etc., *op. cit.*, II, 784–85.

[18] Henry Bouquet, "Papers," Ser. 2, 81.

[19] Fitzpatrick, *op. cit.*, II, 191–92.

149

chester from Fort Frederick bearing two scalps which the Raven presented to Washington with a demand for a reward. Other Cherokees at the base knew the scalps as spurious—probably those of the whites killed on the Catawba path to avenge the Edisto murders. Indignant, they alerted the young Colonel, who rejected the Raven's demand. The disappointed trickster departed southward from Winchester, perhaps, as Washington thought, in a consciousness of guilt and the dread of being called to severe account by his countrymen; but not before Christopher Gist, who feared the Indian would give bad talks on the path, had sweetened him with presents.[20]

About this time Cherokees approaching Winchester met some of their disgruntled countrymen coming away and turned back with them, saying that the English were rogues and the French and Shawnees good people.[21] And on April 13 the Augusta county court had indicted one Hugh McNamara on suspicion of attempting in the French interest to seduce Cherokees from the English cause.[22] With two large parties of unhappy Cherokees in Virginia, serious trouble was probable.

Nor was it long delayed. About May 1 marauding Cherokees returning from Winchester alarmed settlers on Otter Creek in southwestern Virginia. The Indians entered homes, threatened people, took clothing and household utensils, ripped featherbeds, and carried off plunder on stolen horses. Settlers flocked from the region in panic. When sterner souls followed the thieves to retrieve their stolen goods, the Indians fired upon them.[23] The whites fled but, reinforced, soon returned, eleven in number, amongst them one William Verdiman. The official report of what followed states that when the pursuers came to Staunton River they

. . . heard the Indians war halloo on the other side . . . . when they

[20] *Ibid.*, II, 201.

[21] Hamilton, *op. cit.*, II, 312–14.

[22] J. Waddell, *Annals of Augusta County, Virginia*, 78–79.

[23] Hamilton, *op. cit.*, II, 307, 310–11.

got over . . . they found a small fire just kindled and at some small distance . . . the enemy. William Verdiman aged about sixty went foremost . . . when they came up to the enemy they found they had tied their horses . . . to the bushes, that most of the Indians were painted . . . others painting, some black, some red but mostly black . . . . Old Verdiman pulled off his hat, bowed and accosted them . . . and said Gentlemen we came in brotherly fashion to ask you for our horses and other goods . . . . the Indians gave a kind of grunt and determined for mischief, stripped themselves . . . struck their tomahawks into trees and demanded . . . if they would fight. . . . whilst Verdiman was still . . . bowing and treating . . . the Indians attempted to environ them and actually got into a half circle before [the whites] were aware. . . . [the whites] all retreated . . . with their faces toward the enemy and took to the trees . . . . The Indians threw tomahawks . . . one of them would have hit old Verdiman but luckily he parried it with an elder stick . . . and the Indians pursuing and they retreating . . . they were nearly pushed to the river bank . . . a gun was fired upon which the engagement ensued . . . in which [one of the whites] fell . . . mortally wounded . . . three Indians fell.[24]

Out of ammunition, the whites retired. Militiamen rallied and went after the Indians. On May 10, eight or nine miles from Bedford, thirty-five Virginians encountered a large party of Cherokees. As the Virginians reported it:

A captain and a lieutenant . . . went up to talk with ye Indians . . . and desired to be in friendship with them. The Indians answered "no brothers, no Cherokees," they were Shawnees [who] took the cap of[f] the Lt. . . . and stripped and beat them. They were glad to get of[f] naked . . . on which the rest of the men pursued and got before the Indians and had a scrimmage with them. But ye . . . Indians computed 60 or 70 and ye white men about forty and sum [sic] part of ye white men run before a gun fired. Others broke soon after without being of any service[.] The Indians kept the ground.[25]

[24] IBSC, VI, 154–56.
[25] Hamilton, *op. cit.*, II, 296–98, 309.

Altogether seventeen or eighteen Cherokees, Middle Settlements and Lower Townsmen, were killed in the two encounters, a heavy toll to lose to an ally.[26]

The bad effects of the episodes were cushioned and delayed. The Indians in British service heard the news first from the English; and, far from home and among potential enemies, they behaved. When the Cherokees with Colonel Byrd learned the story at Bedford, they raged for vengeance and threatened to go home, but Byrd induced them to continue on to Winchester and sent a messenger to McIntosh at Fort Prince George with the bad news. To prevent further clashes Virginia ordered three hundred militiamen to patrol Cherokee routes but to refrain from warfare, and appealed to Lyttelton to restrain the Cherokees.[27] No more incidents occurred that spring.

But the crest of the Cherokee participation in the Forbes expedition had passed. Cherokee war parties seldom stayed from home more than three or four months. Accustomed to taking the warpath in early spring, they became contemptuous of the midsummer redcoats and their General who in three months' time had made no contact with the enemy and were not halfway to their objective. In May there had been four hundred Cherokees in the British service, but their number began to dwindle in June. British officers, accustomed to specific terms of enlistment, regarded the departing Indians as deserters. Forbes sent orders to Washington at Winchester to prevent further departures, and the harassed young Colonel even rode out from town to persuade one party which had left to return.[28] But no one could stay Wawhatchee. He had held his warriors at Carlisle all through May awaiting Forbes, but when he learned of the bloody encounters between his countrymen and the Virginians, he left for the Lower Towns in anger.[29] With talks and presents Colonel Bouquet in command of Forbes' advanced forces labored among the remain-

26 IBSC, VI, 165.
27 Journals of the Executive Council of Virginia, May 20, May 29, 1758.
28 Fitzpatrick, *op. cit.*, II, 198–200.
29 Bouquet, *loc. cit.*, Ser. 2, 84.

ing Indians to renew interest in the campaign. Only the arrival of the old South Carolina Indian hand Abraham Bosomworth escorting a warrior band prevented his failure.

First word of the Virginia clashes reached Keowee late in May when the battered warriors who had suffered in Virginia arrived with a letter from Colonel Byrd to McIntosh reporting their disaster and asking that he do something to appease them.[30] The Little Carpenter then at Keowee en route from Charlestown had no sympathy with the injured Indians; for he understood his countrymen and suspected that there had been misbehavior. He very sensibly told McIntosh that whites and Indians having suffered, the matter should be dropped. In Keowee town house he rebuked his countrymen, and he sent orders to the warriors with Forbes to behave themselves until he should come to put things right in Virginia. Then he set out for the Overhills with George Turner, an agent Byrd had left to bring more warriors north. A difficult road lay ahead of him; for at Joree he saw faces painted black in mourning for relatives slain in Virginia and heard violent talks of vengeance.

With each returning war party the nation became more agitated. Without the Little Carpenter's tempering influence bad feeling festered in the Lower Towns. Wawhatchee had returned in a rage. The Overhills became grim, and even the Little Carpenter hesitated to go into dangerous Virginia. Finally he told Turner that the omens were bad and that he could not go. Fearing for Turner's life, he sent him under escort to Keowee from whence the Virginian departed the nation.[31]

But the conciliatory forces were still strong. The Virginia explosion had been unexpected. Horse-stealing was not new to the Cherokees, for on the frontier settlers' horses roamed unfenced until their owners caught them. House-plundering had occurred before when Cherokees believed that Colonials had slighted them, and had gone unpunished. The armed encounters caused surprise and dismay among the headmen, who feared an English

[30] McIntosh to Lyttelton, May 27, 1758, Lyttelton Papers.
[31] IBSC, VI, 151–53, 165.

war. The strong talks Lyttelton sent to Keowee and Chota demanding satisfaction for English losses led Tistoe and the Wolf to take a conciliatory line.[32] They blamed Wawhatchee for the bad talk. Old Hop, accusing the warriors of Overhill Settico, apologized to Paul Demere; and when Wawhatchee, seeking support for his vengeful mood, went to the Valley, the Fire King forbade anyone's taking the hatchet. Meanwhile a new alarm developed at Keowee. A Georgia trader, who had surreptitiously bought Virginia plunder from the Cherokees, spread a story that Lyttelton conspired with the Creeks to destroy them.[33] The excited Lower Townsmen plotted to attack Fort Prince George, but the Little Carpenter hurriedly sent important Overhill warriors to counsel patience.[34] When in August the Little Carpenter set out for Virginia, it appeared that the incidents could be peacefully settled.

In the north to allay Cherokee apprehensions over the Virginia troubles and to stem the exodus of the tribesmen many old southern Indian hands were employed. Colonel Byrd, though entitled to a regiment, stayed with his fifty-nine Indians. Richard Pearis made repeated journeys between Fort Frederick and Forbes's advance to lead Cherokees into forward positions in the campaign. Abraham Bosomworth remained in Winchester to persuade tribesmen returning from Fort Cumberland to join Forbes in Pennsylvania. Even former Governor Glen was active. By the end of June the few Cherokees remaining seemed to have recovered their spirits. Bouquet saw them doing "what I never heard of any Indian doing before. That is working for us and carrying a quantity of bark to roof our storehouse."[35]

Vexations, however, did not end. Colonel Byrd's party refused to leave Fort Cumberland to join Bouquet at Reastown, giving as their reason that they did not care to march to Fort Duquesne over any road but Braddock's. Interestingly, the

[32] P. Demere to Lyttelton, July 30, 1758, Lyttelton Papers.
[33] McIntosh to Lyttelton, July 28, Aug. 1, 1758, *ibid.*
[34] P. Demere to Lyttelton, July 30, 1758, *ibid.*
[35] Bouquet, *loc. cit.*, Ser. 2, 105.

Cherokee impatience with Forbes's interminable road-building reflected Byrd's and Washington's hostile point of view concerning the feasibility of a new Pennsylvania road when a usable road already existed. Aware of the Fort Cumberland heresy, Bouquet sent Glen to fasten onto any new Indians who came there before they became infected. Cherokees escorted by Richard Pearis to various points tended to collect presents and then follow him when he left.[36] There was also the problem of identification. Indians pretending to be Cherokees killed two wagoners, and Forbes ordered Cherokees to wear "a yellow badge or fillet . . . around their heads or tied about their arms or breast."[37] But as July ended, the likelihood of a Cherokee coming to grief from mistaken identity had lessened considerably; barely forty were with the army.[38] Too few to fight, they were used as scouts. The Virginia partisan Colley Chew depicted one party at work in August near Fort Duquesne:

> We hid ourselves in a thicket until the Indians had congered and painted after which we went down the river to within 3/4s of a mile of the fort then turned to the SE. and went up a stony ridge where the chief warrior took his congering implements and tied them about the necks of the three . . . young Indians . . . and told them they could not be hurt; round my neck he tied the otter skin in which the congering implements had been kipt [*sic*] and round the sgt's neck he tied a bag of paint that had been kipt with the implements, he then told us not one of us could be shot . . . he then made us strip ourselves of all our clothes except our breechcloths and mocasins [*sic*] and then shook hands with us and told us to go fight like men for nothing could hurt us.[39]

The hallowed preparations led, however, to nothing; for the enemy Indians were too numerous about the fort.

Not all the Cherokees in the north that summer were on

36 *Ibid.*, Ser. 2, 113, 121.
37 Hamilton, *op. cit.*, II, 348.
38 Fitzpatrick, *op. cit.*, II, 248.
39 Hamilton, *op. cit.*, III, 39–40.

the warpath. Deputies from Keowee, headed by Moyeman, or Kool, who had been at Fort Johnson in 1757, carried an answer to Teedyuscung and the Six Nations.[40] Agreed to by Chota, it was a pledge to even more ardent war against the French and their Indians. Moyeman arrived in Philadelphia about June 1, but became ill with pleurisy and for two weeks hovered between life and death. Fearing that the business might be delayed, the Pennsylvania authorities persuaded Moyeman to give his talk for the Delawares from his sickbed. A week later, carried to the Statehouse, he dictated the talk he had for the Iroquois. As Henley, his assistant, brought out tokens and implements in their proper order, the sick man gave the talk with full ritual of pipe, wampum, and belts as he had memorized it in Keowee. Learning that the famous Mohawk conjurer, Seneca George, was near, he called him to his bedside. Shortly the authorities received a petition from Moyeman reading, "I desire Seneka George may have two bottles of rum, he thinks it necessary for my service and designs it as an offering."[41]

Effectively doctored, Moyeman proceeded to New York where he taught another set of Colonial officials how to entertain Cherokee deputies. The New Yorkers, wishing to speed the envoys, had engaged a sloop to take the Indians to Albany the day after their arrival. But the Cherokees expected a full ceremonial hearing—a four-day affair with reception by the Governor and council, talks, and gifts. That is what they received, to the extent even of the Governor's visiting the ailing Moyeman in his lodgings. The gifts from the frugal council were, however, disappointing: saucepans, ribbons, gartering, vermilion, and six pounds of soap.[42]

When the Cherokees arrived at Fort Johnson on July 19, Sir William returned from the Lake George frontier to receive them, and with his usual feeling for protocol and dispatch, launched without delay into the proper ceremonial. Condoling with the

[40] IBSC, VI, 117–18.
[41] Sullivan, etc., *op. cit.*, II, 860–64.
[42] New York Council, "Minutes," XXV, 245–48.

Cherokees for their losses in battle, he presented Moyeman with a French scalp taken at Ticonderoga in symbolic replacement of Swallow Warrior killed the year before.

On the twenty-first in the presence of Sir William and Mohawk, Oneida, and Seneca sachems, Moyeman delivered his talk and belts.[43] Iroquois and Cherokees under English auspices sealed their friendship in a pledge to fight the French and thus laid the ghost of the backdoor intrigue for neutrality between Chota and Onondaga. On August 12, the amenities completed, Sir William symbolically cleared the path to enable the Cherokees to depart in peace, and Moyeman and his companions set out on the long path of far return.[44]

Since May in southwestern Virginia there had been no conflicts between settlers and Cherokees. Most parties leaving the Potomac went home by unfrequented routes or else under escort through the province. But for unguided groups there were hazards undreamed of even by Indians.

On August 19, not far from Draper's Meadows on New River, Captain Wade's frontier patrol came upon five Valley Cherokees going toward the Tennessee with horses, possibly stolen. The temptation was too great. Virginia paid a £50 scalp bounty, and none could tell whether a scalp was Shawnee or Cherokee. According to one of the men:

> After the captain heard the opinion of the people he past sentence of death upon them. . . . we overtook and past them because the captain said they were in such order we could not kill them all . . . . They were agoing toward New River . . . the men knew of two fords and they emagined they would cross one of them . . . . We laid an ambuscade at each ford . . . and the captain's orders were to fire at them as they crossed the river . . . . But after we had placed ourselves and sat awhile 2 or 3 of the men came . . . and informed us that the Indians had cross't at the Loer ford and they did not fire because they were all together. So the captain and the men went down toward the Loer ford and as we went along we saw 4 of the

43 Sullivan, etc., *op. cit.*, IX, 945–49.
44 Johnson to Abercrombie, Aug. 12, 1758.

Indians; but we did not fire . . . the captain concluded to ly by for awhile and let them all get together. . . . soon after the other Indian followed them and the captain's orders was for twelve of the best men to follow them. . . . the captain proposed . . . to dog them till night then to ly by until brake of day and then follow them. But we did not approve his skemes . . . we followed them and overtook them at a peach orchard just as they were leaving it . . . and fired at them and followed them up until we killed four of them, and wounded the other. We skelped them that we killed and then followed the other . . . . He bled very much . . . he went into the river and to an island . . . some of the men left looking for him and went down to the fort and some went after the Indians' horses. But myself and four or five more we search't the island until late in the afternoon and when we came to the fort the captain and the men were handling the Indians' goods . . . . Next morning we pack't up in order to return homeward for signs of Indians was plenty and we had little ammunition. But before we left the fort we were sworn not to tell we had ever heard them say they were Cherokees.[45]

It was murder and robbery by forces acting under Virginia commission and intent on perpetrating a fraud on the colony. It was not intended that there be a survivor to report the incident in the nation. But the wounded warrior, who skillfully evaded pursuit, came naked into the Valley with news of the death of three important Valley headmen.[46]

Inflammatory as this incident was, more crucial to the future course of events was the clash which occurred at Bedford about the same time. Settlers, angry over horse-stealing, set upon the Lower Townsmen who had accompanied Colonel Byrd north in the spring. They were returning under escort. According to their interpreter, trader James Beamer's mixed-blood son:

Thirty or forty miles from Winchester they all put their horses into a pasture and that night there was six horses stole out. . . . one of them James Holmes that went out of this nation with an express

[45] W. P. Palmer, S. McRae, and W. H. Fleurnoy, *Calendar of Virginia State Papers*, I, 255–57.
[46] McIntosh to Lyttelton, Sept. 18, 1758, Lyttelton Papers.

to Virginia. . . . the Indians that lost their horses two of them was warriors belonging to this town [Estatoe]. . . . the Indians said since the white people began to steal horses from them first, they would take horses which [young Beamer] as soon as he see them would make the Indians turn loose.

At Bedford Courthouse young Beamer was told that as he went out the next day he would be waylaid by the inhabitants. He sent one of the two white men in his party to ask the inhabitants to refrain from mischief for he would keep the Indians from doing any harm. But at Goose Creek the next day, "the white people all rose up . . . and ordered the Indians to ground their arms which they did and the white people fired on them." Four Indians fell, three dead and one wounded. Beamer and the two white men a little distance behind rode up as fast as they could. The Indians threw off their packs and picked up their guns. By that time Beamer and Holmes were riding back and forth between the whites and Indians and succeeded in preventing further bloodshed. Two of the dead had distinguished themselves but shortly before in a fight against a patrol of French and Indians.[47] The outraged Indians hurried toward the nation. At the time, the Little Carpenter with thirty warriors was on the road to Williamsburg to ask for an adjustment of the spring disorders.[48]

But even as the Second Man went up the path, reports of the new clashes poured into the nation and the towns seethed with hatred of the Virginians. Vengeance-seeking warriors started north, and runners raced toward the Creeks and the Chickasaws to raise them against the whites.[49]

The Lower Towns traders, their lives at stake, worked feverishly to prevent war. Beamer talked earnestly to the Estatoe headmen, and Lachlan McIntosh hurriedly sent to Lyttelton for gifts to meet Wawhatchee's furious demands.[50] On September

[47] J. Beamer to Lyttelton, Sept. 16, 1758, *ibid.*
[48] Jones, *op. cit.*, 230.
[49] S. C. Council Journals, Nov. 16, 1758.
[50] McIntosh to Lyttelton, Oct. 21, 1758, Lyttelton Papers.

26, Lyttelton in a conciliatory message to the Lower Towns headmen invoked the treaty of 1730. Taking a position which he knew the Indians would understand, he asked that the killings on New River and Goose Creek be regarded not as an act of all Virginia but as that of private individuals who would be punished by the proper authorities and that satisfaction would be rendered by Governor Fauquier. Meanwhile, if the war parties were recalled, he would send presents to the relatives of the slain. However, should conciliation fail, South Carolina would embargo goods and ammunition, and Crown and Colony would move against the nation.[51]

Even Wawhatchee quailed before this ominous warning, and seemed disposed to follow the Lower Towns' moderates in accepting Lyttelton's terms.[52] The First Warrior of the Lower Towns by now knew that the Cherokees stood alone; for the Creeks and the Chickasaws both had rejected his appeal for a league against the English.[53] There was even a prospect of war with the Creeks, for Creek guests at a drunken brawl in Keowee had killed two of their hosts. Wawhatchee hastened runners after the Virginia-bound war parties in hopes of overtaking them before they did damage, and Lower Townsmen once again smiled at traders.

Chota, however, expressed its disillusionment with the Virginians by making peace with the Shawnee allies of the French against whom the Cherokees had fought to protect the Virginia frontier. The move led to further Cherokee isolation. Before the year was out it ruptured Catawba-Cherokee friendship. Cherokees returning from Virginia allowed Shawnees to pass them and attack a near-by party of Catawbas.

In the north, a few Cherokees still stayed with Forbes, but they were of little value. When the French and their Indians attacked Bouquet at Loyalhanna, none of the Cherokees would fight.[54] Indeed they all threatened to go home unless they re-

---

51 Wawhatchee to Lyttelton, Sept. 18, 1758, *ibid.*
52 S. C. Council Journals, Nov. 14, 1758.
53 Chandler, *op. cit.*, XXVIII, Pt. 1–A, 242–43.

ceived presents. To the sick General they and their interpreters appeared "imposing rogues" who sought to blackmail him. Evidently he thought that Cherokees, unlike loyal subjects of the crown, should fight for nothing. He grasped eagerly at the Little Carpenter's presence in Virginia to resolve his difficulties and sent Glen to Winchester to divert the Second Man from his Williamsburg mission. The former South Carolina Governor succeeded in bringing the Cherokee to Reastown.[55]

Forbes at first disdained the protocol of presents implicit in the Cherokee headman's visit. He treated the diplomat "with the greatest signs of indifference and disdain" as a mere seeker of bribes.[56] Nevertheless, the Little Carpenter contented himself with a token acknowledgment and agreed to hold his warriors with the army, thereby demonstrating to both English and Cherokee the disposition of Chota to peace.

His services, however, disappointed Forbes. The General could not understand why the Little Carpenter's men refused to join the November advance to capture Fort Duquesne. The reason seems to have been an unwillingness to be allied to an attack which might endanger Shawnees, for the Little Carpenter made peaceful contact with the Shawnees and was informed that the French would abandon the fort. Possibly he also learned from the Shawnees that relations between his countrymen and the Virginians had further deteriorated, and concluded that it was necessary for him to go to Williamsburg as soon as possible. He reported to Forbes that Fort Duquesne would be abandoned, stated that there was grave possibility of a Cherokee war with Virginia, and went off to complete his mission of peace.[57] The General regarded him as a deserter to the enemy and sent couriers to have him seized, stripped of arms, and escorted from post to post from Virginia.[58] To James Glen at Fort Cumber-

---

[54] Jones, *op. cit.*, 226.

[55] S. C. Council Journals, Apr. 17, 1758.

[56] Jones, *op. cit.*, 224.

[57] S. C. Council Journals, Apr. 17, 1759.

[58] Jones, *op. cit.*, 256.

land fell the assignment of subjecting his old antagonist to the humiliating order.

Meanwhile in South Carolina with the approach of the hunting season the Virginia incidents appeared to be moving toward a peaceful resolution. In November, Tistoe and the Wolf of Keowee, the Mankiller of Keowee, Conjurer Jaime of offended Estatoe, and two headmen of Toxaway, having been received with military honors in Charlestown, conferred with Lyttelton. Though the governor blamed the Cherokees, he pointed out that Virginia had now repealed the scalp bounty which had caused the New River episode in August, that she would return all the plunder then taken from the Cherokees, and had taken measures to prevent further outrages. He said that if the Cherokees would recall their war parties and send a peace delegation to Virginia, the King's forces would not attack; but if war came, the Cherokees would stand alone, for no southern Indians would league with them. The headmen informed him that his conditions were in the process of being met. Thereupon Lyttelton promised particular presents to the headmen whose relatives had been slain and that he would not embargo the trade.[59] Seemingly appeased, the headmen set our for home to place before their towns the settlement they had made.

[59] Lyttelton to Amherst, Dec. 27, 1759, Amherst Papers, B.P.R.O., W. O. 34/35.

162

CHAPTER TWELVE

A Divided Nation

IN THE WINTER OF 1758–59, while Cherokee high policy looked to a peaceful resolution of the Virginia trouble, war feeling ran strong among the nativists. Wawhatchee, stirred by fresh English offenses, raged. Moytoy of Hiwassee talked of bitter vengeance. Standing Turkey of Chota, heir-designate of Old Hop, was darkly anti-English.[1] Particular hotbeds of unrest were Lower Towns Estatoe and Overhills Settico. These two towns, related by clan ties, had suffered heavy losses. They fed each other's resentments and were objectives for strong Creek and French propaganda.[2] The Mortar, an anti-English Creek headman who, at French behest, had established a settlement less than a week's journey from the Overhills, frequently visited Settico and chided the Setticoes for their tardiness in avenging their slain. He propagated alarm by reviving the story that the English intended to enslave the Cherokee women and children. He raised hopes that the French might soon come to establish a great trade and to drive the English out of the nation.[3] At Estatoe not only did scheming Creeks urge action but Ensign Belestre, the Frenchman captured in Pennsylvania when the Swallow Warrior fell,[4] had the ear of Seroweh, the Head Warrior of the town, who had taken vengeance for the Edisto murders the year before, and of Conjurer Jaime, the First Man of the town.

[1] Richardson, *loc. cit.*, Jan. 11, Jan. 20, 1759.

[2] S. C. Council Journals, June 20, 1760.

[3] Richardson, *loc. cit.*, Feb. 1, Feb. 6, 1759.

[4] *Virginia Gazette*, June 7, 1760.

The peace party, consisting, in the absence of the Little Carpenter, of Tistoe of Keowee, Round O of Stecoe, Oconostota of Tanase, and Willinawaw of Toquo, were a powerful and restraining minority.[5] But even these wavered and might if given additional provocation go over to the war party; for all parties had heard of Forbes's insult to the Little Carpenter, and they worried for the Little Carpenter's safety in hostile Virginia.

At January's end it began to appear that the whole nation might soon storm out to war, for new troubles had broken out. Carolina settlers had gone thirty or forty miles over the Long Canes' line into the Lower Towns' hunting grounds to kill deer. On news of this, Standing Turkey went about Chota denouncing the English as "thieves and rogues" because they stole the Cherokees' "land, bears, and elks, and beavers." Talk boiled hotly in Chota that an Englishman would die for every Cherokee slain in Virginia. So dark were the looks cast upon white men that the Presbyterian missionary William Richardson, who had come to Chota hoping to make converts, lost his zeal and fled to Keowee. There, save for the members of the Keowee ball team who tried to get him to use his magic on their behalf, his message of Christian love fell on barren ground. Wawhatchee went angrily to Fort Prince George and denounced the English to Ensign Lachlan McIntosh, the commander. Word that Governor Lyttelton, influenced by Forbes's charges, would not receive the Little Carpenter when he returned from Virginia created a furor. Rumor ran that if the French attacked Fort Loudoun, hundreds of disaffected Cherokees would join them.[6]

While the nation glowered, in Virginia the Little Carpenter talked peace with Fauquier. During December and January, fearful of traveling unarmed in Virginia, he had lingered at Winchester; but on January 9, guided by Abraham Smith, he appeared in Williamsburg. Before the cold Governor, the Cherokee diplomat was humble. His people, he said, had at the be-

[5] J. Adair, *History of the American Indians*, 263–64.
[6] Richardson, *loc. cit.*, Jan. 30, Feb. 24, 1759.

ginning acted unjustifiably, "but since later the English had offended," he proposed that the troubles be forgotten. Finally rallying to his mission, he strove to achieve a bargaining position. The path to Virginia, he said, could be made open and clear if Virginia would fulfill her Broad River promises of trade and a garrison. There must, however, be presents.

Though eager to avert a war, Fauquier took a strong stand. Denying presents to his visitor, he accused the Cherokees of violating the Treaty of 1730 by failing to surrender those Indians whose misbehavior had caused the troubles. He stated flatly that the British never again would reward Indians until after they had rendered services. He disavowed any Virginia obligation to garrison the Chota fort, for Virginia had agreed only to co-operate in Carolina's fort-building.[7] Then, surprisingly, he proposed to open the promised Cherokee trade that very spring; for the burgesses in 1757 had agreed to support an official Cherokee trade under a board of commissioners who had already ordered £5,000 in trade goods from England. The Little Carpenter realized that he had won a great victory. Despite the Governor's violent tongue-lashing and his failure to offer presents, Virginia had granted what he desired, peace and trade.[8] The elated diplomat hurried a runner off to inform Tistoe at Keowee and to tell him to go at once to Chota with the good news.

But the Little Carpenter was to be tried as no Cherokee headman before him had been tried in historic times. The nation was plunging toward an English war which even he might not be able to prevent. In Chota town house French-allied Ottawas made overtures for peace and alliance; and, the pro-French Creek headman, the Mortar, delivered a French talk and sought permission to settle on Cherokee lands at Hiwassee Old Town and Old Estatoe.[9] In Settico the Mortar conspired with the Moytoy of that town, who on pretense of making his winter hunt shortly set off to take scalps in Virginia or North Carolina. Even

[7] Journals of the Executive Council of Virginia, Jan. 19, 1759.
[8] Richardson, *loc. cit.*, Mar. 14, 1759.
[9] S. C. Council Journals, Apr. 21, 1759; IBSC, VI, 178.

in the Middle Settlements the war fever burned; for "renegade" Virginians with grudges of their own to settle excited the hot-headed with anti-English talk.

The Little Carpenter, swallowing his anger at a North Carolina attempt to kill him on his way home, held to his purpose of averting what he foresaw as certain calamity to his people.[10] On March 13, unaware of what the Setticoes intended, he stood triumphant in Chota town house to denounce French lies and to lay before the headmen the Virginia talk of peace and trade.[11] Chota, despite Fauquier's failure to give satisfaction for those killed on New River, and unaware of new trouble in the making from forces out of control, eagerly confirmed the peace. Sending Fauquier a promise that all mischief would end, the Little Carpenter set out for Charlestown to reassure Carolina and to allow Lyttelton to make a demonstration over him which would signify friendship.

Lyttelton now desired very much to see the Little Carpenter, for he had heard of both the Virginia peace and the rumored French attack upon Fort Loudoun.[12] But like Fauquier he was determined to be firm. His reception of the ambassador on April 16 was cool. When the Cherokee came into the council chamber bearing a French scalp upon his scalp pole, Lyttelton sternly charged him with having deserted the Forbes army. Only after he heard the headman's lengthly defense did he deign to take his hand. When the Indians returned to their camp, they saw that Carolina had provided but lean fare. Sensitive to the slight, the Little Carpenter next day pleaded in moving terms for Lyttelton's confidence:

> I am not a rogue, nor given that way. Many bad and false talks have been sent your Excellency of the Cherokees and many such have also been sent me of the white people, but I believe them not. My love for my own people and their young ones has always determined me to do everything in my power to prevent their falling

10 Richardson, *loc. cit.*, Mar. 14, 1759.
11 S. C. Council Journals, Apr. 18, 1759.
12 Journals of the Executive Council of Virginia, Apr. 17, 1759.

out with the white people having told them they would be thoroughly destroyed . . . . I am the only one alive of those who went to see the Great King. He told me never to take a Frenchman by the hand nor to have anything to do with them but to take care and to love and to behave well to his children the white people . . . . I have always done so and will always continue to do so . . . . I have brought two strings of wampum to your excellency of equal length. The one denotes the lies that are told to your Excellency; the other the lies that are told to me. I present them to you as a token and pledge of my fidelity to the Great King over the water.[13]

Lyttelton relented and ordered large quantities of provisions sent to the Cherokee camp. He invited the Little Carpenter to his home for dinner and ordered a parade and review of the colony's troops in his honor. Nevertheless, on the last day of the conference, the Governor was a proconsul talking to a vassal. For after asking the Little Carpenter to remain at home that summer to counter anti-English talk and to thwart the Creeks and the French, he put him on probation. Handing him a string of white beads terminated by three black beads connoting the three bad reports he had heard of him, he said, "When you come to see me again I desire you will bring this string with you . . . and if I then find you have acted the part of a good and faithful friend to the English . . . I will pull off these beads with my own hands and leave it all white."[14] Presents, he said, would not be as plentiful as the last time he came down.

Subdued, the Little Carpenter promised to stay the summer in the nation. However, he had little evidence of English esteem to take home with him. It was small consolation that in the final minutes of the conference Lyttelton granted his request that a trader be established at Keowee, where none had been since Richard Smith had left to serve Virginia in 1757. He had been rebuked before his own people, and his leadership did not bring what it had once brought from Carolina.

Meanwhile, events in the nation surged toward a new crisis.

[13] S. C. Council Journals, Apr. 18, 1759.
[14] *Ibid.*, Apr. 21, 1759.

On May 2, Paul Demere received from Oconostota, who had returned from war down the Tennessee, assurance that he would end the bad talk.[15] Everything seemed quiet. Yet even as Demere wrote his report to Lyttelton, terror gripped the North Carolina frontier. Near the Yadkin on April 22, Setticoes killed four persons.[16] On April 25 and 26 they killed at least eleven more on the branches of Broad and Catawba rivers. On May 3, Moytoy of Settico came with twenty-five warriors into the Lower Towns, boasting nineteen scalps taken in the German settlements along Catawba River. He had avenged the Setticoes killed by Virginians.

Lieutenant Coytmore, who had succeeded Ensign McIntosh in command of Fort Prince George, having orders from Lyttelton to keep the peace with the Indians, could only have Moytoy brought before him to hear a bitter rebuke. Wawhatchee, despite his anti-English intrigue, foreseeing the storm to come, hastily assured Coytmore that the Lower Towns had no part in Moytoy's vengeance. Coytmore looked over the hills and worried that Fort Loudoun had but twenty-five days' provisions and that he lacked pack horses to deliver more. He also heard with apprehension that many Creeks visited in the Lower Towns and that a Creek band hunted near Estatoe Old Town where they planted corn preparatory to settling.

On May 9 or 10 the Little Carpenter came into Keowee, unhappy over Lyttelton's treatment of him. He had been humbled before his followers. The terrible news of Settico's vengeance had destroyed his diplomacy and thrown him into uncharted seas. He knew he would be called on to act, that his action must accord with the English alliance, and that the English would demand blood satisfaction. The largest Overhill clan, that which lived at Settico, was out of hand. To yield up Moytoy and his nineteen Settico offenders to execution at the hands of the English, or to require the outraged Setticoes to execute them, was impossible. For other clans to execute them was also impossible.

[15] IBSC, VI, 179.
[16] Fries, *op. cit.*, I, 209.

He had no alternative but to attempt to treat Settico as Great Tellico had been treated, as an erring town to be disciplined by means short of bloodshed. He dispatched a runner to Chota with orders "that nobody should stir from home until he arrived" and that Old Hop should direct Settico to deliver up the scalps of the whites which should be buried. Then leaving two runners at Fort Prince George to await the stern talk he knew Lyttelton would send, he went toward Chota, stopping in the towns on the way to give strong talks for the English.

The onus of the new outbreak was on the Overhills. Keowee, appeased by Lyttelton's promise to establish a trader in the town and concentrating on the spring hunts, wished to be dissociated from it. Tistoe and Wawhatchee sent white beads to Lyttelton affirming their friendship and apologizing for the Setticoes who, they said, "had acted as if they were drunk."[17] The Settico outrage, they pointed out, was after all the act of but one town. Similar sentiments prevailed in the Middle Settlements where the Maryland-feted Round O won a peace pledge from the headmen and a statement that the memory of the bloodshed should be forgotten. He made Joree wipe away its bad thoughts over the previous year's losses and sent Lyttelton a reassuring message of good will.

On May 26 the Little Carpenter arrived at Chota. In the town house sat a hostile Overhill council which had failed to carry out his orders against the Setticoes.[18] From the fort Captain Demere was demanding the lives of the offenders whom the headmen refused to surrender. Demere, however, was aware that he stood on infirm ground; for the Creeks intrigued in the towns about him, and the French threatened to develop the Mortar's settlement at Coosawaithes as a trading or military base from which to penetrate the Cherokees. These circumstances enabled the Little Carpenter to achieve a temporary solution. Prompted by the Second Man, Demere ordered the trader at Settico to withdraw from the offending town, thus effecting a limited em-

17 IBSC, VI, 180, 184, 190–91.
18 S. C. Council Journals, June 6, 1759.

bargo; and the Setticoes delivered to him eleven of the English scalps they had taken. They retained another eleven. Then, despite his promise to Lyttelton, the Little Carpenter, having done what he could in the nation where even Old Hop was prone to give the malcontents comfort, determined to go himself to war against the French and their northern Indians.

Perhaps the move was the only device by which he could counter the pro-French. Certainly as long as he warred on the French, Chota must remain officially at peace with the English. Ordering the people to behave themselves in his absence, he set off down the Tennessee.[19] If his intention was to keep his people busy with the northern Indians, he succeeded; for in a few weeks his activities caused the Wabash River Twightwees to retaliate with a raid to within twenty miles of Fort Loudoun.

As soon as the Little Carpenter had left, the Overhills under the leadership of Old Hop and Oconostota reopened communication with the French. The Tellico situation of 1756–57 was being repeated, but this time it had broader support in high places. With the English trade already denied Settico and Charlestown's reaction to the Settico compromise uncertain, a Carolina trade embargo, if not worse, was a possibility. Chota began to cast about for support. The Slave Catcher of Chota, an intimate of the Mortar, carrying a red pipe from Old Hop and Standing Turkey and messages from Osteneco and Oconostota, left for the south.[20] Picking up the Mortar at Etowah, he went to Fort Toulouse. The French greeted him enthusiastically and gave him abundant presents, but pressing for a trade, he received only promises. These failed to satisfy Oconostota, who would not trust the French until they produced goods.

Charlestown had no desire for a Cherokee war. When the news of Moytoy's outrage arrived, there was anger and the inevitable distrust of the Little Carpenter because treaty violations had occurred even while he had talked with Lyttelton. The council, however, decided to await formal report from Governor

19 *South Carolina Gazette*, Aug. 4, 1759.
20 *Ibid.,* July 21, 1759.

Dobbs of North Carolina before acting.[21] Lyttelton, pleased with the friendly talks of Tistoe and Wawhatchee, acknowledged them with white beads, but to Old Hop he sent a strong protest.

The bad news had not all been heard; for behind the official face of peace in the Lower Towns dangerous sentiment had built up. All winter and spring pro-French Creeks had labored to fan the smouldering grudge against the Virginians into a holocaust. Creeks visited each of the aggrieved towns—Hiwassee, Settico, and Estatoe—harping on revenge, hoping to push Cherokees into aggressive acts which would provoke English retaliation. Settico had proved fertile ground; but its overt acts had as yet provoked no hasty English counteraction. Indeed the Little Carpenter and Paul Demere appeared for the moment to have muffled the explosion. Estatoe's unsatisfied vengeance alone remained to be exploited. In Estatoe numbers of Creeks, among them Ishenpoaphi of Coweta, brother of the dead Malatchi,[22] had poisoned the air already tainted by the Frenchman Belestre, now living in the family of the dead Swallow Warrior. Rumor of an English attempt to weave an anti-Cherokee plot permeated the town, and possibly the women of the town demanded blood satisfaction for the injuries done the clan.[23] Finally in June, fired by rum smuggled in from the Carolina Broad River settlements, Seroweh, the Young Warrior of Estatoe, authorized Yachtanno, a leading warrior, to take English scalps. Early in July he killed three Englishmen on Pacolet River. On July 20 he brought his reeking trophies home and presented them to a woman—perhaps a clan official—"in revenge for a relative of hers killed by the whites." When Coytmore went in person to demand the hair, the woman palmed off upon him a single old scalp. Like Settico, Estatoe was not to be robbed of its satisfaction.

At this point Governor Lyttelton should have acted vigorously; but the Carolina Governor who had delegated Indian

[21] S. C. Council Journals, May 21, 1759.

[22] McIntosh to Lyttelton, Mar. 31, 1759; Outerbridge to Lyttelton, July 2, 1759, Lyttelton Papers.

[23] Outerbridge to Lyttelton, July 2, 1759, Lyttelton Papers.

discipline to the commanders of the two forts, did nothing. Virginia's Governor Fauquier, however, was of a different temperament. On news from North Carolina of the Settico murders, he hesitated to open the trade promised the Little Carpenter in January until the Cherokees gave satisfaction. On July 2, Coytmore called the Lower Towns headmen to Fort Prince George to hear Fauquier's message. Sternly the Lieutenant offered Wawhatchee the alternative of punishing Estatoe or suffering a trade embargo. Wawhatchee indignantly refused to surrender the guilty Estatoes and withdrew from the fort to meet with certain of the more belligerent headmen in his home. There the angry headmen affirmed their determination never to give satisfaction for the blood that had been spilled, and they considered striking before the expected English retaliation should come.[24] With visiting Overhill dissidents and loitering Creeks they talked of a possible Cherokee-Creek uprising supported by the Alabama French and the French Indians above the Ohio to assault the Virginia and Carolina English.[25] However, the officials of the peace phalanx still hoped that the situation would be glossed over. But instead of appealing to Lyttelton, they sent deputies to Fauquier with white beads to ask that the outrages be forgotten and to give promises of future good behavior.[26] The Creeks, too, were an uncertain quantity, as events would prove.

When Edmund Atkin, bent on quashing the French intrigue among the Creeks, arrived in the Creek country in June, he found a critical situation. The Mortar's conspiracy was far advanced. "Scalps of his majesty's subjects" (obviously some of those taken by the Setticoes) "had been received in the public square of the Oakhoys . . . and of Coweta."[27] The conspirators planned the assassination of the Creek first man and an alliance with the French at Mobile to take Fort Loudoun and destroy the pro-English Chickasaws. To defeat the scheme, Atkin, escorted

[24] Coytmore to Lyttelton, July 23, 1759, *ibid.*
[25] B.P.R.O., C.O. 1328, p. 287.
[26] *Maryland Gazette*, Aug. 30, 1759.
[27] G. S. Kimball, *Correspondence of William Pitt*, I, 268.

by his company of uniformed guards, went from town square to town square threatening to withdraw the trade and bolstering the pro-English or neutral headmen. His success in negotiating on July 18 a trade treaty with the French-allied Choctaws demonstrated to the Creeks and Cherokees the French inability to bring trade goods through the British blockade.[28]

Frustrated by Atkin and spurred by the desperate French, the Mortar and his faction strove harder to impel the Cherokees into further anti-English action. On July 28 in Keowee town house the conspirator Nehalatchco, son of the dead Malatchi of Coweta, and his confederate the Young Twin offered the Lower Townsmen French ammunition and support. The Lower Townsmen agreed to go to war if the Creeks would join them.[29] On August 3 two Lower Towns deputies left for Coweta town with Nehalatchco. Their intent was to trigger a Creek-Cherokee uprising to kill the English among them on August 24.[30] War parties from Toxaway, Conasatchee, and Estatoe began to steal into the woods toward the North Carolina frontier.

The Cherokee parties took scalps on Broad and Pacolet rivers; but the Creek up-rising failed to materialize. Warned by Lyttelton, who had Coytmore's report of the plot, Atkin and neutral Creek headmen stifled the effort to stampede the Cowetas.[31]

With the collapse of Creek support, Wawhatchee sought peace with the English. He sent to Georgia Governor Ellis urging him to come into the woods to talk over Cherokee grievances.[32] The Indian's move appears to have been an effort to circumvent Coytmore, who controlled communications with Charlestown. The Lower Towns had developed a great dislike for the Lieutenant, who in July had taken a firm line with them. They accused him of rumming up and painting himself in the warrior's fashion

---

[28] *Ibid.*

[29] *South Carolina Gazette*, Sept. 22, 1759.

[30] *Maryland Gazette*, Sept. 20, 1759.

[31] *South Carolina Gazette*, Sept. 1, 1759.

[32] Chandler, *op. cit.*, XXVIII, Pt. 1-A, 313–14.

and coming into Keowee to stomp and boast and to play with the Indian women.[33]

Actually Wawhatchee had no quarrel with Lyttelton at the time he entered into the conspiracy with the Creeks; for Lyttelton had taken no action to embargo the Cherokee trade. Not until August 14 did the Governor order ammunition cut off from the nation and a reinforcement prepared for Coytmore and Demere.[34] It was Coytmore, carrying out his duty, who was forcing the situation. He held out for the surrender of the Estatoe murderers, and, prying into Wawhatchee's councils with informants, occasioned distrust.

In the nation hostility heightened by report of the ammunition embargo coincided with the unceasing efforts of the conspiracy to precipitate war. Near Great Tellico, young Setticoes under the warrior Tuscoloso ambushed a convoy carrying flour to Fort Loudoun and killed a straggling pack-horse man.[35] Near Fort Prince George a white man was shot at.

In the new tension Round O of Stecoe, hearing of the bad behavior in the Lower Towns, went down to Keowee and gave the headmen there a stiff dressing out. Asserting his friendship for the English, he asked the Keowees what they thought they were about. "Had they found a mountain of powder? Had their women learned to make clothes and their men to make knives? Hatchets? . . . where was their store? He would like to come and deal with them if perhaps the southern Indians [the Mortar's gang, some of whom were present] can supply you."[36] Having thus stated the classic case for peace with the English, Round O warned the Lower Towns to mend their ways or he would start a Creek war by killing all their Creek visitors.[37] Returning to Stecoe, he caused two of his young men who had joined with Conasatchees in raiding the whites to be scratched from head to foot.

[33] S. C. Council Journals, Oct. 19, 1759.
[34] *South Carolina Gazette*, Sept. 22, 1759.
[35] P. Demere to Lyttelton, Sept. 13, 1759, Lyttelton Papers.
[36] *South Carolina Gazette*, Sept. 22, 1759.
[37] Beamer to Lyttelton, Sept. 10, 1759, Lyttelton Papers.

For the next few days the surface of life at Keowee took on a better aspect. Round O had bolstered the antiwar group. Shortly that faction gained added strength from Lyttelton's seeming offer of a peaceful escape from diffculty by a conference in Charlestown. Informed by Governor Ellis of Wawhatchee's message, Lyttelton had merely sent to Wawhatchee reminding him that he should make his complaints to Charlestown rather than to Savannah.

Yet the stoppage of ammunition, affecting as it did the fall hunts, had fueled the Overhill war faction. Old Hop with difficulty withheld the hatchet from the young men. The anti-English party, now supported by Osteneco, asserted everywhere that things would be as bad as the French had prophesied, that the English would soon set about destroying the nation.[38] On the last day of the green-corn dance Setticoes killed a soldier two hundred yards from Fort Loudoun, and the next day the Chota headmen came to the fort to insist that ammunition be supplied their people. On September 12, inspired by Osteneco, extremists killed Chilhowee trader William Neal. They attempted to drive off the garrison's cattle; and Demere, realizing his vulnerability, butchered and salted the beeves against possible siege. He sent for Old Hop, Oconostota, and Standing Turkey and charged their people with starting a war. They at first denied the accusation but made no offer of satisfaction. Then Oconostota boldly stated that the English embargo on ammunition had occasioned the hostile acts and that future trouble could only be avoided by lifting the ban.[39] Demere pointed out that the embargo had been caused by Lower Towns' misbehavior and that the Great Warrior should carry his ammunition problem to Coytmore at Fort Prince George. The Great Warrior, accompanied by Osteneco, then set out for Fort Prince George.

Oconostota, knowing that the French could not supply the nation in event of war, adhered to the English alliance. But he soon had knowledge that the Slave Catcher of Chota, Tuscoloso

---

[38] S. C. Council Journals, Sept. 17, Oct. 18, 1759.
[39] *South Carolina Gazette*, Oct. 6, 1759.

of Settico, Seroweh of Estatoe, and possibly Moytoy of Hiwassee planned with the Creeks another attempt to force the situation. About September 20, while the Great Warrior stopped at Hiwassee, traders began to receive tips to make a quick getaway.[40] A few delayed, unwilling to leave their goods and deerskin take behind, but most fled. Already the conspirators guarded the passes. Piloted by Indian wives, mistresses, and relatives the fleeing traders detoured the ambushed spots and joined a constantly growing caravan which moved toward the Lower Towns under Oconostota's protection. On September 24 the frightened crowd tumbled into Fort Prince George. Oconostota and Osteneco stopped at Keowee where that day Creek emissaries had arrived, perhaps to enlist Wawhatchee.

At Fort Prince George tension mounted swiftly. Though Keowee seemed quiet and Oconostota and Osteneco came to deliver a letter from Demere, the panicky whites felt isolated in a hostile country. Four Cherokee war parties were rumored to have gone against the frontier.[41] Stuart, who had arrived from Charlestown on the twenty-second with the reinforcement, at night dispatched a warning to the settlers. In a few hours his courier, Isaac Atwood, returned. Indians, blocking the path, had fired on him. Warriors from Settico had cut off Fort Prince George. Coytmore sat down and wrote Lyttelton that the Cherokees made "absolutely open war" and entrusted the message to one McLamore who, having many Cherokee friends and relatives, was guided by devious paths around the blockade.[42]

Again the stage was set for massacre. On September 28, as Atkin talked to Creek headmen beneath an arbor in the Tukabatchis' square, the Cussita warrior Totscadater struck him from behind with a pipe hatchet.[43] Bleeding, the Superintendent fell. But the blows, impeded by an overhead beam and Atkin's upraised arms, had failed to kill him. As friendly Creeks rushed

[40] *Maryland Gazette*, Oct. 6, Nov. 15, 1759.
[41] *South Carolina Gazette*, Oct. 6, 1759; S. C. Council Journals, Oct. 18, 1759.
[42] Enc. No. 12, B.P.R.O., 92, C.O. 5/57.
[43] Atkin to Lyttelton, Oct. 2, 1759, Lyttelton Papers.

to his aid and his guards leaped on Totscadater, threw him down, and tied him, the Superintendent struggled to his feet. "Had the aimed blow succeeded," writes James Adair, "the savages would have immediately put up the war whoop, destroyed most of the white people on the spot and set off in great bodies both to the Cherokee country and to our own valuable settlements."[44] The next day Atkin, bandaged, summoned the headmen and renewed his talk at the point of interruption as if nothing had occurred. The plot had come to naught. Pro-English and neutral Creeks disclaimed the attempt and tightened their grip upon their people.[45] Among the Cherokees, the warning to the traders and Oconostota's timely arrival at Keowee appear to have prevented action.

[44] Adair, *op. cit.*, 266.
[45] Kimball, *op. cit.*, I, 271.

177

CHAPTER THIRTEEN

Lyttelton's Peace

THE SEPTEMBER 28 coup having failed, the Lower Towns peace deputies appointed earlier were free to go to Charlestown to attempt a settlement. Refused ammunition and advised by Coytmore to talk with Lyttelton, Oconostota and Osteneco decided to go also; on October 2 with Wawhatchee, Seroweh of Estatoe, and a crowd of Lower Towns people they set out. Shortly, Osteneco returned to keep order in the nation while the deputies treated with the English. Three days later Tistoe and the Wolf with a few others went down the path. On October 5, Round O of Stecoe, on his way with trader Aaron Price to buy hunting ammunition at Ninety-Six, stopped at Fort Prince George and was persuaded to follow the mission to Charlestown.[1] Thus in mid-October many important Cherokees were accepting the risk of entering deep into English territory to make a peace, and it is not an unreasonable assumption that Stuart and Coytmore were fully aware that while these men were in Carolina, the nation would not make war on the English.[2]

All the peacemakers knew that they must try to nullify that provision of the Treaty of 1730 which required the surrender of Indians who had killed whites. To prevent embargo and war all they could offer was some solution such as Glen had been forced to accept for the Oconees murders in 1751: "That every murderer should be sent out in quest of a French scalp or prisoner

---

[1] Coytmore to Lyttelton, Oct. 7, 1759, Lyttelton Papers.
[2] *Maryland Gazette*, Dec. 6, 1759.

for every white man they had killed."[3] It was a sane and honorable resolution of a difcult situation; for it would prevent division in the nation by protecting the vengeance takers, and it would use their energies to destroy the French alliance they had sought to achieve. But Charlestown, intent on punishment, saw only evasion.

Apparently on Oconostota's orders, hostiles withdrew from the Carolina frontier. The Setticoes who had blocked the Carolina path from Fort Prince George went home, and the raiders against North Carolina returned without inflicting damage.[4] However, war parties directed at Virginia may have traveled too far to have been overtaken in time to prevent trouble. Had Lyttelton exercised as much energy and tact with the Cherokees as Atkin used with the Creeks, or had he received the full co-operation of his Commons House, the war which soon burst upon Carolina might have been averted; for by now the peace forces among the Cherokees were strong. But influenced by reports from his captains in the wilderness, particularly those of Coytmore, who, frightened by the conspiracy around him, distrusted the peace elements, the Governor thought only in terms of punishing the Cherokees.

When on September 30 he received Coytmore's account of recent Cherokee hostilities, he determined to march against the Cherokees with 150 regulars and sizable drafts of militia, and exact satisfaction or make war as circumstance required.[5] He sent to Atkin among the Creeks to arouse the Chickasaws against the Cherokees; ordered the Virginia caravan of trade goods, which on Fauquier's acceptance of the Lower Towns' July overture had already started toward the nation, to be halted in North Carolina; and asked his Commons House for funds to finance his military expedition.[6] The Commons, fearful of war, refused him a free hand and limited his expedition to three months.[7] It

[3] *South Carolina Gazette*, Nov. 24, 1759.
[4] Coytmore to Lyttelton, Oct. 16, 1759.
[5] S. C. Commons House Journals, Oct. 5, 1759.
[6] S. C. Council Journals, Oct. 7, 1759.
[7] Lyttelton to Amherst, Oct. 16, 1759, Amherst Papers, B.P.R.O., W.O. 34/35.

was much too brief a period to raise and supply 1,500 men, march them 300 miles, and bring the Cherokees to terms. Despite this limitation, and reports that Cherokee war parties had withdrawn from the frontier and that a peace mission was on the way, Lyttelton remained enamored of his military solution. What appealed to him in the dispatches was the hint that as long as the English had the Cherokee deputies in their power, the nation would refrain from hostilities. On advice of his council, he determined to hold Oconostota and his companions as hostages for a peace which he would make in the nation at the head of an army. Oconostota, assured by Stuart and Coytmore of safe conduct and relying on Lyttelton's ambiguous August message to Wawhatchee, walked into a trap, baited with what was later to appear to him to have been double talk. Possibly it was, for Stuart and Coytmore were not artless men.

The Cherokees arrived in Charlestown on October 17, and on the next day Lyttelton received them in the council chamber. He did not offer to shake hands. When he asked Oconostota his mission, the Great Warrior replied that he had come only to hear the Governor talk. Lyttelton then said he had no talk to give, that he had merely suggested that the Cherokees come if they had grievances to discuss. The Indians withdrew to consider their reply. On the nineteenth Oconostota expressed a desire for peace, disclaimed responsibility for the bad things that had been done, and asserted his respect for the English. For himself, he said:

> I am a warrior and want no war with the English . . . . My desire is to have the path clear and open for goods to go to the nation . . . . Your warriors [meaning the Virginians] have carried the hatchet of war against us, we have done the same against them; and both have acted like boys. I am willing to make clear weather once more and bury the hatchet of my young people.[8]

Lacking the customary string of white beads to attest the sincerity of his talk, the Great Warrior placed a deerskin at Lyttelton's feet. The Governor refused to pick up the honored symbol

8 S. C. Council Journals, Oct. 15, Oct. 19, 1759.

of the bond which had held the two peoples together for over half a century.

Lyttelton, meeting with his council, decided that murderers of the King's subjects must be surrendered in numbers to be determined when the Governor arrived at Keowee. Meanwhile, the Cherokee peace delegation must be held as hostages. Holding fresh dispatches which reported that Setticoes had gone against the English and that Lower Towns Indians had threatened a soldier hunting for a horse, Lyttelton grimly faced Oconostota and asserted that atrocities having been committed since the deputies had their authorization, the deputies were now men without a mission. However, he said that because they had been assured protection if they came down, he would provide it. He himself must go to the nation and they must accompany him. Abruptly he terminated the conference. The Cherokees filed from the room in the terrifying knowledge that since they lacked freedom to leave town at their will, they were captives.[9]

Under escort of the provincial regiment and the regulars of the Charlestown garrison the Cherokees left Charlestown on October 23. On the twenty-sixth they arrived at Moncks Corner to rendezvous with the Governor and the low-country militia. When Lyttelton visited them and detailed the satisfaction he intended to ask, the submissive headmen replied that "they were content that their countrymen should be compelled to give satisfaction."[10]

On October 30 the Governor and his cavalry, several days in advance of his captives who were required to travel with the wagon train, met Round O's party of forty-five Middle Settlements Indians. He greeted the unsuspecting red men cordially, but informed the leader of his intention to demand satisfaction. Round O could only express his approval and join the Carolina march. But at the Congarees he found himself forced to encamp under heavy guard next to the Governor's quarters.

After five days in Lyttelton's hands, four of Round O's men

[9] *Ibid.*, Oct. 22, 1759.
[10] *Maryland Gazette*, Dec. 6, 1759.

181

slipped away at night. Lyttelton doubled the guard and explained to Round O that he feared "deserters" might go to the nation, misrepresent affairs, and make the people think that his and Oconostota's parties were ill-treated and in danger. Round O blandly suggested sending two deputies to counter the bad effects the four runaways might create, and Lyttelton agreed. He delegated Elliott, now withdrawn from Chota and established in trade near Keowee, to accompany Round O's deputies with dispatches to Coytmore, Stuart, and the Lower Towns headmen.

Late that afternoon Oconostota's party with the wagon train overtook the Governor. As they passed Round O's camp, they raised a shout of recognition to which the Middle Settlements men gave vigorous reply; but they were not allowed to meet. That night Elliott left the army with "the Raven," who carried Round O's reassuranace to the Lower Towns that he was well treated and approached the nation "hand in hand" with his brother. By Elliott the Governor conveyed a promise that he intended to distinguish between friend and foe.

Lyttelton had reason to worry. Only two days after Oconostota had left Charlestown under guard, some Conasatchees, who in mid-October had bravely gone out against Carolina, slunk home with talk of militia rallying. Panic spread on the arrival in Keowee of the four escapees from Round O's camp. A grim runner sped the long path to the Overhills, and another raced to the Creek country with "a painted tomahawk" and a demand for immediate Creek help. Cherokee young men talked of death rather than submission; and Fort Prince George heard that the army would be assaulted as it forded a creek twelve miles below Keowee. Nor did Round O's "Raven" message calm the fever. Its public reassurances had undercover repercussions which "put all the nation in a ferment." Five Creeks hurriedly departed Keowee to reinforce the Cherokee demand for Creek help, and numbers of Lower Townsmen went down the path "to hunt."

On the march Lyttelton redoubled the guard over his Indian "guests"; and when on November 17 forty Silver Springs Chickasaws joined the army, guards prevented their making contact

with the Cherokees. At Ninety-Six one of the Cherokee "hunters," Tistoe's brother Chenallotehee, walked into the English
camp and was permitted to see for himself that his brother was
well. The two Indians rejoiced in each other's company; and
when the guard came to separate them, the brothers were said
by an interpreter to have been discussing how to deliver the
murderers to the Governor.

On November 23, Elliott returned. In twelve days the ener-
getic little man had made the four-hundred-mile round trip to
Fort Loudoun. He reported the nation divided: the Middle Settlements clearly for peace, the Overhills mostly so, and the
Lower Towns but partially. Settico, Chilhowee, and Telassie
among the Overhills, and Estatoe and Conasatchee among the
Lower Towns openly prepared for war. The latter group alone
mustered near five hundred men.[11] Elliott also brought news
that the Little Carpenter had returned from a successful foray
into the Illinois country between Fort Chartres and Fort de
l'Assomption. On September 18 the Little Carpenter's scouts
had spotted near the Mississippi eight Frenchmen seated about
a fire eating buffalo steaks. The Cherokees crept up on them,
fired, and rushed, taking eight scalps and losing one man. They
finished the meal themselves with great satisfaction. They also
fired from ambush upon a boat which came close to shore.[12] At
the end of October they had come into Fort Loudoun, displayed
their scalps, told their story, and received presents. To hear the
Little Carpenter talk was to believe that old times had come
again. On Elliott's arrival at Fort Loudoun on November 15,
the Little Carpenter came to express his concern at the Carolina measures and to send word that he would meet Lyttelton
at Keowee.

Unfortunately for Lyttelton's plans the Mortar was also to
be nearby during the conference at Keowee. After the September
28 fiasco the Mortar, standing almost alone in his pro-French
activities, was informed by Atkin that the price of English good

[11] *South Carolina Gazette*, Nov. 10, Nov. 17, Nov. 24, Dec. 8, 1759.
[12] *Maryland Gazette*, Jan. 10, 1760.

will would be his endeavoring to bring the Cherokees to terms. The artful Creek went to Keowee bearing Atkin's message that, abandoned by the Creeks, Choctaws, and Chickasaws, the Cherokees should "lay down the hatchet immediately" and come to Augusta to talk with the Superintendent. Thus on November 24 the Mortar was legitimately in the Cherokee country, but he would be of no help to the peace.

While Lyttelton's army rested at Ninety-Six, confusion of council prevailed at Keowee. Chenallotehee urged immediate delivery of the killers demanded by the Governor. The war faction adamantly opposed him, encouraged by the Georgia smuggler Williams who, with ammunition to sell, spread the story that Carolina proposed to destroy the nation. The young men and many of the warriors talked of waylaying the army in some brushy hollow, but the Governor's detaining so many important headmen deterred them. Finally they agreed to stand with wary eyes behind a show of peace. They sent the Governor white beads, a British flag, and a talk; but Lyttelton, warned by Coytmore that the deputies were spies, turned them back.

On November 29 the army consisting of 1,299 effectives marched from Ninety-Six. On the road the Governor practiced his troops for surprise battle with right and left wheels into line. Apprehensive that the maneuver presaged an attack upon the towns, the captive headmen told the Governor that "every man of them had come to a resolution to die by the Governor but he should have the satisfaction he required."[13] Oconostota said that he would see that every man in the nation who had committed a murder or an intrigue would be delivered up to his excellency; and, Lyttelton, concealing his own fears, assured them that he intended them no harm.

As the army neared the Cherokee towns, desertions ceased. Soldiers regarded the forests as unsafe for stray whites. Yet Captain Grennan's horsemen, scouting ahead, saw no signs of enemy. The only disturbance to the marching men was occasioned by deer racing out of the thickets and knocking men down

[13] *South Carolina Gazette*, Dec. 8, Dec. 18, Jan. 5, Jan. 12, 1760.

as they leaped for the woods across the road. On December 7 they crossed the difficult ford of Twelve Mile Creek where steep banks and deepish water made them most vulnerable. The next night they bivouacked beneath the stars on the hills within six miles of Fort Prince George. In the still winter cold they could hear the distant singing and dancing of the Cherokees in their villages.

At eleven o'clock on the morning of December 9, as knots of Indians gazed from the wooded hills across Keowee River, the army trooped into the flats beside Fort Prince George. The roar of saluting cannons and the answering rattle of musketry mingled as acrid gunpowder smoke rolled from the valley. While the soldiers prepared their camp, the Governor summoned his unwilling guests and sent fifty of them home. Twenty-eight of the most prominent, including Oconostota, Tistoe, Round O, and Wawhatchee, "who seemed inclined to promote the satisfaction his excellency required," he detained at the fort.

On December 10 when the Keowees requested permission to visit the fort, Lyttelton, fearing the smallpox he heard was in the town, permitted but one to come over. As scores of warriors stood on their side of the river and fired a salute, the Second Man of Conasatchee brought a talk stating that the Little Carpenter would soon come and that the Lower Towns would abide by the agreements he and the Governor made.

Difficult days of waiting ensued. Concerned over the smallpox, Lyttelton ordered his men to stay on the fort side of the river. On his advice the Cherokees carried the sick from the town and burned the houses they had occupied. But the fatigues of the march and the bad camp hygiene took a toll of the army. Shortly a measles epidemic broke out and desertions began. Lyttelton's effectives dwindled, and every sunrise brought nearer January 1, the date of formal dissolution of the expedition. On the fifteenth the Mortar, encamped near Keowee, sent a threat that if harm befell the Cherokees held hostage, the Creeks would avenge them. Lyttelton scanned the horizon for reinforcements: two hundred men under Colonel Singleton and Colonel Waddell's promised North Carolinians. Before a week had passed, the Chickasaws, reprimanded for entering Keowee, had left in disgust.[14]

Over the hills the Little Carpenter, opposed by all the forces of hate in the nation, had fought the battle of his career to prevent the Overhills from plunging the nation into an English war. When he had heard Elliott's translation of Lyttelton's demands for surrender of those who had killed whites, he had wept, knowing that these men had acted by the basic law of family and clan and that now he must deliver them to death in order to bring peace. He had faced nativist accusations of servility to the English for having accepted presents at Fort Loudoun and Charlestown.[15] In Chota council house, Old Hop had called him a traitor to his people and had threatened him with death should he ever go against the French again.[16] In great anger he had turned his back on the Fire King and had taken the unprecedented step of announcing to the council that he as Second Man would fill the role of First Beloved Man, or head of the nation. What had happened was that the First Beloved Man in supporting a war with the English had deserted his kingly duty as keeper of the peace, his fundamental religious and civil role. The Little Carpenter in determining to maintain the peace had assumed the First Beloved Man's duty in this respect. First Beloved Man the Little Carpenter could not be unless elected by the nation. But when he announced his decision at Fort Loudoun, Stuart, who had arrived some time before with reinforcements, welcomed the idea and conceived the notion that he could have Carolina declare the Little Carpenter the emperor of the Cherokees. Since this was an English office and granted by them to the Cherokee they chose for recognition as head of the nation, the Little Carpenter, who needed the confidence of Demere, Stuart, and Lyttelton, left the two Captains at the fort with the impression that he was their man and aspired to the appointment they held out.

[14] *Ibid.*, Dec. 29, Jan. 12, 1759.
[15] Stuart to Lyttelton, Nov. 22, Dec. 3, 1759, Lyttelton Papers.
[16] P. Demere to Lyttelton, Dec. 4, 1759, *ibid.*

His position as negotiator with Lyttelton was nevertheless anomalous, for he lacked proper authorization to confer. Lyttelton through oversight had not invited him;[17] and Chota and Old Hop, distrusting him, had failed to give him the talk of the council.[18] Minor figures carried Old Hop's empty talk to Keowee. The Little Carpenter, however, was not without standing. The Middle Settlements deputies had invited him to accompany them, and as Second Man of the Overhills, and Right Hand Man of the King. he ranked highest among the Cherokee conferees.[19]

On December 19, the Little Carpenter, carrying an English flag and accompanied by Old Hop's deputies Ocayula of Chota and Ucanokeach, arrived at Fort Prince George. The conference opened at once. As proof of loyalty to his pledged word, the Little Carpenter bore scalps of eight Frenchmen, and Lyttelton took from his outstretched hand the string of beads he had given him in April and drew from it the three black beads which had signified English displeasure. Formal talks began the next day.

The Cherokees were in no position to bargain. Lyttelton held twenty-eight of their most prominent headmen and had an army behind him. The Little Carpenter's problem was to release the headmen and get rid of the army as soon as possible. Lyttelton spoke at length of French inability to supply the Cherokees; and, reading the provisions of the Treaty of 1730 which related to the punishment of murderers, he recalled that the Little Carpenter and five other Cherokees had put their hands to it in London. Finally he demanded that the Cherokees deliver twenty-four of their warriors who had killed whites in North and South Carolina.

From among the hostages, Oconostota responded by pointing out that since many of the guilty were over the hills or out hunting, compliance with the Governor's demand could be difficult. It was an important point and true. Delivery of all the guilty would be impossible for some of the culprits, forewarned, might

---

[17] Stuart to Lyttelton, Nov. 15, Dec. 3, Dec. 7, 1759, *ibid.*

[18] Lyttelton's Memorandum, Dec. 18, 1759, *ibid.*

[19] Stuart to Lyttelton, Nov. 22, 1759, *ibid.*

fade far away. With this the conference adjourned until the twenty-first and the Little Carpenter stayed behind to confer with Oconostota.

On the twenty-first the Governor and the Little Carpenter sat long in conference, and at the conclusion of their talks, Tistoe of Keowee and Seroweh of Estatoe were released. On their return to Keowee, the English flag rose to the top of the town house. The next morning two of the killers, the Young Twin and the Slave Catcher of Conasatchee, were delivered at the fort. On the twenty-third the Little Carpenter came once more, soon to be followed by the Good Warrior of Estatoe who stated that he held three of the killers at Estatoe and would come the next day to report his further progress. But the next day no headmen came, for the three killers had been rescued by Indians determined that they should not be surrendered. Chenallotehee came down to Keowee River to shout over Keowee's complaint that the Governor had not kept faith, that for the two Conasatchees they had previously delivered he should release two men of Conasatchee whom he held. Lyttelton replied that when all the murderers were delivered to him he would free all the hostages. When two more days passed and still the Little Carpenter did not come, Lyttelton sent him an ultimatum that unless he came to the fort the next day, the army would attack Estatoe.

But the next day, despite the arrival of Singleton's reinforcement, the army was in no mood to attack. On rumor that smallpox had struck the camp, three-quarters of the army were ready to desert. As the morning wore on and the Little Carpenter failed to appear, Oconostota was prevailed upon to contact Keowee and ask that Chenallotehee or some other headman come over. But none of the Keowees dared come. They feared that Lyttelton in anger at the jail delivery of the guilty Estatoes would seize them. When finally, to the relief of everyone, the Little Carpenter appeared, the twenty-six hostages were brought into the Governor's presence and the conference was renewed. The Little Carpenter, sensing that the Governor's position had weakened, pointed out that for the twenty-two Indians still to be sur-

188

rendered, the English held too many hostages. Lyttelton thereupon released Oconostota, Kittagusta, his brother, Round O, and Killianca of Hiwassee. Then he presented for signature a treaty the Little Carpenter had agreed to in private conference.

It provided that there be peace and friendship between the Cherokees and the English; that the Treaty of 1730 be strictly observed; that twenty-four of those guilty of the murders perpetrated by the Cherokees since November 9, 1758, be surrendered at Fort Prince George; that twenty-two designated Cherokees, chief among them Wawhatchee, stay at Fort George as hostages for the guilty, and that the hostages be freed as the killers were delivered; that the licensed traders should return to the nation at once; that the Cherokees put to death French emissaries who came to them; and that any white man or Indian who attempted to put the Cherokees at variance with the English should be apprehended and reported to the Governor. To this treaty Attakullaculla, Oconostota, Round O, Kittagusta, Oconeca the Wolf of Keowee, and Killianca set their marks.[20]

The Little Carpenter had effected the release of leading men friendly to his point of view, but he had been unable to extricate twenty-two other important Cherokees. More significantly, he had negotiated a treaty repugnant to the majority of his people. Unratified by Chota it would be no better than the disposition and ability of the men who signed it to enforce it. His position had become impossible; several important Cherokees owed their freedom to him, but he was hated for the terms by which he had freed them.

The treaty ceremonies completed, Lyttelton showed the red men the presents he had brought to seal the compact but which would not be given out until all the killers had been surrendered. They consisted of articles of which the Cherokees stood in great need: woolens, several cases of muskets, three tons of powder and ball in proportion, and numerous minor articles.[21]

The headmen who had signed the treaty then walked from the

[20] *South Carolina Gazette*, Jan. 12, 1760.
[21] Bull to Amherst, Oct. 19, 1760.

189

fort free men—except for Round O, who grieving that his son was still held and, wishing to show his faith in the English, returned to be a voluntary prisoner and to die of smallpox.[22] Lyttelton, confident that his terms would be met and that he had disciplined the Cherokees, prepared to take his army out of its precarious situation.

On the twenty-eighth the smallpox panic among the Carolinians became so intense that Lyttelton intimated that all who feared the disease could go. Within an hour half the force had stampeded down the path toward home. The next morning more left, and the independent company of regulars marched away, with the three killers already surrendered. On the last day of December, Lyttelton and his staff rode off at the head of the remnants of his army.[23] In Fort Prince George he left as dangerous a set of explosives as decaying log walls ever held: a smallpox epidemic; twenty-two important hostages awaiting an exchange which the Cherokees were in no mood to make; and a wealth of ammunition, which under the circumstances was only obtainable by force. He also left behind him a Cherokee nation inflamed against the English.

[22] Encl. 30, B.P.R.O., 92, C.O. 5/57.
[23] *South Carolina Gazette*, Jan. 12, 1760.

CHAPTER FOURTEEN

The Cherokee Rebellion

As CHARLESTOWN REJOICED in disaster averted and victory won, the Cherokees seethed with anger. They refused to understand the holding as hostages of persons unrelated to the guilty and resident in towns guiltless of aggression, but they did understand treachery. Headmen who had gone to Charlestown had been tricked into confinement. Relatives of the hostages, once friends of the English, nourished deep resentments, and the augmented anti-English faction moved for vengeance.

While Charlestown feted Lyttelton, Cherokees wrecked the treaty he had made. Hiwassees and Nottelies killed trader John Kelly, quartered his body, and set his head and hands on stakes near Hiwassee town house. Elliott, bearing dispatches to Fort Loudoun, on hearing of Kelly's death, entrusted his mission to one McCormack, a renegade, and fled back to Fort Prince George. On the way he heard that the Middle Settlements, roused by the imprisonment of guiltless men, marched in force to effect a delivery. On January 15, Tellicoes advanced on a similar errand, and blood-hungry Setticoes poured through the Twenty-Four Mountains. On the seventeenth Cornelius Dougherty, James Baldridge, and Henry Lucas, whom Indian friends had spirited from their trading posts, galloped into Fort Prince George. Coytmore learned that Seroweh of Estatoe planned to gain access to the fort and rescue the hostages.

On January 19, as heavy rains slanted, Seroweh and a crowd of blanketed warriors demanded admission to the fort ostensibly to exchange killers for hostages. Coytmore, his garrison under arms and his hostages locked up, agreed to admit three or four of the Indians. As soldiers held the gates ajar, Cherokees surged forward. Before the guards could shove the gates together, a dozen warriors had squeezed in. Each of them had under his blanket a tomahawk, a pistol, or a knife.[1] Imperturbable, Seroweh parleyed with Coytmore but finally asserted that in the press he had left his prisoners outside and must go after them. He and his companions were let out. Then it developed that the killers had "escaped," and Seroweh and his gang left for Estatoe.

A few miles away Cherokees had already commenced the war. Before Seroweh had reached the fort, thirty Indians had attacked Elliott's trading house at New Keowee. Of the dozen whites about the place when the Estatoes struck, several fell in the first fire. Two or three were seized. Others, running, were shot down. The hated Elliott, tomahawked, raced a mile before his pursuers felled him. Ten others, including James May, the Joree trader, died. Seroweh's men, returning, joined the looting and rum-drinking at Elliott's.[2]

Seroweh sent runners through the nation to proclaim the war. In the Middle Settlements, Tuckaseigee Cherokees killed traders James Russell and James Crawford. The Nequassee Mankiller, however, intervened to save trader John Downing's life. From Cheoah in the Snowbirds, James Miller escaped to Fort Loudoun. But Overhill Oconostota, supporting the Little Carpenter, refused Seroweh's bloody hatchet and trader's scalp and with the Second Man visited Fort Loudoun and professed loyalty. Nevertheless, hostiles blocked the mountain paths between Fort Loudoun and Fort Prince George. Vengeance-seeking Setticoes headed for Virginia, and in the last week of January hundreds of warriors blockaded Fort Prince George or advanced upon Carolina and Georgia.

Warning reached the Georgia frontier on the twenty-ninth

[1] Amherst to Pitt, Mar. 8, 1760, Encl. 30, Amherst Papers, B.P.R.O., C.O. 5/57.
[2] Fort Prince George Journals, Jan. 13–Feb. 28, 1760, Lyttelton Papers.

192

when John Downing, Bernard Hughes, and other fleeing Middle Settlements traders, bypassing the Lower Towns, arrived at John Vann's on Georgia's Broad River.[3] On the thirtieth Aaron Price, who had stolen from Fort Prince George, warned Ninety-Six.[4]

But warning failed to avert disaster at the hated Long Canes settlements. On Sunday, February 1, a host of Cherokees struck 150 settlers fleeing toward Fort More. Caught with their wagons in a stream crossing, the men ran in terror. The Cherokees raged unchecked among the women and children, shooting, scalping, and taking prisoners. Many fled into the woods, and for days after search parties brought in stunned survivors to Forts More and Augusta. The Cherokees took 23 scalps and as many prisoners.[5] Later on Stevens Creek the John Davis party of 23 women and children was massacred.[6]

On the Georgia frontier the Cherokee assault failed when John Vann escaped the attack upon his home and roused the militia. Creek Indians interfered. Their hunting parties filled the forests; and, though not hostile to the Cherokees, they refused to be allies. Unwilling to have their trade spoiled by undiscriminating whites, they warned the Cherokees to be careful.[7] Though six Georgians were killed, Georgia was spared the long war which followed.

On their left wing the Cherokees also failed. On February 3, Ninety-Six beat off forty warriors who took prisoner a boy, a woman, and a slave, and burned Goudy's house.[8] Thirty miles south William Miller's fort repulsed a four-hour assault.[9]

Though the main body of Cherokees drew back to celebrate their prisoners and scalps, sporadic raids continued. Near Fort More eighteen warriors with private grudges to settle hunted

[3] *Maryland Gazette*, Mar. 13, Mar. 20, 1760.
[4] S. C. Council Journals, Feb. 2, 1760.
[5] *South Carolina Gazette*, Feb. 9, 1760.
[6] *Maryland Gazette*, Mar. 20, 1760.
[7] *South Carolina Gazette*, Mar. 22, 1760.
[8] *Maryland Gazette*, Mar. 20, 1760.
[9] E. Musgrove to Lyttelton, Feb. 6, 1760, Lyttelton Papers.

scalps.[10] Sometimes they were disappointed at having killed the wrong man, as in the case of Ulric Tobler shot while riding with three others to his father's stockade. Near Germany's above Augusta they killed and scalped two men, but failed in their attack on Lachlan McGillivray's slaves working the fields.

Throughout January at Chota, the Little Carpenter struggled for peace. He restrained Oconostota's indignation over his recent captivity, and he prevented the Chota council from taking hostile action against Fort Loudoun and the pack-horse men living in the towns. He finally even prevailed upon Demere to send for Lyttelton's approval of a compromise solution: that guilty Cherokees join the English against one of the French forts.[11] Then Old Hop died, and the inveterate nativist Standing Turkey was elevated to the office of Fire King.[12] Even the Little Carpenter could not stand against his argument that guiltless Chotas were captives in Fort Prince George on terms that the Second Man had made. In a despairing effort to keep Chota from making the fatal decision for war, he consented to accompany Oconostota to the Lower Towns and demand that Coytmore release the five Chotas he held.[13]

On February 14 the two headmen encamped three miles from smallpox-infested Keowee, and Oconostota went to Fort Prince George. There, too, smallpox raged, taking off several soldiers and five hostages, among them the peace-loving Round O. The Great Warrior did not approach the gates; but standing in the fields, he called Coytmore to the ramparts and demanded the Chotas' release. The Lieutenant firmly replied that he could not comply until the Cherokees surrendered guilty persons to take their places. Oconostota yelled his repudiation of the treaty he had signed and stalked angrily away. That night he went into Keowee. The next morning he confronted the Little Carpenter

10 *Maryland Gazette*, Apr. 3, 1760.
11 P. Demere to Lyttelton, Jan. 26, 1760, Lyttelton Papers.
12 *Maryland Gazette*, Mar. 16, 1760.
13 P. Demere to Lyttelton, Jan. 26, 1760, Lyttelton Papers.

Courtesy the British Museum

William Henry Lyttelton

AUSTENACO, Great Warriour,
Commander in Chief of the Cherokee Nation.

From the Royal Magazine of London *(July, 1762)*

Osteneco, on his visit to London, 1762. Osteneco was not
Great Warrior but Second Warrior of the Cherokees.

with the terrible news of the Lower Town's raids into Carolina. The two men had come to a parting.

On the morning of February 16, Oconostota, having placed an ambush in the thickets beside the river, stood at Keowee ford and summoned Coytmore. Accompanied by Cornelius Dougherty, Ensign Bell, and an interpreter, Coytmore came down to the ford. Oconostota called over that he wanted a white man to accompany him to Charlestown to see the Governor. When Coytmore agreed, the Great Warrior shouted he would catch a horse and, turning, swung the bridle over his head. Musket fire spurted from the thickets and Coytmore fell. Soldiers rushed from the fort and bore the Lieutenant inside as shots sung by them. Hastily manned, the cannon of the fort belched, scattering the Indians and knocking down houses in Keowee. But the Indians did not attack. When Coytmore died that afternoon in the fort, the soldiers, according to Ensign Milne, his successor, turned on the twenty-two hostages confined among them. Swearing bitterly that they would kill every Indian in the fort, they fixed their bayonets. Milne later maintained that he tried to stop them, but failed. The hostages, armed with weapons smuggled to them during their captivity, fought back in desperation.[14]

Near eight o'clock that evening a crowd of Indians appeared on the hills across the river and fired two shots as if to signal to their countrymen in the fort. "Fight strong and we will deliver you," they shouted. But their battle cry brought no response. All the hostages were dead, and the garrison manned the walls to repulse the expected attack. The Great Warrior, in uncontrollable hatred of Coytmore for encouraging him to walk into Lyttelton's trap, had signaled the final disaster to the hostages and calamity to his people. The Little Carpenter, defeated, went home to Tomatly, from whence he shortly withdrew his immediate family into the woods. Remaining true to the treaties he had signed, symbolically and actually he separated himself from the Chota council, which was now launched on a course he did not wish to be even thought to tolerate.

[14] Fort Prince George Journal, Feb. 14, Feb. 24, 1760, *ibid*.

Still no assault was made on Fort Loudoun. Indian women continued to enter it and to barter provisions for goods. But Paul Demere kept details from his two-hundred-man garrison busy strengthening its walls. Looking at the formidable work, the Chotas felt the need of allies. They sent deputies to the northern Indians, and Oconostota's brother went to Fort Toulouse with English prisoners and scalps given the Great Warrior at Keowee.[15] Soon Oconostota, well aware of the Cherokee need of supplies and reinforcement, followed. Early in February, Demere sent two Irishmen, Fitzgerald and McCormack, to warn the Virginia frontier and to obtain help from Fauquier. To Tanase trader Sam Benn's trustworthy Negro slave Abraham, he gave dispatches for Lyttelton. Promised freedom should he succeed in his mission, Abraham, a skilled woodsman, passed around the Cherokee watches in the mountain gaps and eventually reached Charlestown.[16]

By February 10, Indian alarms and killings occurred in North Carolina. For a month the Wachovia–Fort Dobbs–Salisbury region experienced constant attack, and refugees swarmed into the stockade of the Moravian settlement at Bethania.[17] At Fort Dobbs on February 27 between eight and nine at night, Major Waddell, suspecting by the barking of dogs that Indians were near, took out a patrol and was hit by sixty or seventy Cherokees. Another large party assaulted the fort. The Major's men killed ten or a dozen Indians, and the Major himself was nearly captured before the Indians drew off with but one English scalp and the garrison's horse herd.[18] Near Bethabara two settlers were killed and another wounded. Though the militia sallied, they were too few to drive off the assailants, and fifteen settlers died before the marauders withdrew.[19] One Cherokee party, however, suffered heavily. Having raided along the Catawba River, it was caught by a vengeful pursuit near Broad River and

[15] *South Carolina Gazette*, Mar. 20, 1760.
[16] *Maryland Gazette*, Mar. 20, 1760.
[17] Fries, *op. cit.*, I, 228.
[18] *South Carolina Gazette*, Apr. 12, 1760.
[19] Fries, *op. cit.*, I, 228.

lost thirteen men. By April 1, the North Carolina frontier had quieted.

In March, Cherokees, probably from Settico, Chilhowee, and Telassie, forayed into southwestern Virginia. In Halifax County at the confluence of the Dan and Mayo rivers many whites were killed or taken.[20] Eighty Cherokees pillaged in Augusta County but took only two scalps.[21] Panic ruled in the country out to Reed Creek, once protected from the Shawnees by Osteneco; and settlers, abandoning their plantations, fled eastward. The old Indian hands, Andrew Lewis and Nathaniel Gist, commanded the forces sent to repel the raiders.

Also in March a second Cherokee thrust reached deeply into South Carolina, penetrating to within six or eight miles of the Congarees. For thirty-six hours on March 2 and 3, 250 warriors fired on the wooden walls of Ninety-Six. Cockily confident, the garrison attempted to lure the besiegers into an assault by hoisting a Cherokee scalp to the top of the flagpole; but the Indians were wary. On the third in a smart rain a small reinforcement fought its way hand to hand through the warriors and entered the stockade. The next day, leaving numerous ambuscades in the neighborhood, the Indians struck down Saluda Valley, burning and destroying. Near Turner's Fort they encountered six men, killed two and took two, and showed themselves en masse before the fort as if daring the garrison to sortie. For miles around they burned houses and killed cattle. A few days later on the forks of Edisto, they killed or captured twenty-five settlers. Others killed two men in Saxe-Gotha township. At Ruhl's Fort raiders took a scalp and lost two men to the garrison's sally. By the twenty-second most of the warriors had returned to the Lower Towns, bringing at least fifteen prisoners.[22] On the twenty-first Tellicoes brought in ten scalps from the Congarees, and on the twenty-third Seroweh returned to Estatoe to rejoice in the bloody harvest.

[20] Journals of the Executive Council of Virginia, Apr. 10, 1760.
[21] *Maryland Gazette*, May 1, 1760.
[22] *South Carolina Gazette*, Mar. 15, Mar. 22, Apr. 19, 1760.

In two onslaughts against South Carolina the Cherokees had killed several score settlers and taken as many prisoners. They had destroyed hundreds of buildings and thousands of head of livestock. They had depopulated the region between Ninety-Six and Fort More and had set the frontier line back nearly one hundred miles to between the Congarees and Orangeburg. They had isolated the two English forts in the nation with garrisons of over three hundred men. And for all this after two months of raiding, they had seen little indication of Carolina retaliation.

Emboldened, Osteneco, in the absence of Oconostota, attacked Fort Loudoun. On March 20 the Overhills, bitterly convinced that the hostages at Fort Prince George were dead, ringed the Tennessee fort cutting off its provisions. For ninety-six hours, day and night, they fired upon it.[23] Then, as abruptly as he had begun the siege, Osteneco broke it off. Soon after he set out with three hundred men for the Lower Towns.

The next week Oconostota returned from down the Tennessee and sent into Fort Loudoun by McCormack, Demere's Virginia messenger, the disheartening news that the Virginia mission had failed. Piankashaws had captured the messengers, but McCormack had escaped and, wandering in the forest, had stumbled upon Oconostota's party.[24] Nevertheless, Oconostota hesitated to attack Fort Loudoun. Indian women came once more to barter corn, chickens, and pigs for the clothing the men wore. But it was apparent to all that a determined siege meant starvation, and Demere cut the corn allotment to one pint per man a day. Still the garrison hoped for relief.

Osteneco's departure for Keowee had been caused by a rumor that a retaliatory force assembled at Ninety-Six. The Cherokee warriors, bold from success, planned its destruction and concentrated near Keowee.

When Lyttelton learned that his Cherokee treaty had failed, he determined to exact full satisfaction from the insurgent nation. But his December force had disintegrated, and the prov-

23 *Maryland Gazette*, June 5, 1760.
24 *South Carolina Gazette*, May 3, 1760.

198

ince held less than 200 soldiers. Lacking faith in the militia, he sent to Amherst in New York for 1,500 or 2,000 regulars and asked Fauquier to send a Virginia force to relieve Fort Loudoun.[25] From his assembly he obtained authorization for seven ranger companies of 45 horsemen each, scalp bounties of £25 a head, and a new provincial regiment of 1,000 men.[26] The ranger companies filled quickly, but enlistment in the provincials lagged. In the face of scalp-mad warriors, Carolinians lacked enthusiasm for foot warfare in the Indian country.

Since the regulars could not arrive for two months, Lyttelton planned to supply Fort Prince George under cover of a volunteer diversion against the Lower Towns. Fort Loudoun would have to await Virginia action or the regulars. But the scheme never materialized. Colonel Richard Richardson, dispatched to Ninety-Six to raise 500 men to go against the Lower Towns, found the frontiersmen unwilling to volunteer for so hazardous an undertaking.[27] They were wise. Rumor of the effort had concentrated almost 1,000 warriors at Keowee.

Entirely different forces lightened the pressure at Fort Prince George. What the Cherokees could not take by strength they hoped to win by guile. On March 11 the garrison saw a white flag flying over Keowee town house and received a peace offer from Tistoe. In a few days Moytoy of Hiwassee sent a captured messenger from Fort Loudoun to invite Dougherty to the riverbank for a talk. Dougherty, remembering Coytmore's disaster, refused; but Keowee continued the show of peace. Indians moved freely about the town and up and down the Overhill path or repaired houses wrecked by cannon shot. They even allowed their young women to visit the fort. One of these reported that Moytoy had taken 240 warriors toward Carolina; another said that the Little Carpenter had led the Fort Loudoun garrison to Virginia. Tistoe sent saying that none of the Keowees had been to war and that he had forbidden war parties to enter the town.

[25] S. C. Council Journals, Feb. 9, 1760.
[26] S. C. Commons House Journals, Feb. 9, 1760.
[27] S. C. Council Journals, Mar. 6, 1760.

Fort Loudoun, he said, had been evacuated three weeks before (at that moment Osteneco had it under fire.) There was even prospect that prisoners might be released; for the friendly Mankiller of Nequassee would come soon bringing one Robert Scott.

With this prelude, a girl brought from Tistoe an offer that should the garrison be short of provisions he would be glad to escort it to Carolina. However, Milne's counter-intelligence informed him that Fort Loudoun still held and that war parties moved freely through the Lower Towns.

But the Cherokees continued their friendly talks. Standing Turkey was reported to be coming with Stuart to make a peace similar to that enjoyed by Fort Loudoun. The next day the Mankiller of Nequassee came with Half Breed Tom, the Rat, and the prisoner Robert Scott. Though active in the war the Mankiller appeared as an apostle of peace. He desired, he said, to dispel the cloud which hung over his town. On the thirtieth after a council with visiting Overhills, perhaps Osteneco's following, the Keowees sent over the May Apple, with the Mankiller, Half Breed Tom, and the Rat, bearing a flag of peace and a seductive message that Keowee desired "that the chain of friendshhip might be brightened [and] the path might once more be cleared for the white and the red people to be travelled as before. . . . It was dreadful to think of their brethren shut up in the fort that they could not speak to them . . .[28] that the flag at the fort [should be] hauled down and a red one run up."

Milne did not relax his vigilance. He knew that scalping parties had gone against Virginia and that more would go. An Indian girl informed him that the Mankiller intended what Seroweh had tried in January: to take the fort from the inside. Should this fail, the Indians would ask a truce to plant their crops and re-establish a trade. Then with ammunition replenished and crops harvested, they would renew the war. Since Milne expected Richardson's relief any day, he prolonged the talks to throw the Indians off their guard.

He invited Tistoe to dictate a message to Lyttelton and re-

[28] *South Carolina Gazette*, Apr. 19, 1760.

lease a prisoner to carry it under escort to the settlements. The Union Jack he refused to pull down.

Tistoe came the next day, his first visit since he had come with Seroweh's hostile gang on January 21. He radiated peace and consideration. He would send a truce talk through all the nation and keep his white flag flying the while. Milne should also raise a white flag and there would be no more war. After all, said the scheming Tistoe, it was Seroweh's war; and Seroweh was at home and would be quiet. He hoped the Keowee women and children would now live in safety. He would even send letters to Fort Loudoun and bring back messages; and in three days he would bring a white man to carry his letter to the Governor.

Listening with wary interest, Milne took the opportunity to contact Fort Loudoun. He also asked that Tistoe recall the scalping parties still out. Though the Keowee headman neither brought a prisoner nor recalled the war parties from Carolina, he continued the truce. He sent to Fort Loudoun as he had promised; and his people, as the Indian must have planned, planted the corn fields about Keowee without menace of cannon shot.

But on April 1 the Lower Towns had a shock. Within sight of the Keowee cornfields strange Indians killed three people. The Cherokees feared the English had enlisted the Chickasaws or, more appallingly, the Creeks. Mindful of the rumored Carolina concentrations at Ninety-Six, they mended their sprawling vulnerability by abandoning Keowee and Toxaway and concentrating at Conasatchee and Estatoe which they stockaded.

Cherokees and English vied for Creek support. In mid-February Cherokee deputies bore an English scalp and a bloody hatchet to Coweta town to arouse the Young Twin. But older Creek headmen insisted upon watchful waiting;[29] and, divided, the Creeks perforce held to their traditional trade and neutrality. Georgia's Governor Ellis attempted to prevail on "straggling parties of Creeks," hoping "by their means to embroil their

[29] *Ibid.*, Apr. 2, Apr. 19, May 3, 1760.

201

nation insensibly . . . against their will."[30] Aided by Lachlan Mc-Gillivray, the commander at Augusta, Ellis induced a few small bands to go scalping among the Cherokees. On March 12, We-offki, the Long Warrior of the Creeks, crossed the Savannah above Augusta to open hostilities. George Cornel, brother of a Creek trader, induced four stray Cowetas and Oakfuskees to take up the hatchet; but his attempt to recruit Chickasaws from New Savannah failed, though later Chickasaws burned abandoned Keowee town house. It was Weoffki's party which took scalps near Keowee.

While the dubious truce prevailed at Fort Prince George, the Cherokees pushed their war on Carolina, confident, perhaps, that the colony would seek peace. Throughout early May parties of from eight to sixty men ranged toward Fort More, Orangeburg, and Ninety-Six. Reports mention as many as 240 warriors leaving the Lower Towns during the truce talks to attack North Carolina and Virginia; and in mid-April, despite earlier reverses, Overhill Chilhowees and Telassees moved on Virginia. By the beginning of May "scalping parties more numerous than ever" worked from Little Saluda to Salisbury, North Carolina.

No sieges marked these raids, though the Indians, still expecting Richardson's attack upon the Lower Towns, kept watch on Ninety-Six. On April 6 four of Lazarus Brown's rangers, having strayed from the main body to hunt turkeys, were killed and another, one Hawthorne, was captured. The next day Hawthorne came into Ninety-Six, having escaped from two Cherokees "while they were asleep and laying upon two cords which they had fastened about his neck and body." He reported the Cherokees to have had five white and two Negro scalps. On April 7 in the forks of Edisto, Indians surrounded Gavin Pou's company of twenty-three scouts, wounding three while losing one of their own before they retired into a swamp where Pou's men could not reach them. On April 17 scalping parties near Ninety-Six killed James Francis' son and captured Tuckaseigee trader John Downing. The boy's scalp was vengeance on his

[30] Chandler, *op. cit.*, XXVIII, Pt. 1-A, 370.

father for the Justice's part in the 1751 disturbances. Downing they took to Estatoe, where they cut off his feet and burned him at the stake.

Reacting to the Chickasaw-Creek threat, the Cherokees renewed operations on Savannah River. A mixed force of Chickasaws, Creeks, and Georgia rangers moved against them without success. When Chickasaws urged an assault upon Estatoe, the Creeks demurred; for some of their countrymen were in the town. Other Chickasaws brought two Cherokee scalps into Augusta. On the twenty-first not far from Augusta fifteen Cherokees fought seven Euchees raiding for the English, and lost their leader before the Euchees ran. At Long Canes Creek, Cherokees killed two white men looking for strayed cattle; and on Wilson's Creek, seventeen Cherokees killed two of four men rounding up stock and took a boy prisoner. Apparently the Cherokees also sought cattle, beef being an acceptable substitute for deer meat.

On May 4 two large war parties, one of sixty men, were seen near Glover's and Ford's cowpens in the forks of Edisto, but they feared to attack; and on May 8 near Ninety-Six, Goudy's son was taken. Surprisingly, a week later he came home, released by Old Caesar of Chatuga, who said "he would quit his nation with his family and take up his residence amongst his brothers the white people."[31] In May, Cherokees approached Bethabara in North Carolina and killed one man and wounded another.[32] In southwestern Virginia, as Cherokee pressure increased, Lewis and Gist were steadily reinforced.

Though three waves of war parties had now scourged the English settlements, and over sixty Cherokees had been killed, Chota still maintained the face of peace toward Fort Loudoun. Oconostota, awaiting French aid, neither assaulted Fort Loudoun nor checked the barter which women, encouraged by the Little Carpenter, maintained with the garrison. Nor did he join the Overhill war parties against the English frontier. Osteneco, op-

[31] *South Carolina Gazette*, Mar. 29, Apr. 12, Apr. 19, Apr. 26, May 3, May 10, May 17, May 24, May 28, June 7, 1760.
[32] Fries, *op. cit.*, I, 231.

erating from Tomatly, had directed the March attack upon the fort; but Standing Turkey, the new First Beloved Man, asserted to Demere that he had halted it. He even hinted that overtures from Charlestown would be welcome.

The Cherokee peace moves appear to have been an effort to gain time and to win something by guile. The nativists aimed to eliminate the two English forts and halt English settlement at the Long Canes–Ninety-Six line, but to succeed they needed allies and munitions. The munitions problem had already become acute. The English peacetime trade muskets, neither powerful nor substantial, easily broke down, and the Cherokees lacked the skill and tools to repair them. In February the Overhill war parties had but two to six guns for every eight or twelve men.[33] Armed with knives, tomahawks, and bows, the gunless relied upon their luck and prowess in battle to obtain firearms.

Milne believed this circumstance a factor in the truce at Fort Prince George. The Cherokees knew that the fort contained scores of muskets and tons of powder and lead. Failing to capture the place in January and March, they fondly dreamed that it and its contents would be given to them in a peace settlement.[34]

While the Mankiller of Nequassee, Tistoe, and Standing Turkey schemed to take the powder at Fort Prince George, Oconostota's mission arrived at Fort Toulouse seeking munitions and trade goods.[35] Save for what occasional New England sea captains could smuggle in, the French had no trade goods; for the English navy blocked Louisiana from France.[36] Fort Toulouse could spare no ammunition. The Cherokee deputies received only promises, including one that a great force of Canadians and northern Indians would reach the Overhills in May or June to take Fort Loudoun.

Cherokee diplomacy failed to raise up allies from the tribes.

---

[33] *South Carolina Gazette*, May 3, Aug. 23, 1760.

[34] Bull to Amherst, Oct. 19, 1760, Amherst Papers, B.P.R.O., W.O. 34/34, Microfilm, Pt. 2.

[35] Paris, France, Archives Nationales Colonies, C13 A42, Vols. 58–60.

[36] Saunders, *op. cit.*, VI, 259–62.

The Shawnees were now at peace with the English and the Ottawas and Wyandots feared to take up the hatchet.[37] The contest for the Creeks was intense. Supported by the Mortar, Cherokee deputies went to the Cowetas urging them to keep their previous summer's promise of aid. At Fort Toulouse they held protracted conferences with nearly all the important Creek headmen, but the Creeks could not be stampeded into war.[38] Even the Gun Merchant, under Atkin's pressure, announced for neutrality and warned the Cherokees against attempts to hi-jack trader pack trains bound for the Creeks.

Feeling ran high. Pro-Cherokee headmen countered the Gun Merchant by threatening to kill any Creek who killed a Cherokee.[39] In reply pro-English elements assaulted the Cherokee deputies, beat them, and took away their horses.[40] On May 14 the clash of wills reached a climax. Among the Upper Creeks pro-Cherokees killed eleven English traders.[41] Headmen, aware of French weakness and honoring English subsidization, throttled the attempt to make the massacre of whites general and escorted the surviving traders from the country. The Georgia Governor resisted his impulse to take punitive action, which would have thrown the Creeks into the war.

In mid-May, as Cherokee war parties came home to celebrate their triumphs, hostilities quieted. Chota must by then have learned the disheartening results of its French, Creek, and northern missions. The Little Carpenter had returned from the woods to live in Fort Loudoun to insure it immunity from attack. At his behest Indian women continued to barter food to the garrison for such trumpery as the soldiers could offer.[42] Standing Turkey awaited Lyttelton's answer to his peace talk.

Ensign Milne's trickily managed coup at Fort Prince George also gave pause. Milne had little faith in the truce. Tistoe had

---

[37] Bull to Amherst, May 8, 1760, Amherst Papers, B.P.R.O., W.O. 34/35.

[38] *South Carolina Gazette*, May 3, 1760.

[39] Bull to Amherst, May 29, 1760, Amherst Papers, B.P.R.O., W.O. 34/35.

[40] Montgomery to Amherst, May 24, 1760, *ibid.*, W.O. 34/47.

[41] Bull to Amherst, May 29, 1760, *ibid.*, W.O. 34/35.

[42] Saunders, *op. cit.*, VI, 259–62.

failed to bring the promised prisoner to carry Standing Turkey's message to Ninety-Six; but Milne did not know that Tistoe had it placed in a cleft stick outside Ninety-Six where it was sighted and taken in. Having only reports that war parties continued to bring in scalps and that the Cherokees daily tortured and burned prisoners, he determined to enforce the truce and to protect the white prisoners in the nation.

When on the morning of May 9 two hundred mounted Cherokees, perhaps by Milne's prearrangement, rode up to the Keowee end of the ford, Milne invited them to send over deputies. Eight headmen, including Tistoe, laid aside their weapons and crossed, to sit outside the fort and smoke and talk of peace with Milne. Finally the Ensign invited them to dinner. Soldiers erected a marquee, opening toward the fort gate. As the headmen were about to sit at the table, Seroweh came in and joined them. Dougherty reached as if to take the bow which hung on Seroweh's shoulders, but grabbed him about the body. Other whites seized the headmen near them, and soldiers ran to help and propelled the captives into the fort.

Late in the day, Milne released the Wolf of Keowee to inform Standing Turkey that he would free the headmen when Standing Turkey delivered to the fort a like number of Cherokee-held prisoners; that if Fort Loudoun were fired upon, the hostages would be killed; and that all Cherokee-held English must be well treated. When the Indians across the river heard the Wolf's report, they went away subdued and in a few days brought four captives for whom Milne exchanged but two hostages.[43]

The headmen thus caught must have been led to believe that the English desired peace before the war ran to further destruction. The English will to peace, however, put chastisement first, and it was marching sternly up the path from Carolina to the swing of kilts and the skirl of pipes.

[43] *South Carolina Gazette*, May 3, May 24, June 7, June 17, 1760.

CHAPTER FIFTEEN

Montgomery's Expedition

On February 24, 1760, Amherst, commander in chief of the British forces in North America, assigned Colonel Archibald Montgomery of the Seventy-seventh Regiment twelve companies of highlanders, totaling 1,312 officers and men, to the expedition against the Cherokees. The force included a battalion of the Royal Scots under Major Hamilton; a battalion of the Seventy-seventh under Major James Grant; and four separate companies, two of light infantry and two of grenadiers drawn from the same regiment.[1] Heavily armed, they were presumed from their rugged Scottish background and their campaigns in western Pennsylvania, upper New York, and Canada to be expert in wilderness warfare.

Amherst contemplated a swift and stunning blow against the Cherokees, whom he regarded as having committed "an infamous breach of the peace." But he begrudged the use of his troops in this unexpected Indian war and contemplated having them return to New York soon for deployment elsewhere. He so informed Montgomery and to this end refrained from instructing him to remain in the field until the Cherokees made peace, though he allowed him to hold all or part of his force in Carolina until mid-October should an emergency arise.[2]

The troops embarked from New York and Perth Amboy on March 16 and 24 and on April 5 and 6 debarked on the banks of

[1] Amherst to Pitt, Mar. 2, 1760, B.P.R.O., C.O. 5/57.
[2] Amherst to Montgomery, Mar. 6, 1760, *ibid.*

Cooper River above Charlestown. They waited two weeks at Moncks Corner for Carolina to assemble transport for their baggage and provisions. Impatient with the delay in this operation, Montgomery started upcountry on April 23 with what wagons he had and reached the Congarees 110 miles from Charlestown on May 2. There he paused for two weeks to gather more wagons and to send back those he had to Moncks Corner to bring up additional supplies.

The weather had already turned hot. To avoid the heat the troops commenced a day's march soon after midnight; but the slow, horse-drawn vehicles and the beef herd entered the night encampment late in the day. The army arrived at Ninety-Six on May 24; and, its horses worn and its cattle thin, it halted for several days to round up replacements and several hundred more beeves. Finally on May 28, accompanied by 295 rangers, 40 picked men of the provincials, about 12 guides, and 40 or 50 Catawbas, the highlanders set out for Fort Prince George. The force now numbered 1,650, exclusive of Indians and pack-horse men.

Moving rapidly, with Catawbas scouting ahead, the army made Twelve Mile Creek before noon of June 1. Here it expected a Cherokee assault. Troops and wagons must go down a steep bank to the ford and up over rocks to regain the road level. But the crossing proceeded without interruption, and Montgomery believed the Cherokees to be unaware of his approach. He did not know that Milne held them to peace with hostages. He thought "that after one or two of their towns had been burnt," the Indians would "be very desirous to come to terms."[3] Though his army had already marched twenty miles that day, he decided to strike Estatoe, twenty-five miles away, that night. To deceive the Indians he had his troops set up their tents in the usual square not far from the creek. When later in the day the wagons came up, the soldiers helped the tired and straining horses trundle them up the steep banks, and placed them with the cattle inside the square.

[3] Montgomery to Amherst, May 24, 1760, Amherst Papers, B.P.R.O., W.O. 34/47.

At eight o'clock in the evening, leaving a small camp guard of regulars and rangers, Montgomery with 1,400 men struck up back paths through the forest toward Estatoe, bypassing Fort Prince George. His guides had forgotten that the dead Elliott's New Keowee hamlet lay in his route. At 2:00 A.M., as the British advance raced across the single log bridging Crow Creek a quarter of a mile from the houses, Indian scouts fired upon them. What Montgomery had hoped would be a quiet affair of bayonets became noisy as the troops returned the fire. The soldiers quickly surrounded the few houses and killed all the men in them; but Estatoe was warned in time for its inhabitants to clear out before the highlanders stormed in by early dawnlight. A pretty town of two hundred houses, it was well supplied with corn, ammunition, bearskins, and plunder from the English settlements. The troops looted and burned every house and killed a dozen persons who had lingered. From Estatoe the army hurried on to give Qualareetchee, Conasatchee, and Toxaway the same treatment. Nowhere after New Keowee did the Cherokees resist; and by four o'clock in the afternoon the tired soldiers had bivouacked under brush bowers beside Fort Prince George. In the thirty-six hours since the early morning of June 1 the troops had marched more than sixty miles, assaulted and burned five Indian villages, killed sixty to eighty Cherokees, and taken forty prisoners. The Colonel was justly proud of this brilliant stroke which he believed would be sufficient. To Amherst he wrote: "The Lower Cherokees who were the most guilty have been effectually corrected."[4] Major Grant, depicting the disconsolate Cherokees on the hills watching flames destroy their villages and the looting soldiers running from house to house, wrote: "The correction you'll allow has been pretty severe. I dare say the whole nation will readily come to terms and will not be very fond of breaking them."[5]

Montgomery undertook to encourage the Cherokees to make peace. In the fort he found the headmen whom Milne had seized

[4] *Ibid.*, June 4, 1760.
[5] *Maryland Gazette*, July 10, 1760.

on May 9—"improperly," so the gentlemanly Montgomery thought—oblivious to the fact that Milne's deed had prevented an attack upon the army as it entered the Cherokee country. From these hostages Montgomery selected Tistoe of Keowee and Ecuwe, the Good Warrior of Estatoe, to be his messengers. Ecuwe was to seek out the Lower Townsmen—they had fled to the Middle Settlements—and tell them to bring in all their white prisoners. Tistoe was to inform the Overhills that for the sake of the Little Carpenter, Montgomery would spare them provided Little Carpenter came to him within ten days. Should the Second Man fail to come, Montgomery intended to destroy both the Middle and the Overhill towns.[6]

Ten days passed and the diplomat did not come; nor did the messengers return to Fort Prince George. On June 15, Tistoe sent to ask for an extension of time. Montgomery gave him six more days.[7] But Tistoe's mission, if carried out, was fruitless. The Little Carpenter had left Fort Loudoun and had gone again into seclusion, and Oconostota had laid siege to the place. Osteneco proclaimed that he was so angry over the death of the hostages in February and Milne's seizure of new hostages in May that, make peace who would, he would never keep it.[8] A similar temper dominated the Lower Cherokees smarting under the destruction of their towns. Small parties of warriors hung on the outskirts of Fort Prince George and the British camp taking pot shots at exposed details and rushing lone sentries at night.

Despite their reverses, the Cherokees were contemptuous of the British soldier. He had shown himself in his northern campaigns to be ponderously slow. Futhermore, the Cherokees knew that when the regular had fought Indians at Braddock's Field and at Loyalhannon, he had been defeated. The Cherokees themselves had little reason to doubt their own prowess. As allies of the English against the French they had a long string of minor

---

[6] Montgomery to Amherst, June 4, 1760, Amherst Papers, B.P.R.O., W.O. 34/47; *South Carolina Gazette*, June 21, 1760.

[7] *Maryland Gazette*, July 21, 1760.

[8] *South Carolina Gazette*, June 21, 1760.

William de Brahm's own profile of his projected Fort Loudoun
and the surrounding country.

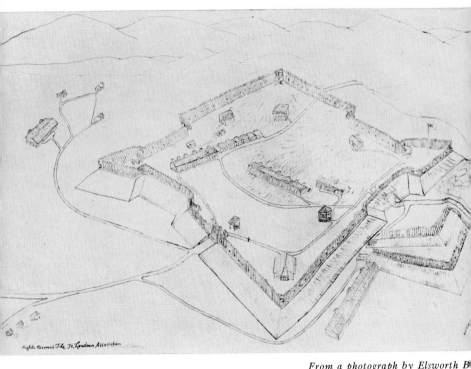

From a photograph by Elsworth B
Courtesy The Fort Loudoun Associ

Sketch of reconstructed Fort Loudoun by Colonel Claude A. Black.

successes, and now as enemies of the English in Carolina their assaults had gone unchecked for half a year. Their towns were full of plunder, settlers' horses, and captive colonials; and scores of scalps hung from their belts. In their own minds they were formidable warriors.

Montgomery, unaware of the high morale of his foe, hoped that after his bitter treatment of the Lower Towns, a show of good will would inspire the Cherokee headmen to come in and make a peace. For three weeks, save for Catawbas and provincials scavenging among the burned towns, no move came from the army. The Colonel released four more of Milne's hostages, among them Seroweh whom he told that to obtain peace the Cherokees need only display a white flag.[9] The gesture brought no response. Seroweh, outraged by Milne's treachery, effectually ended talk of peace by telling his countrymen that the British overture was a feint to draw the headmen together in order to put them to death.[10]

As the grace period expired without a reply, Montgomery realized that, though he believed a mountain campaign impossible, he must carry out his threat of fire and sword. He blamed Milne, writing Amherst that the Cherokee "fear of our not keeping faith with them prevents the peace from being made and obliges me to march further into their country."[11]

The army was unprepared for a long campaign in the mountains where no vehicles could go. Montgomery, therefore, improvised. From ropes, bearskins, and pieces of wagon harness, his troops made pack saddles for the draft horses which had hauled the wagons; and from their tents they fashioned provision sacks to be slung upon the makeshift saddles.[12]

On June 23, with the provincial rangers ahead, the army crossed Keowee River and marched up the path toward the Middle Settlements sixty miles away. That night they encamped

[9] *Maryland Gazette*, July 31, 1760.
[10] Grant to Amherst, Jan. 17, 1760, Amherst Papers, B.P.R.O., W.O. 34/47.
[11] Montgomery to Amherst, June 23, 1760, *ibid*.
[12] *Ibid*.

at Oconee Old Fields and the next day at Tuckareetchee on War Woman's Creek. On the twenty-sixth they stopped at Stecoe old town.[13]

On the twenty-seventh, though they had seen no Indians in their march, the troops were certain the Cherokees would fight. Etchoe, the first of the Middle Settlements, lay but eighteen miles away. They moved from their bivouacs at dawn, prepared for battle, the rangers in advance. Shortly they came to the northward-rushing waters of the Little Tennessee along which their route lay. Near nine o'clock, about twelve miles out, the advance flushed three Indians and took one of them prisoner. About half an hour later, five miles below Etchoe, the rangers entered "a plain covered with wood and brush so thick that one could scarce see three yards distance with an ugly muddy river defended by steep clay banks in the middle of it, overlooked on one side by a high mountain and on the other by hilly uneven ground."[14] The place was called Tessuntee old town.

As the rangers moved into the area, shots spurted from the thickets. The rangers pressed ahead and at once were hotly engaged with arrows slanting and bullets whining among them. Six hundred or more Lower and Middle Cherokees led by Tistoe and Seroweh, Milne's recent captives, lay concealed in the thick growth. Under heavy fire the rangers drew back. Captain Morrison, their leader, was shot and killed.[15] Captain Manly Williams, a favorite of the army, moved forward with the Royal Scots company of light infantry to support the rangers. He was a conspicuous figure as he rallied the highlanders to the fight, and the Indians, mistaking him for Montgomery, concentrated their fire upon him. He fell in a storm of bullets and from the ground cried, "Advance, my brave boys, never mind me." Some of his men rushed to help him, and three were shot down over him. It is probable that at this stage of the battle the fighting was close in and the Scots were in confusion as Indians strove to

---

13 *Maryland Gazette*, Aug. 7, 1760.
14 *Gentlemen's Magazine*, 30:442. (Sept., 1760).
15 *Maryland Gazette*, Aug. 7, 1760.

take scalps and prisoners, for the Cherokees took a drum and captured a piper and his pipes.[16]

Yet this was no Braddock's field. The Cherokees had no Frenchmen to lead them, and the officers and men of the Seventy-seventh had seen this sort of action before. Eventually the Royal Scots formed in line to receive the attack and responded to the wild Cherokee cries with "three whirras and three waves" of their bonnets.[17] With their quarry at bay, scalp-hungry warriors rushed upon the Scots; but the highlanders did not panic, and the attack soon lost momentum and died down to sporadic shooting from bush and tree. Then the battalions moved against their hidden foe. In the openings and above the low brush the long frontal lines of redcoats made brilliant targets, and Scots fell left and right.[18] But the Cherokees, as they were driven from cover, stole away, and the troops soon formed again in column and marched toward the now deserted town of Etchoe.

As the column advanced, the Cherokees hit the long pack train which followed, shooting down horses or cutting them out for their own use. But the rear guard and rangers with the help of a reinforcement soon remedied this; and the train, fetching along the wounded from Tessuntee field, made Etchoe in safety. The British losses that day were for the regulars seventeen killed and sixty-six wounded, and for the provincials and rangers the unstated number comprised in the words "several" and "a few."[19]

All the next day, June 28, the army rested at Etchoe, caring for its wounded. Late in the afternoon Cherokees fired from a near-by hill into the camp, but when a company of the Seventy-seventh crossed the Little Tennessee and delivered several volleys at them, they fled. Montgomery spent the day taking stock of his situation. He had marched through "passes the most dan-

[16] *South Carolina Gazette*, July 19, Aug. 14, Aug. 23, 1760; *Maryland Gazette*, Aug. 7, 1760.

[17] *Maryland Gazette*, Aug. 7, 1760.

[18] *South Carolina Gazette*, Oct. 25, 1760.

[19] *Maryland Gazette*, Aug. 7, 1760; Montgomery to Amherst, July 2, 1760, Amherst Papers, B.P.R.O., W.O. 34/47.

gerous man ever had to penetrate."[20] He had fought an action in which his losses, though not crippling, had been severe. He was sixty miles from his base, in an enemy country with three-score or more wounded. Around him rose mountains in the like of which a British force had never before campaigned. He could not carry his wounded forward without sacrificing the provisions necessary for sustaining his army in the field. To leave the wounded behind at Etchoe meant dividing his force. The road back was long and tortuous, and to lose a battle in that wild country meant to lose all. So the Colonel who had won his field made the decision which lost him his campaign. "Convinced," he reported to Amherst, "we had done so much as you intended," he directed that a retreat commence that very night.[21]

The troops jettisoned bags of flour to make room for the wounded on the pack horses, and, leaving lights in the houses of Etchoe, moved swiftly back over the road they had come. Passing the battlefield where they saw the scalped bodies of Williams, Morrison, and the others, they marched twenty-eight miles before they camped at Tuckareetchee Old Fields. The next day they pushed on to Oconee, halting only while a detachment dislodged some Indians on a hill near the line of march. On July 1 the army reached its old campsite near Fort Prince George. After a day of rest, leaving six months' provisions and forty head of cattle, along with two wounded sergeants and twenty-four privates at the fort, it marched rapidly downcountry toward its waiting ships.

In Montgomery's summary of the campaign he wrote: "We succeeded in everything we have attempted but 'tis impossible for this detachment to extirpate them and they will not treat with us for fear of being made prisoners for which reason a peace is impracticable."[22] The accuracy of this appraisal hinges to some extent upon what the Colonel thought he had attempted

[20] *Gentlemen's Magazine, loc. cit.,* 30:442.
[21] Montgomery to Amherst, July 2, 1760, Amherst Papers, B.P.R.O., W.O. 34/47.
[22] *South Carolina Gazette*, Oct. 25, 1760.

in his march to Etchoe. He had failed to reduce the Middle and Overhill towns to ashes as he had threatened if the Cherokees did not heed his ultimatum. He had left behind him a nation of Indians which had challenged him to battle and believed that he feared them. The precipitate retreat downcountry from Fort Prince George strengthened that impression. The Overhills pressed the siege of Fort Loudoun with vigor.

CHAPTER SIXTEEN

Triumph in the Mountains

MONTGOMERY'S EXPEDITION temporarily freed the southern frontier from Cherokee attack. Their towns destroyed, the Lower Cherokees remained in the Middle Settlements where they celebrated the trophies taken at Etchoe, erected two temporary villages, and engaged in summer hunts to supplement the food supply of their overcrowded relatives. When the new corn filled, they surrendered themselves to the ecstacies of the several day green-corn feast. From mid-May until mid-August the Carolina and Georgia settlers were undisturbed.

The army gone, Fort Prince George renewed its lonely and uneasy vigil. The luxuriant gardens and the unburned corn bins of the ruined towns drew Indians from the Middle Settlements to eat and to spy on the fort. The day after the army left prowlers appeared. A provincial soldier, picking over the trampled campsite, was shot and scalped before aid could reach him. The garrison again began to feel hemmed in.

Respite, however, came the next day in the persons of Captains John Brown and James Adair with fifty-six men, thirteen whites dressed as Indians and forty-three Chickasaws.[1] Learning that the army had retired, they stayed ten days scavenging the blackened townsites, burning houses and corn bins the British had missed, and seeking scalps for which Carolina had raised its offer to £50 each. Now and then they flushed a few Cherokee food seekers; but they netted merely an occasional stray horse

[1] *Maryland Gazette*, Aug. 14, Sept. 11, 1760.

and only a single scalp. By July 14, disgusted, they had all left to return to Augusta.

Fort Prince George settled down to wait out the war. On June 16, a messenger who had slipped away from Fort Loudoun came in on his way to Charlestown. On the eighteenth from across the river shots spat at the walls. The garrison replied with cannon, and the shooting ceased.[2] Then followed long summer days of empty watching for an enemy who at any moment might spring from the brush to attack a work detail or appear on the ridges to renew the siege.

The Little Carpenter continued through May to work for peace, if only for the Overhills. When he heard of Montgomery's march on Keowee, he expressed pleasure that the Lower Towns, cause of all the trouble, would be chastised.[3] He sat with the Chota council and reported its proceedings to Demere. Unhappy with his countrymen, he thought a little of Montgomery's chastising would do the Overhills good also. However, with the moderates, he believed he could check Chota.[4] When Demere expressed fear that the Mortar's Creeks planned a Trojan-horse capture of the fort, he promised to give him ample warning.

When the Mortar's gang did not materialize, gloom permeated the Overhills. Some spoke of possible attacks by English-allied Indians. On news of Montgomery's march the peaceably inclined talked more loudly. Others planned to run.[5]

With the passing days the supply problems at Fort Loudoun became more acute. The corn ration remained the pint a day prescribed on March 20. Barter with the Indian women became so costly that the men were stripping themselves and their wives of clothing to purchase food. On May 21, Negro Abraham arrived by devious mountain paths with a packet of ribbons and gauds which Lieutenant Governor Bull, Lyttelton's successor, had selected as compact materials a man could carry unob-

[2] *South Carolina Gazette*, Aug. 23, 1760.

[3] *Maryland Gazette*, July 21, 1760; *South Carolina Gazette*, Aug. 23, 1760.

[4] Bull to Amherst, May 21, 1760.

[5] *South Carolina Gazette*, June 14, 1760.

trusively on his back into the hostile nation. They did not purchase much. The Overhill corn supply ran low and was forbidden the Little Carpenter's confederates. When on June 5 or 6 the women ceased to come, Demere again reduced the corn ration. Four beeves brought by a friendly Indian were the last food the garrison received from the Cherokees.

The Little Carpenter's picture to Demere of Overhill fears, doubts, and divisions misrepresented realities. The plain truth was that on news of Milne's seizing new hostages, the Overhills burned with a bitter will to war reinforced by knowledge that the Creeks, having killed their own traders, might join them. On May 27, Henry Lucas going express to Fort Prince George was fired on at Great Tellico and turned back. On June 2 the Chota headmen banished the Little Carpenter from their meetings with threats of death. The next day Lieutenant Anderson and a pack-horse man walking outside the fort were shot and scalped. The sorties sent to help them raced into the fort as slugs hammered into the pickets. The siege, directed by Oconostota, was on. In Chota town house the warriors rejoiced over the scalps they had just taken. On June 5 the Little Carpenter walked through the besiegers for his last visit with Demere.[6] He said that the Great Warrior planned to burn the walls and storm the fort, and that Montgomery had attacked the Lower Towns. Creek runners reported that a host of southerners were on their way to help the Overhills. Oconostota forbade the Indian women to deal with the whites on pain of death. On the night of June 9, James Branham stole away with messages for Charlestown; and on June 10, Demere reduced the corn ration to one quart a day for every three men.

Convinced that Montgomery's forces would come, the garrison countered the insolent Cherokee story of a great victory at Etchoe with disbelief.[7] On July 16, when but two or three weeks of scanty provisions remained, they began to supplement

[6] *Maryland Gazette*, July 31, Sept. 11, 1760.
[7] *South Carolina Gazette*, Aug. 13, 1760.

their diet with the flesh of horses which strayed near the walls. The Indians ceased firing at the fort and merely watched to prevent wood and water details from emerging, Indian women from entering, and horses from approaching. Now and then Oconostota visibly surrounded the place with crowds of warriors to show Demere the hopelessness of his position. Demere, confident of eventual relief, several times spoke for a truce; but the headmen refused to negotiate. They knew that Montgomery's retreat had made relief impossible and that the garrison must starve. By July 27 the English were "without hope" and "miserable beyond belief," and finally men had begun to sneak over the walls at night to risk captivity or death rather than endure further hunger.[8] Four of these, traders and pack-horse men, found their way to Colonel Byrd in southwestern Virginia.[9] On the nights of August 4 and 5 sizable parties deserted, and the entire garrison threatened to leave the officers. At a council of war the next day the officers agreed to capitulate; and in Chota town house on August 7, Captain Stuart and Lieutenant Adamson arranged the terms. In return for surrendering Fort Loudoun, its guns, furniture, and ammunition "without fraud," the Indians promised that the garrison could march out under arms, each man carrying a few rounds of ammunition, and go without molestation to Fort Prince George or to Virginia as the officers chose. Sick or enfeebled soldiers would be cared for in the town until they recovered and then would be delivered to Fort Prince George. Finally, "all thoughts of further hostilities were to be laid aside and an accommodation heartily set about."[10]

Gratified, Demere wrote Bull of his capitulation and on August 9 hauled down the flag and evacuated the fort. Each soldier possessed eight rounds of ammunition prepared for use, a full powder horn, and buckshot. As the garrison marched out, the Indians swarmed in and under the direction of the headmen took

[8] *Maryland Gazette*, Sept. 11, 1760.
[9] *South Carolina Gazette*, Sept. 11, 1760.
[10] *Maryland Gazette*, Sept. 25, 1760.

the store of powder, a disappointing half-ton, and carried it to Chota town house. The other plunder they divided among the towns.

Accounts of what followed disagree. The renegade McLamore, carrying Demere's last dispatches to Lieutenant Governor Bull, said that Oconostota accompanied the marching garrison. John Stephens, a soldier, testified later that Oconostota, who promised to escort the troops, failed to appear, and that Osteneco stayed but a short time with them as they encamped ten miles from the fort at Ball Play Creek.

That night the Overhill warriors met in secret council. On the morning of August 10 at Ball Play Creek the storm struck. According to Shephens:

> After the beating of reveille, while [the soldiers] were preparing to march, two guns were fired at Captain Demere who was wounded by one of the shots . . . . Lt. Adamson, who stood beside him and viewed the two Indians returned their fire and wounded one . . . the war whoop was . . . set up and vollies of small arms with showers of arrows poured in . . . [from] 700 Indians, who, as they advanced surrounded the whole garrison and put them into the greatest confusion . . . they called out to one another not to fire and surrendered. . . . Some endeavored to escape but . . . the Indians rushed upon them with such impetuosity that it was in vain. By this time all the officers except Stuart [who was during the assault seized by an Indian, perhaps by the Little Carpenter's arrangement, and carried to the other side of the creek] were killed with between thirty and forty privates [later reports said twenty-five] and three women and others wounded.[11]

Vengeful warriors scalped Demere while he was yet alive and made him get up and dance before he died.[12]

The survivors became captives of those Indians who had seized them and led them away. Some were beaten in the face with raw scalps to hasten their movement. Parading the captives

---

[11] *South Carolina Gazette*, Aug. 23, Oct. 18, 1760.
[12] *Maryland Gazette*, Nov. 6, 1760.

through each of the river towns, the warriors herded them into the chunky yards near the town house, and, flailing them with switches and clubs, made them dance.

Cherokee apologists later gave many reasons for the violation of the capitulation. Some said Setticoes angered by the uneven distribution of plunder had caused it. Others, that Demere had gone contrary to agreement by carrying off a bag of gunpowder, as indeed he had in permitting his men to fill their powder horns. McLamore told Milne that Oconostota had opposed the planned massacre saying that "he himself would kill . . . the first Indian that should hurt a white man."[13] But Oconostota killed no Indians at Ball Play Creek or afterward. Indeed settlers heard that Oconostota had signaled the attack by turning back from the morning march to look for his matchcoat.[14] However that may be, the number of dead included all the officers but Stuart and totaled a near equivalent to those Cherokees who had died within Fort Prince George. That such was intended appears from Lieutenant Governor Bull's information and from Cherokee tradition.[15]

With the repulse of Montgomery's expedition and the taking of Fort Loudoun, the Indians had gone a long way toward achieving their war aim of eliminating the English garrisons from the nation. By taking Fort Prince George they could complete their triumph. To effect this they stopped abusing their prisoners and fed them well to strengthen them for the task of dragging the Fort Loudoun cannon over the mountains for use against Milne and his garrison.[16] They offered Captain Stuart his freedom should he manage the cannon for them. But the Little Carpenter, who from his retreat must have regarded the proceedings with dismay, took the Captain into the woods on a pretext of hunting and led him to Colonel Byrd.[17]

[13] *South Carolina Gazette*, Aug. 31, Sept. 27, Oct. 18, 1760.

[14] *Maryland Gazette*, Nov. 6, 1760.

[15] Bull to Amherst, Oct. 19, 1760, Amherst Papers, B.P.R.O., W.O. 34/35; Payne, MSS, VII, 19.

[16] Bull to Amherst, Oct. 19, 1760, Amherst Papers, B.P.R.O., W.O. 34/35.

[17] *Maryland Gazette*, Nov. 6, 1760.

No Creeks aided in the capture of Fort Loudoun; but as soon as the fort fell, the Overhills sent runners to the southerners and the French. Near the end of August rumors again circulated that large numbers of Creeks and northern Indians marched to assist in the capture of Fort Prince George. But only the Mortar came with a dozen of his henchmen. At Chota on September 1 they saw a sight no southern Indian had seen since D'Artaguette's defeat by the Chickasaws twenty years before: two hundred white soldiers dancing as captives of red men.[18] Cherokee prowess at that moment stood at its zenith; never again was the nation to enjoy such a triumph.

With Montgomery's failure Carolina went on the defensive. Since the regulars would return to New York and the unpaid rangers and provincials were disbanding, the colony was naked.[19] Pressed by panicky Carolina authorities, Montgomery detailed his Royal Scots battalion to duty at the Congarees, but with orders not to undertake an offensive.[20] Not until August 1 did Carolina pay its rangers and put them again to patrolling a protective arc from the Catawba to the Savannah.[21] To the few provincials fell the duty of convoying supplies to Ninety-Six, Carolina's farthest outpost. Near the end of August the Carolina assembly, hoping eventually to punish the Cherokees, authorized a new provincial regiment. The pattern of defense, while preventing further raids on Carolina, did nothing for Fort Prince George which lay open to Chota's contemplated offensive.

In the spring it had been assumed that Virginia and North Carolina would match Montgomery's assault with attacks in other quarters.[22] Though the Governors of both provinces promised help, they encountered delay. Dobbs of North Carolina wrestled with two assembly sessions over the paper-money question before in June he received authorization to raise three hun-

[18] *South Carolina Gazette*, Sept. 13, Oct. 18, 1760.

[19] Montgomery to Amherst, Sept. 23, 1760, Amherst Papers, B.P.R.O., W.O. 34/37.

[20] Montgomery to Hamilton, Aug. 15, 1760, *ibid.*

[21] S. C. Commons House Journals, Aug. 14, 1760.

[22] S. C. Council Journals, Apr. 12, 1760.

dred men.[23] The North Carolinians would not be in the field until autumn. The Virginia burgesses worked speedily when they assembled in May, but the one thousand troops they authorized would be too late to act with Montgomery.[24] Colonel Byrd, chosen to command them, would not leave the British in Pennsylvania until the Virginia council overrode his demurrers. Finally on the job with nine hundred men, he emulated the 1758 road- and fort-building advance of Forbes toward the forks of the Ohio by constructing forts at twenty-five-mile intervals all the way to the great Island of the Holston.

Montgomery's retirement left Byrd's laboring corps in the air. Byrd nevertheless worried over the peace terms he expected soon to be offering the Cherokees.[25] But Governor Bull of South Carolina sent him orders to leave peacemaking to Montgomery and push on toward Fort Loudoun. Byrd attempted to carry out the orders, but heavy rains bogged him down three hundred miles from the fort when Demere was less than a week from surrender.[26] In the next two months the Virginians advanced fewer than one hundred miles. On news of Montgomery's retreat Fauquier directed Byrd to hold back;[27] but escaped pack-horse men reported that Fort Loudoun was about to yield, and the Colonel sent Andrew Lewis with three hundred men to within eighty miles of the place to rescue escapees.

On September 8 the Little Carpenter with Captain John Stuart met this force at Spring Hill and reported the surrender of Fort Loudoun.[28] Byrd relayed the news to Governor Fauquier with a request for further orders and took stock of his situation.[29] By November 1 the enlistments of most of his men would expire. If Fauquier ordered him to advance, he had still 220 miles to cover and several forts to build.

[23] Saunders, *op. cit.*, VI, 426.

[24] McIlwaine, *op. cit.*, May 23–24, 1760.

[25] Journals of the Executive Council of Virginia, June 11, July 23, 1760.

[26] *Maryland Gazette*, Sept. 11, 1760.

[27] Fauquier to Lords of Trade, Sept. 17, 1760, in McIlwaine, *op. cit.*, Appendix.

[28] *South Carolina Gazette*, Oct. 11, 1760.

[29] Journals of the Executive Council of Virginia, Sept. 16, 1760.

The Little Carpenter insisted that the Overhills had a strong will to peace and that Byrd should do something about it before his force evaporated and the Cherokees captured the great store of ammunition at Fort Prince George.[30] Though the Cherokees held the British in contempt, said the Little Carpenter, they feared the Virginians. Byrd decided that despite orders, he must undertake a peace.[31]

With the Little Carpenter's connivance, he dispatched a strong talk to Standing Turkey and Oconostota, stating the Virginia power and threatening that unless the Cherokees delivered their prisoners at once, he would not "leave one Indian alive; one town standing; or one grain of corn in all their country." The King's army would:

> . . . drive the French southward . . . . Then who will supply you with goods to keep yourselves and your families warm? Who will let you have ammunition to kill deer; or knives, or salt, or any necessaries of life? Our people know the way into your nation. They are as numerous as the fish in the seas . . . they will destroy your corn in your granaries and will build forts in your hunting grounds; and will at last drive you into the South Seas. Think on these things, Cherokees . . . . Call in your warriors directly, come down and talk with me and bring me your prisoners . . . and I will believe you friends and brothers again and procure you a good peace.[32]

The Little Carpenter was to follow this message to Chota and display the fine gifts which Byrd would give the Cherokees who came to him. He also would present the harsh peace terms he had worked up with Byrd to the effect that the murderers demanded by Lyttelton were to be surrendered; all English prisoners to be given up; Fort Loudoun to be returned intact; Virginia or Carolina to build such forts as they pleased in the nation; Frenchmen to be banned; the Little Carpenter to be acknowledged governor of the nation; and His Majesty to pardon the

[30] S. C. Council Journals, Oct. 6, 1760.
[31] Bull to Amherst, Oct. 19, 1760, Amherst Papers, B.P.R.O., W.O. 34/35.
[32] *Maryland Gazette*, Nov. 27, 1760.

nation, return all prisoners, and send traders in the spring.[33] Impressed by the Little Carpenter's statement that "a patched up peace" would not do because the Indians would declare war again, Byrd planned, if the nation refused the terms, to seize the deputies who brought the reply.

If not a party to Byrd's intentions, the Little Carpenter had his own dark schemes to force a Cherokee peace with the English. He would have some of his friends murder any French emissaries who came to the nation, and would force a Creek war on his countrymen. His henchmen would secretly attack the Creeks and leave Cherokee symbols.[34] Vindictive, longing to direct his people's fortunes, he desired a complete rout of his triumphant old associates. On September 20, he left Byrd's camp for Chota.

Early in August the Cherokees themselves had commenced a peace offensive. The Middle Settlements, their food and ammunition taxed by two thousand refugee Lower Townsmen, had lost enthusiasm for the war. On August 2 at Watoga, headed by the Mankiller of Nequassee and Chistocohea, they composed a talk to Bull "to cleanse the path of blood and to brighten the chain of friendship." They blamed the battle of Tessuntee upon the Lower Towns. The Lower Towns, too, were unhappy. With winter ahead they thought to rebuild their burned-out towns and to harvest the corn the English had failed to destroy in the fields. They were willing to talk peace, but peace without victory was far from Seroweh's thoughts. He proposed that the English evacuate the forts, send only traders into the nation, halt the frontier at Ninety-Six, and that Carolina prove her peaceful intentions by returning one of the murderers surrendered to Lyttelton. In return the Cherokees were to give up all the English they held. Should Carolina reject the peace, Seroweh would give his war talk in all the towns.[35]

Rachel of Keowee and mixed-blood George Downing, son of

---

33 Byrd to Amherst, Sept. 17, 1760, Amherst Papers, B.P.R.O., W.O. 34/35.
34 S. C. Council Journals, Oct. 6, 1760.
35 *South Carolina Gazette*, Aug. 23, 1760.

the trader burned in April, delivered the talks to Milne on August 14; and Milne forwarded them to Bull with the comment that they were not to be trusted.[36] Someone else in the garrison, less partisan, wrote Bull in a different vein: "My private opinion is that the Indians have some just complaints to make; that they have often been misused, imposed upon, misrepresented . . . they have an equal right to justice . . . . I therefore wish they may be heard, peace restored, and a well regulated trade established."[37]

Charlestown received the peace overtures on August 19 with Demere's report of the capitulation of Fort Loudoun. Optimistically Demere had written on the eve of his death, "Only the Indians' desire for peace could have saved us," and "the Indians expect immediately upon our arrival at Keowee the prisoners confined there shall be released . . . that a firm peace and well regulated trade may be established."[38]

Bull hastened to inform Byrd by courier of the peace talk but cautioned him to keep the field "till the disposition of the Cherokees prove satisfactory." By McLamore, Demere's messenger, he sent a talk to Oconostota, Standing Turkey, and the headmen of the Middle Settlements indicating a willingness to listen to peace overtures, inviting the headmen to Charlestown, and promising to halt hostilities when the Indians did.[39] Sanguine, he stopped recruiting for the Carolina regiment.

But in the nation news that Fort Loudoun had fallen and that the garrison had been massacred dispelled all thought of peace. Wild with success, belligerents dominated the nation's councils. On August 18 at Fort Prince George, Setticoes seized two soldiers outside to gather fruit. One they burned and the other they gave Chota for questioning. On the twenty-ninth a wood detail was attacked and one man killed.

In the crowded Middle Settlements the mood also changed. Fired by the Overhill success, Seroweh and the Mankiller of

36 *Maryland Gazette*, Aug. 7, 1760.
37 *South Carolina Gazette*, Aug. 23, 1760.
38 *Maryland Gazette*, Sept. 25, 1760.
39 S. C. Council Journals, Aug. 20, Aug. 22, 1760.

Nequassee devised stratagems for the taking of Fort Prince George. A sentry plucked their message from a cleft stick in the ground outside the walls reporting the capture of Fort Loudoun, the massacre of the garrison, and the approach of three thousand warriors with a cannon. If the garrison left immediately, Seroweh guaranteed safe passage.

With foreboding Milne looked at the deteriorating supplies left by Montgomery and his orders to hold fast to his post. When McLamore came in with Bull's reply to the earlier peace proposal, the Ensign hurried him toward Nequassee and Chota.

Though the threatened great force of assailants never appeared, Seroweh and the Mankiller came to Keowee with a large gang to harvest corn and to prevent reinforcements and supplies from entering the fort. On September 5 the Mankiller, first having sent an Indian girl to learn if he would be welcome, came to see Milne and scout the fort. He depicted himself as an emissary of peace. He said he would stay at Keowee until McLamore returned with Oconostota's answer to Bull; and, if it were good, he would go to Charlestown with the deputies he thought could be sent. After he left, other signs of a friendly disposition appeared. An old Indian brought a leg of mutton, and Indian women smuggled green corn into the fort for barter. But on September 7, Thomas Hawkins, a renegade, styled "the Indian's secretary of state" by reason of his transcribing into English their talks, came to Keowee ford and called out that the Overhills with three cannons were coming. The garrison also heard that two thousand Cherokees, confident that the fort would be abandoned, lay in wait at Twelve Mile Creek. The next day the Mankiller came again. He warned Milne that Cold Weather, an Overhill from Chilhowee, lay in the grass near by to take a scalp. He said that he himself had been up all night looking for hostile Chickasaws, but Milne surmised he had been blockading the fort.

While the Mankiller talked to Milne, Cherokees took scalps in Carolina. A man was scalped at Goudy's, and soon after a woman and her daughter were killed at Fishing Creek. Shortly

227

the fort itself was in straits. The Mankiller ceased his visits and ordered Indian women to stay away on pain of death. The garrison subsisted on scant allowances of horse meat and sour corn.[40] On September 12, Milne employed McGunningham's knowledge of bypaths to inform Bull that "the Cherokees have actually blockaded us up like a parcel of cattle for slaughter."[41]

Nevertheless, the Cherokees would have made peace that autumn had Carolina seriously sought it; for as the Lower Townsmen ate corn and besieged Fort Prince George, Chota's mood changed. On September 7, as the Overhills prepared to march on the fort, Chota heard McLamore read Bull's peace talk. It made no impression until the messenger spread a story that powder mines sufficient to blow one thousand Cherokees to bits ringed Fort Prince George. Thereupon Oconostota and Osteneco listened to McLamore's arguments for their going to Charlestown. They ordered the Overhills to stay away from Keowee and appointed the Wolf of Keowee and the Corntassel of Toquo deputies to interview Bull. McLamore escorted the emissaries to Fort Prince George, which they understood from McLamore was to be the site of a big peace conference when the Wolf and the Corntassel returned from Carolina. There the Cherokees would deliver their English prisoners in exchange for their countrymen held in Charlestown.

The investment of Fort Prince George was lifted. As the Cherokee emissaries crossed Keowee river, besiegers rose from the thickets and made off. Seroweh and the Mankiller agreed to abide by Oconostota's decision. Milne, correctly appraising the Cherokee desire for revenge upon him personally as one "which neither time, treaties, nor presents" would eradicate, hesitated to believe that the Indians had given up the siege. But every day events demonstrated that there was a truce. An Overhill brought John Stephens of the Fort Loudoun garrison and traded him for a heap of goods. After the Overhill left, Coosah-Ekah, the second man of Sugar (Conasatchee), and Thomas Hawkins

[40] *South Carolina Gazette*, Sept. 13, 1760.
[41] *Maryland Gazette*, Nov. 6, 1760.

228

came for a social call. The next day Coosah-Ekah warned Milne that the Mortar and his gang lurked nearby to take a scalp. Milne knew that every day he gained improved the prospect of relief. He asked that the Cherokee order the Mortar to leave lest he ruin the chance for peace. When Coosah-Ekah complied, the Mortar, indignant, departed, telling the Lower Townsmen not to call on him again for help.

It is, however, doubtful that even had the Mortar been encouraged, the Creeks would have helped the Cherokees. Though on news of the fall of Fort Loudoun some of the Creeks had sent a bloody hatchet to the Cherokees, had warned that the English peace talk was a trap, and had promised Creek help for continuing the war, other Creeks had frustrated their designs by killing two Nequassees.

The truce at Fort Prince George, being Oconostota's, stood. While some of the Lower Townsmen murmured against Chota's commands, fearing that they would not be properly indemnified for their burned towns, and others hovered hostilely about the fort at night, a dominant note of friendliness prevailed. Coosah-Ekah visited often. Half-blood Nancy (perhaps the Nancy Butler who had been Demere's informant three years before), whose information Milne valued, moved freely in and out. Old Caesar of Chatuga came to deliver two of the Fort Loudoun men and stay the night in a visit which created complications. Milne had concealed from him four Chickasaws who had stolen into the fort. To permit them to escape, the Ensign inveigled Old Caesar into mounting the ramparts at dark and ordering all skulking Cherokees to leave. At midnight the Chickasaws sneaked out, and the Cherokees missed an opportunity to accuse Milne of violating the truce.

More menacing was the death of two Cherokees, members of a hunting party trapped by Dorgan's rangers. Seroweh demanded of Milne if Carolina sincerely wanted peace. Milne suggested he forget the deaths, that all white men did not know that a peace mission was in Charlestown. Seroweh suavely replied that Indian vengeance parties were out, but that since he, too, desired peace, any scalps they took should be overlooked "as a thing done in the dark."[42]

On September 22, certain that Carolina would talk, the Overhills marched in force and pride to the expected conference at Keowee. At Nequassee, Oconostota and Ostenaco hoisting a British flag, talked peace to two thousand warriors.[43] While they lingered in the Middle Settlements the Little Carpenter's runner caught up with them and delivered Byrd's thunderous message, but not his terms. Oconostota concluded that he was right in talking peace and dispatched a runner to Milne announcing his approach. "I am well pleased," he said, "with the governor's letter and Colonel Byrd's. We come to meet in peace, not in war." Ostenaco sent word that he hoped the trade would be restored; for "we can find none to supply us with what we want, but [the English] only."[44]

Arrived at Keowee on October 1 and wary of once more being entrapped within English walls, Oconostota sent the Mankiller of Nequassee and the Raven of Chota to smoke vicariously for him from the great pipe Glen had sent Old Hop years before.[45] He permitted the women to renew their barter, and fresh meat and vegetables again appeased the garrison's appetite. Settling at Sugar, he daily sent representatives to the fort: the Mankiller of Nequassee to be Milne's day-and-night guest, Standing Turkey's son with a captured piper, to entertain the garrison. He also quieted the Seed of Settico, who at Estatoe uttered bitterness against the English and the proposed peace.[46]

But peace was never more distant than at the moment Oconostota and Ostenaco seriously considered Bull's August message. Carolina, outraged by the Fort Loudoun massacre, had determined to reduce the Cherokees to "a state of subjection."[47] The war was to go on whatever the price. Bull planned that while

[42] *Ibid.*, Nov. 6, Dec. 18, 1760.
[43] *South Carolina Gazette*, Oct. 25, 1760.
[44] *Maryland Gazette*, Nov. 27, 1760.
[45] *South Carolina Gazette*, Oct. 18, 1760.
[46] *Maryland Gazette*, Nov. 27, 1760.
[47] S. C. Council Journals, Sept. 9, 1760.

the Virginians threatened the Overhills he would send two thousand men to the relief of Fort Prince George. To conceal the relief operation he intended to lull the Cherokees with peace talk which he hoped would cause them to release the three hundred whites they held.[48]

When McLamore and the deputies came into Charlestown on September 22, they encountered a cold but polite atmosphere. The Carolina council demanded that the Cherokees deliver all their captives to Ninety-Six if they wished peace, and gave the deputies a note for Oconostota to that effect.[49]

Two weeks later Oconostota heard the note and realized that it was not what he had been led to expect. Disappointed, but mindful of Byrd's threats, he decided to withdraw to Chota. Before he left Sugar he repeated the peace talk he had given at Nequassee and enjoined the Lower Towns not to molest any Englishman who should come to the nation. He sent the Creeks white beads, released all the prisoners he had brought down, and announced that he returned to the Overhills to get the remaining prisoners. He replied to Bull with the assurance that "we are now done and I desire nothing but peace."[50]

By chance his withdrawal enabled Major Thompson with 268 picked men to put supplies and a large amount of firewood into Fort Prince George.[51]

Though the relief came and went unmolested and friendly Indians visited the fort, not all Cherokees obeyed Oconostota's orders. Vengeance was exacted for the Cherokees killed during the truce. Three days after the Great Warrior left, Seroweh fired on soldiers sitting outside the fort, and on Enoree River the Seed of Settico took prisoners and scalps. To Carolina the attack was another instance of the Cherokees' treachery and Oconostota's insincerity.

Arriving at Chota, Oconostota found the Little Carpenter

[48] Bull to Amherst, Oct. 19, 1760, Amherst Papers, B.P.R.O., W.O. 34/35.
[49] S. C. Council Journals, Sept. 25, 1760.
[50] *Maryland Gazette*, Nov. 27, 1760.
[51] Bull to Amherst, Oct. 19, 1760, Amherst Papers, B.P.R.O., W.O. 34/35.

waiting with Byrd's terms. The alarmed Chotas made ready to meet the Virginian and comply with his demands. The Great Warrior, learning that Great Tellico burned prisoners, ordered the burnings stopped.[52] Suddenly, however, Chota's tractable disposition altered; news arrived that a French mission approached. But since the French overture needed time to develop, Chota did not reject the Virginia terms outright. It sent ten prisoners to Byrd with a promise that if he would come no nearer and permitted their emissaries to return unharmed, it would keep the peace until the new moon of March when a treaty for permanent peace would be entered into.[53] The war was suspended while both sides played for time.

The French mission was occasioned by Oconostota's message to Mobile and New Orleans. In late spring or early summer Great Elk, the French Seneca living among the Overhills, and Bellestre, released from captivity at Estatoe, had gone down the Tennessee to Fort de l'Assomption to obtain help for the Cherokees.[54] Two Cherokees, the Old Warrior and the Wolf King, visited New Orleans to speak their people's cause.[55] In June, Kerlerec, visiting Mobile, heard that in order to keep the Cherokees at war with the English he must send them something.[56] Therefore in October under the former Carolina trader Lantagnac a French mission came to Chota from Fort de l'Assomption. Though, according to the Little Carpenter, they brought only "one keg of rum, a little brandy, and a few knives," they made a tremendous impression. The Little Carpenter could not carry out his promise to destroy them; for certain Cherokees informed him that if he touched the French, they would kill all the English prisoners. The Little Carpenter again found it desirable to withdraw from the nation. With Willinawaw and the

---

52 *South Carolina Gazette*, Nov. 1, Nov. 29, Dec. 6, 1760.

53 Journals of the Executive Council of Virginia, Nov. 19, 1760.

54 *South Carolina Gazette*, Nov. 29, 1760.

55 S. C. Council Journals, Oct. 6, Nov. 1, 1760.

56 Paris, France, Archives Nationales Colonies, C12, A42, Vols. LVIII–LX.

ten whites released by Oconostota, he returned to Colonel Byrd, leaving Chota to Lantagnac.[57]

Lantagnac made the most of his opportunity. Shortly before November 1 to Standing Turkey, Oconostota, Osteneco, and Seroweh he presented an invitation from the commander of Fort de l'Assomption. In a masterly fashion he misinterpreted a message Seroweh had brought from Milne. Then he pulled from his belt a bloody hatchet, drove it into a log, and cried, "Where is the man who will take up that for the French?" Seroweh leaped up and whipped the hatchet from the log, shouting, "I am not tired of war yet. I shall give them more of it." In a frenzy he began the war dance into which a yelling crowd joined.[58] With a promise to return with cannons to reduce Fort Prince George, some of Lantagnac's party left for Fort de l'Assomption. Oconostota and a great many warriors accompanied them. Lantagnac with the Seed of Settico and a dozen or more Cherokees went to Fort Toulouse.[59]

Seroweh returned to the Lower Towns where on November 2 and 3 at Estatoe, rebuilt during the truce, he gave the war talk. He accepted white beads from a band of Creeks near by and passed out ammunition.[60] Angered by half-blood Nancy, who reported events almost daily to Milne, he threatened to cut off her hair and have her whipped and, shaking a string of black beads under her nose, he ordered her confined. The girl escaped and took refuge in the fort. On November 8, with a band of five, he went out to war. Credible rumor, however, said he had gone to guard the path to facilitate the delivery of contraband goods.

As the second winter without a trade approached, the nation felt shortages, particularly of salt. The English traders among the Creeks provided a small illegal trade, but a more sizable operation was carried on from the Congarees, the Carolina base held by the Royal Scots. Milne believed that the frequent visits

[57] *South Carolina Gazette*, Nov. 29, 1760, Feb. 26, 1761.
[58] *Maryland Gazette*, Jan. 8, 1761.
[59] *South Carolina Gazette*, Dec. 6, 1760, Jan. 31, 1761.
[60] *Maryland Gazette*, Jan. 8, 1761.

of the Mankiller of Nequassee to Fort Prince George were a vigil for the return of half-blood George Downing with contraband for which he had taken four horseloads of deerskins to the settlements.[61] That autumn most of the renegade whites—McLamore, McGunningham, Hawkins, and Torrens in particular—visited Carolina on one pretext or another and with gold and silver taken by the Cherokees in their raids purchased goods for the nation.

In November, Captain Gordon of the Royal Scots, advised by some of his men who had found a parcel of trade goods hidden in the woods, seized half a dozen traders and pack-horse men. Cross-examination revealed the goods to be Downing's. Gordon arrested Downing and sent him to Charlestown.[62] About this time "Secretary of State" Hawkins was reported to have enlisted with the provincials at Ninety-Six, "with no other end in view than to procure Indian goods."

Though Seroweh did not meet McGunningham on the path early in November, his excursion proved fruitful in other ways. On November 15 at Halfway Swamp near Ninety-Six he surprised and took two men. One later escaped, but the other was tortured and burned to death at Estatoe. Seroweh sent word to Milne that the burning avenged the letter misinterpreted by Lantagnac which Milne had him carry to Osteneco. Derisively the Cherokee warrior desired to know if the commander of Fort Prince George was "for peace or for war."

Milne attempted to maintain the truce Oconostota had left. He entertained visitors who brought food as gifts or for trade and used Cherokee young women to spy on the towns. From his feeble battlements he could see what he took to be war parties going down the Carolina path, but some were foragers bent upon collecting stray beef cattle near the abandoned settlements.[63] Twice before the end of the year rangers without interruption put provisions and firewood into the fort. In December they took

[61] *South Carolina Gazette*, Nov. 29, 1761, Jan. 31, 1761.
[62] S. C. Council Journals, Nov. 15, 1760.
[63] *South Carolina Gazette*, Nov. 29, Dec. 6, 1760, Jan. 31, 1761.

away 150 trade guns and most of the gunpowder Lyttelton had left.

Winter came and the war from Georgia to Virginia was quiescent. The Little Carpenter and Willinaw arrived at Byrd's camp at Sawyer's on November 1.[64] Since six hundred of his men had gone home, Byrd had no choice but to accept Chota's truce. He made splendid gifts to the Little Carpenter's followers and penned a talk to be given at Chota. Then, putting his remaining three hundred men into winter quarters, he went north to enjoy a social winter in Philadelphia and New York.

In Carolina, Bull's plan for a great winter co-operative assault had folded. He had sent all the Cherokees he held to the Congarees, hoping to exchange them at Ninety-Six for the Cherokee-held English;[65] but by mid-November, convinced that the exchange would not occur, he had ordered them back to Charlestown. Advised by Amherst against a winter campaign, he abandoned a project to send six hundred provincials and four hundred rangers to harry the Lower Towns.[66] He then ordered the South Carolina regiment under Colonel Thomas Middleton into winter quarters at the Congarees.[67]

[64] Journals of the Executive Council of Virginia, Nov. 19, 1760.
[65] S. C. Council Journals, Nov. 15, 1760.
[66] Bull to Amherst, Dec. 27, 1760, Amherst Papers, B.P.R.O., W.O. 34/35.
[67] S. C. Council Journals, Dec. 25, 1760.

CHAPTER SEVENTEEN

"His Majesty's Displeasure"

THE WINTER OF 1760–61 was difficult for the Cherokees. Deep snow lay in the mountains and the cold was intense. Plagued by rumors of attack, uncertain of French help, and distressed by shortages of food and clothing, the Cherokee councils vacillated between peace and war. Until the Little Carpenter returned they would not know that Byrd had accepted their truce. Creeks and renegade whites who had visited Charlestown reported that Governor Bull intended a winter offensive against the Lower Towns.[1] For safety the Overhills sent large numbers of women and children to Hiwassee Old Fields, seventy miles west of the Valley. Their warriors scouted the Virginia path. To the Lower Towns they sent powder and lead and warning to watch the Carolina path.[2] Rabid elements proposed to kill all the prisoners if the English came; and Setticoes, irritated by the vituperation of an aged white woman, tied her to a stake and shot her full of arrows to die a slow death.[3]

December brought a measure of relief to the Overhills. The Little Carpenter returned from the Virginia camp with goods and ammunition and a reassuring talk from Byrd. Though the Virginia Colonel blustered that not all the prisoners had been delivered to him and threatened destruction in the spring unless

[1] Bull to Amherst, Nov. 8, 1760, Amherst Papers, B.P.R.O., W.O. 34/35.

[2] *South Carolina Gazette*, Jan. 31, 1761.

[3] *Maryland Gazette*, Feb. 26, 1761; *South Carolina Gazette*, Jan. 31, 1761.

the prisoners were then brought in, he accepted the truce until March 1.

The Little Carpenter displayed his presents before the goods-hungry Indians. Diplomatically he gave Chota three kegs of the rum he had brought. In the ensuing orgy one Cherokee died and another was badly burned in the town house fire. It was a triumph of sorts for the English. Soon the French had their turn, for Lantagnac returned from Fort Toulouse loaded with English goods provided by the contraband trade with Yankee skippers on the Gulf Coast.[4] But the Seed of Settico had died from a distemper contracted among the French.

Encouraged by Byrd's truce and the French tangibles, Osteneco, war leader in Oconostota's absence, worried only about the Carolina threat. He warned Seroweh not to break the truce and urged vigilance against Carolina. To check Carolina he advised Milne of Byrd's talk and encouraged him to believe that he would soon send all the prisoners to Fort Prince George.

Though Seroweh had taken the French hatchet, he respected the Lower Towns' truce with the fort and permitted Thomson's rangers again to provision it. Yet rumor of impending Carolina attack kept him alert and uneasy. He placed scouts on the Carolina and Catawba paths and sent spies from the Middle Settlements people to visit Milne. The Mankiller of Nequassee came often to peer after his contraband hopes while he talked peace and the surrender of prisoners.[5] He presented Milne with a string of white beads terminated by a black one, signifying Seroweh, to be plucked off and cast into the fire. Even when Downing failed to materialize, he continued to visit, ostensibly awaiting Bull's answer to his peace talk. But on December 22, Half Breed Will, the Mankiller's henchman, bluntly asked Milne if any army were coming from Carolina. Both Milne and the Cherokees appear to have known that Bull intended to attack that very week. As tension mounted, Seroweh himself went

[4] *South Carolina Gazette*, Jan. 31, Mar. 7, Mar. 14, 1761; Kimball, *op. cit.*, II, 395.

[5] *South Carolina Gazette*, Dec. 23, 1760, Jan. 31, 1761.

down the Carolina path to intercept couriers to the fort and killed two horsemen at Beaver Dam Creek.[6]

Peace talk continued to flow about Milne. On the thirty-first the Mankiller came again to talk of Byrd's truce and the Little Carpenter; and the next day the Pigeon, an Overhill, brought peace talks from Seroweh and Ostenaco. The Pigeon stayed near by a few days awaiting Carolina news. On January 6, Robinson, the courier, rode wildly into the fort, having seen a scalped body on the path. Seroweh had set an ambuscade for him, but had mistakenly killed another man. Shortly the Mankiller came to ask the news. A heavy snowstorm forced him to remain the night, and in the morning he begged for salt, saying that Downing had betrayed him.

On the tenth, in twenty-five or thirty inches of snow and severe cold, Half Breed Will came to assure Milne that Seroweh desired peace and intended to behave; but the next day when Robinson set out for Carolina, he found both fords on Twelve Mile Creek guarded and he returned. That afternoon Seroweh sent word to the fort that it was not his fault that the path was waylaid, that he acted on orders from Chota, but that there would be no more trouble for he was taking his people to join the Creeks.[7]

Cherokee girls who lived at the fort soon learned, however, that Seroweh was not softening.[8] These fond creatures visited relatives in the towns to hear the news and to pick up food for their friends of the garrison. But in mid-January the Lower Towns rejected them. The Estatoes stripped one of the girls naked of her English clothes and literally kicked her out into the snow. A wench who went to Toxaway for food for her baby was turned away with a terrible command to go see Seroweh. On the twenty-first Cherokee bitterness sparked more viciously. Two soldiers cutting wood in a gully near the fort were killed and scalped. As the assailants darted away, one of them cried out in

---

[6] *Maryland Gazette*, Feb. 26, 1761.

[7] *South Carolina Gazette*, Jan. 31, 1761.

[8] S. C. Commons House Journals Jan. 23 1761.

Creek and dropped a wooden hatchet symbolical of war. The Tail of Estatoe, who spoke fluent Creek, and Moytoy of Keowee had perpetrated the bloody trick.

Neither fear of the English nor hunger motivated Seroweh's departure from Estatoe. None of the other towns went away; and Estatoe possessed a large herd of English beef driven off from the untended ranges of Ninety-Six and Long Canes. But seventeen tradeless months had reduced the Cherokees to rags. Increasing numbers made deer- and bear-skin clothing and tipped their arrows with bone points instead of trader's brass. To remedy their condition Seroweh's people, driving their beef herd, went off through the winter snow to the woods northwest of Augusta where bands of Creeks entertained Georgia smugglers. The Cherokees were very welcome.

Meanwhile Overhills, to meet their needs, joined anti-English Creeks to plunder traders' storehouses at the Sugatspoges and the Hillabees in the Creek country, and even attempted to highjack Chickasaw-bound pack trains in western Alabama. Others exchanged their captives to the English traders among the Creeks or to the French at Fort de l'Assomption on the Ohio and Fort Chartres in Illinois for goods.[9] Milne, on hearing of these transactions, recommended that Carolina provide ransoms for all the prisoners; and shortly goods to the value of £6,000 provincial money were on the way to Fort Prince George.[10]

Chota now played for time. While the Little Carpenter talked peace to a doubting audience in Chota, Oconostota at New Orleans made an alliance with the French.[11] Waiting for Oconostota's report, Standing Turkey renewed his bids to Carolina and Virginia, and Osteneco sent word to Bull "that he thought it was ordained by the Great Man Above that we should talk peace."[12]

[9] *South Carolina Gazette*, Jan. 31, Feb. 7, Mar. 7, Mar. 14, 1761; Depositions of Benedict Thomas and Francis Dayton, B.P.R.O., C.O. 5/20, 153–54.

[10] S. C. Commons House Journals, Jan. 22, 1761.

[11] Paris, France, Archives Nationales Colonies, AC C13 42:27; U. S., National Archives, Rec. Gp. No. 59, Gen. Rec. Dept. State, Misc. Acc. 161, Item 35.

[12] *South Carolina Gazette*, Mar. 7, 1761.

But the Lower Towns, inveterate even without Seroweh, were under no such compulsions. Soon after February 1 their warriors appeared on the Carolina frontier to forage for pork and beef near abandoned farms and to take scalps. On the sixth on Hard Labour Creek they assaulted settlers engaged in rounding up cattle and pursued them to Ninety-Six where they killed a man and captured a straggler from one of the ranger companies. About the twenty-first they were scouting one hundred miles farther downcountry near the Congarees. Isolated Fort Prince George lived nervously. Scalp hunters lurked in the thickets outside, and occasional long shots whistled by those who exposed themselves in the works. There was a brief respite on the nineteenth when Thomson's rangers rode up with supplies.

On the twenty-first Seroweh came back from Georgia to achieve one of his more notable coups. As the rangers, returning from the fort, encamped one night, he stole upon them and stampeded their horses. Several score Carolinians accustomed to riding walked eighty miles back to Ninety-Six, while Seroweh laughed and boasted at Estatoe, and his people feasted on horse flesh.

Thomson's relief had brought Fort Prince George the Carolina goods for ransoming captives, and a new commander, Lachlan McIntosh, to replace the hated Milne.[13] Milne feared the Cherokees, whom he had twice betrayed, and was accused in Charlestown of having kept the war alive by feeding Seroweh's animosity.[14] McIntosh had been so popular with the Cherokees in his previous tenure at Fort Prince George that it is possible had he continued in command, the war could have been averted. The Cherokees trusted him. Now he sent talks throughout the nation that he had goods with which to ransom captives.[15] Headmen who before had feared seizure replied with promises to deliver their prisoners.

---

[13] *Ibid.*, Jan. 31, Feb. 21, Mar. 7, 1761.

[14] *Maryland Gazette*, Apr. 16, 1761; Grant to Amherst, Jan. 17, 1761, Amherst Papers, B.P.R.O., W.O. 34/47.

[15] *South Carolina Gazette*, Mar. 28, 1761.

Alarms, however, slowed the new dispensation. Chickasaws following cattle raiders from Long Canes captured a Cherokee, took a scalp, and made the neighborhood of Long Canes unsafe for Cherokees.[16] Then, too, Seroweh had one hundred men foraging on each side of Savannah River near Augusta.[17] They maimed horses, drove off beeves, and killed a woman and a boy.[18] Near Ninety-Six, Conasatchees stole cattle and took a scalp. So successful were these forays that large herds were driven to the Middle Settlements, and Seroweh sold or gave McIntosh a score or more beeves.[19]

But by April 1 events took a new turn. Cattle raids ceased, prisoners were offered for ransom, and peace talk became more serious. The change may have been due in part to Cherokee knowledge that the season was getting right for English vengeance. Partly it stemmed from the efforts of McIntosh and the Little Carpenter.

On news of McIntosh's arrival at Fort Prince George with the power to offer ransoms, the Little Carpenter delegated to Willinawaw his mission to Byrd. As Willinawaw went early in March with a few Fort Loudoun men to Fort Chiswell in southwestern Virginia, the Second Man, his brother Tistoe, the Wolf of Keowee, and five hundred others arrived at Fort Prince George. They brought 12 captives.[20] Beneath an arbor erected outside the fort the familiar cadences of the Cherokee orator rolled out to the crescent of seated Indians, as with white beads in his hand he told McIntosh that the "leading headmen and the generality of Cherokees were for peace."[21] Should the Governor send up one of the Cherokees held captive in Charlestown, the Indian fear that Carolina put captives to death would be allayed.[22] Should all be released, demands for blood satisfaction would

[16] *Maryland Gazette*, Apr. 16, 1761.

[17] *South Carolina Gazette*, Mar. 28, 1761.

[18] *Maryland Gazette*, May 21, 1761.

[19] *South Carolina Gazette*, Mar. 21, Apr. 11, Apr. 18, 1761.

[20] *Maryland Gazette*, Apr. 30, 1761.

[21] *South Carolina Gazette*, Mar. 28, 1761.

[22] S. C. Council Journals, Mar. 25, 1761.

cease and distrust of the English would quiet. McIntosh, without other instructions than to obtain the release of as many whites as possible and to hold the Indians quiet, could only promise to send the Little Carpenter's talk to his superior. He gave the Little Carpenter substantial presents, which the Indian diplomatically distributed among his followers.[23] In private conversation the Cherokee told McIntosh of his people's distress and held out hope that they would surrender most of their whites.[24] Tistoe and the Wolf of Keowee asked that their people be allowed to resettle Keowee in time to plant their corn. The delivery within a month of 113 whites attested to the Little Carpenter's sincerity and influence.[25] But these were all. Some Indians would not yield their prisoners, and policy dictated that 35 or 40 be held to ensure the return of English-held Cherokees.[26]

Nevertheless, even Seroweh showed a disposition to peace. He sent McIntosh a message admitting guilt, pleading repentance, asserting that others were as guilty as he, and blaming Coytmore. "It is true," he said, "I was at the beginning of the mischief, but it was owing to the bad talks and ill usage my people and I got several times in the fort . . . . When you were here, when did you know me a bad friend of the white people."[27] Despite Oconostota's French treaty, the war could have been brought to an end that spring.

But in Charlestown peace talk was unpopular. The colony had suffered heavily, and the crown, bent on punishing the Cherokees, only waited until the upcountry grass could support the livestock of its expeditionary force. Meanwhile, Bull worked for the release of captive settlers before the Indians killed them in spite.[28] On March 31 he favored the Little Carpenter with an

---

[23] *Maryland Gazette*, Apr. 30, 1761.

[24] *South Carolina Gazette*, Mar. 28, 1761.

[25] *Maryland Gazette*, Apr. 30, May 21, 1761.

[26] *South Carolina Gazette*, June 20, 1761.

[27] Talk of the Young Warrior, Mar. 31, 1761, Amherst Papers, B.P.R.O., W.O. 34/47.

[28] S. C. Council Journals, Mar. 25, 1761.

extended message praising him for his loyalty, but stating that peace could not be had until all the captives had been released, that Cherokees who did not wish to be hurt should separate from those who wanted war, that Tistoe could live in peace on the fort side of Keowee river, but that the warlike should beware the King's men who would bring a terrible vengeance.[29]

Bull's message, however, effected little. The Cherokees had surrendered all they intended unless Carolina made a definite peace overture. The amnesty granted Tistoe brought but few young men and a thin trickle of women and children to the fort side of the Keowee River. Tistoe and the Wolf deserted them, and Seroweh went to the Middle Settlements, leaving the Tail as his deputy to use the Keowee people as cover for anti-English activity.[30] The war faction intended to keep itself intact for later action if need be. Even the Little Carpenter paused. His overture having achieved nothing, he awaited developments. Willinawaw in Virginia might effect a peace or at least stall off an English attack; on the other hand Overhill deputies sent to the Senecas might achieve the long-dreamed-of all-western Indian coalition against the land-hungry whites which, with Oconostota's success at New Orleans, could mean offensive war.[31]

Not until mid-May did the Little Carpenter move again. By then the Cherokee position was desperate. Chota's overtures to the Senecas had as yet no reply. Oconostota had returned from the French with a commission as *"Captaine grand chef medaille de la fond"* but without the trade or the military help which could sustain the Cherokees in war.[32] As a powerful English force under Colonel James Grant advanced up the path from Carolina to assault the nation, in Chota town house empty-handed Oconostota was no match for the keen-minded Little

[29] Bull to Little Carpenter, Mar. 31, 1761, Amherst Papers, B.P.R.O., W.O. 34/47.

[30] *South Carolina Gazette*, June 20, 1761.

[31] Sullivan, etc., *op. cit.*, III, 439ff.

[32] U. S., National Archives, Rec. Gp. No. 59, Gen. Rec. Dept. State, Misc. Acc. 161, Item 35.

Carpenter, who insisted that the war be ended.[33] Nevertheless the burden of proof that an honorable peace could be had lay heavy on the Second Man. With time running short the Little Carpenter set out again for Fort Prince George, hoping to stay the English vengeance.

His mission did not succeed. He conferred with McIntosh for several days; but when the British expedition failed to arrive, he gave McIntosh a message to forward to Grant and left for home.[34] Grant was but fifty miles from Fort Prince George when he received the message, and he replied promptly. He wrote appreciatively of the Little Carpenter's fidelity and indignantly of Cherokee treachery to the Fort Loudoun garrison. He repeated the familiar terms: no peace until all the captives had been surrendered and Oconostota came himself to ask it of Grant. The British would march into the nation. Those Indians desiring to avoid punishment must remain quietly at home, for any Cherokee found at large would be treated as enemy.[35] Grant's courier was shot at, but he reached the fort; and McIntosh sent after the Little Carpenter, who returned at once.

On the morning of May 27, Indians loitering about the fort were startled to see a long file of buckskin-clad men striding up the path from Carolina. It was Grant's advance guard, Quentin Kennedy's "Indian Corps." Most of the Cherokees fled.[36] Only the Little Carpenter and his escort remained.

That afternoon in a lengthy formal speech the Cherokee asked the Scot to delay punitive action while he went to Chota for the other headmen. Grant listened courteously but refused to stay his hand. He would march into the nation as soon as his men had prepared an entrenchment near the fort for his wagon train. The Little Carpenter pleaded for a twelve-day respite. "No, Attacullaculla," Grant replied, "I will not lose half an hour wait-

---

33 Little Carpenter to Grant, May 27, 1761, Amherst Papers, B.P.R.O., W.O. 34/47.

34 Grant to Amherst, June 2, 1761, *ibid.*

35 Grant to Little Carpenter, May 23, 1761, *ibid.*

36 *South Carolina Gazette*, June 30, 1761.

ing here for your people."[37] The Indian importuned, but Grant's orders permitted no other reply. When the unhappy Little Carpenter departed, he carried the bad news that once again a British army was poised at Keowee to strike into the Middle Settlements.

James Grant was a humane man. His harshness was official, not personal. It derived from Amherst in New York, who, angered by the violation of the Fort Loudoun capitulation, had determined to punish the Cherokees. The Commander in Chief regarded the Cherokees as "a vile and fickle crew" upon whom "the weight of his majesty's displeasure" should fall so heavily as to prevent "all further outrages and encroachments."[38] On December 15 he had ordered Grant "to chastise the Cherokees [and] reduce them to the absolute necessity of suing for pardon." However, upon arriving in Charlestown, Grant had become convinced that "If both sides were heard . . . the Indians have been the worst used . . . the greatest part are sorry for what has been done and would be glad to make a peace if they knew how to bring it about." He believed that ever since September the war had existed primarily in "the heated imaginations of an independent and two provincial officers at Fort Prince George." These men, one of whom must have been Milne, he said kept up a continual alarm because the war was popular in Charlestown, where "some think it will bring money into the province [and] others are anxious about their frontier plantations."[39] The Scottish Colonel, whose judgment the evidence appears to support, did not find a receptive listener in Amherst. The General replied, "That the greatest part of the Indians are sorry . . . I can scarce credit . . . punished therefore they must be and that severely, too, before peace is granted them."[40] Thus enjoined, Grant put aside his private opinions to carry out his assignment as promptly and efficiently as circumstances allowed.

He had already delayed long. Amherst had envisioned a late

[37] Laurens Papers, No. 49, p. 112.
[38] Amherst to Bull, Nov. 27, 1760, Amherst Papers, B.P.R.O., W.O. 34/46.
[39] Grant to Amherst, Jan. 17, 1761, *ibid.*, W.O. 34/47.
[40] Amherst to Grant, Feb. 13, 1761, *ibid.*, W.O. 34/48.

winter or early spring campaign. The 1,100 or 1,200 regulars from New York with the battalion of Royal Scots wintering in Carolina should complete their task before the summer's heat.[41] But when, in January, Grant landed in Charlestown, the severity of the weather upcountry and the lack of forage for his stock caused him to place his troops in barracks to await better weather.[42] The regulars left Charlestown on March 20, halting for three weeks at Moncks Corner for field-conditioning after their winter's rest. On April 22 at the Congarees the Carolina provincial regiment under Colonel Thomas Middleton and Hamilton's Royal Scots joined them.[43] On May 18 at Ninety-Six they picked up Thomson's rangers. They then numbered 2,828 officers and men. The regulars, consisting of the Royal Scots, four companies each from the Seventeenth and Twenty-second regiments, and two newly raised independent battalions, known as Burton's, numbered 1,400; the provincials, 689; the rangers, 401; the wagoners, 240; the Indians, 57; and the Negroes, 81. The Indian auxiliaries—six Mohawks led by the famous Silver Heels who had visited Keowee in 1757, and some Stockbridges, Catawbas, and Chickasaws—were augmented on May 25 and 26 by a score each of Chickasaws and Catawbas. These with fifty or sixty volunteers from provincials, rangers, and regulars Grant formed into an Indian corps after the system of Rogers' Rangers so effective in the north, and placed under the command of Captain Quentin Kennedy.[44] This corps scouted the flanks and advance as in the last days of May the expeditionary force marched from Ninety-Six toward Fort Prince George.

For eleven days the army encamped in a great square of tents on the flats under the guns of the fort. The troops reorganized their equipment, constructed an entrenched park for the wagons, and made provision sacks and pack saddles for the march into

41 Amherst to Grant, Dec. 15, 1761, *ibid.*
42 Grant to Amherst, Jan. 17, 1761, *ibid.*, W.O. 34/47.
43 Grant to Amherst, Mar. 15, 1761, *ibid.*
44 *South Carolina Gazette*, May 23, May 30, June 20, 1761.

the Indian country.[45] "Friendly" Cherokees moved among them, particularly the Tail of Estatoe. This charlatan, professing weariness of the war, had asked amnesty; but among Grant's Indian auxiliaries he prophesied doom for the army in the dark forests and mountains beyond Keowee River. Grant called him in, dressed him down, and issued scare headlines of his own.[46] But neither side was impressed with the other. The Cherokee warriors knew that a British army had turned away from them once, and they were confident that this one could be defeated. Seroweh and his warriors had already gone to the Middle Settlements to concert measures for its destruction. The English knew that the Cherokees had not beaten them the summer before and believed that their fresh and stronger force could smash anything the Indians could throw at them.

On June 7, Grant's army, "2,600 strong," in a column two miles long began the march of over sixty miles to the Middle Settlements.[47] In front and along its flanks, guarding against surprise, ranged the Indian corps. Carolina rangers and British light infantry composed the advance guard. In the center marched the three heavy regular battalions—the Royal Scots and Burton's—followed by the provincials. After them came a mile-long train of 600 pack horses in companies of forty, carrying baggage, ammunition, and thirty days' flour supply, guarded by rangers and light infantry. A herd of beeves handled by cowboys and rangers brought up the rear.

For two days Grant hurried his men over the traders' path to penetrate the narrow defiles beyond Oconee Mountain and along War Woman's Creek before the Cherokees could strike. On June 9 they bivouacked at Estatoe Old Fields, not far from Montgomery's campsite of a year before. Etchoe, from which Montgomery had retreated, lay northward seventeen miles.

The next morning, as the army fell into marching formation

[45] Grant to Amherst, June 2, 1761, Amherst Papers, B.P.R.O., W.O. 34/47.
[46] *South Carolina Gazette*, June 20, 1761.
[47] *Maryland Gazette*, Aug. 12, 1761.

on the wide flats surrounded by sugar-loaf mountains, the soldiers sensed that the day of battle had come.[48] The previous afternoon the advance had seen Indians fading into the thickets ahead; and scouts had found, emblazoned on a tree, freshly carved figures depicting warriors dragging an English soldier into captivity.[49] It was obvious to everyone that if the Cherokees wished to defeat Grant before he plunged into their settlements, they must hit him on the narrow stretch of road upon which they had struck Montgomery. Before the march, Grant increased the cattle and pack-horse guards and ordered every man to load his musket. Preparations completed, he dispatched the Indian corps to scout the way ahead. Then the army advanced up the path. As the rear units of the cattle guard left the campground, a sharp spurt of musketry gave foretaste of battle. Spying Cherokees had essayed contemptuous shots at the rear of the invading host.

For an hour and a half the troops marched freely through the bright morning. Four or five miles up the path the way narrowed between high hills and the brushy banks of the swift-flowing Little Tennessee. Ahead loomed the high blue wall of the Cowee Mountains. Near eight o'clock Kennedy's men perceived a large body of Indians on high ground to the right of the path. Shots crackled. The wild scream of the Cherokee war cry rose on both flanks of the column. Seroweh's host had challenged, and the musketry became heavy. But the Cherokee fire was largely ineffectual, and Grant ordered the Indian corps, light infantry, and rangers to clear the slopes.[50] The Indians melted away before them, while Grant pushed his column ahead to seek more advantageous ground for battle. From both sides arrows and bullets sang through the ranks. Frequent detachments probed the thickets; and once a battalion halted, faced left, and sent a volley crashing into the forest beyond the stream beside their way.[51]

[48] Grant to Amherst, July 10, 1761, Amherst Papers, B.P.R.O., W.O. 34/40.

[49] French, June 9, 1761, *loc. cit.*, Bk. II, 100–101.

[50] *Maryland Gazette*, Aug. 13, 1761; Grant to Amherst, July 10, 1761, Amherst Papers, B.P.R.O., W.O. 34/40.

In half a mile the advance reached the first ford. The volume of fire increased, and Grant decided that there he must make his fight. He sent light infantry over the river to occupy rising ground which covered his crossing and then, under steadily mounting resistance, passed his troops over and formed them into battle line on more open ground.[52]

As the movement proceeded, the Colonel received word that the Indians were also throwing weight against his weakest element, the pack train now filing through the area of first contact. Cherokee success there could wreck the expedition; for if supplies and ammunition were lost in that remote wilderness, the army must retreat or be destroyed. Grant ordered 175 of Middleton's provincials back to help the embattled defenders of the train. The hurrying provincials came upon a scene of confusion. Stabbing musket fire lighted the frightened faces of pack-horse men crouching in the forest gloom. Horses reared and screamed and tumbled kicking in the dust raised from cracked and spilling flour sacks. But in a few hot minutes the reinforcement had the situation under control. Their opportunity gone, the Cherokees drew off, and soon the cattle and horses were re-formed and again underway. Six men were killed, numbers wounded, and two or three score horses were lost in this phase of the battle.

The forward movement through the wooded narrows, the crossing of the Little Tennessee, and the rescue of the pack train were the crucial phases of the battle; for, though the army stood for three hours under fire in the savannas across the river, the Cherokees lacked the will to make a frontal assault upon the firm battle lines of the King's men.[53] For two hours after the firing died down the British held the field, tending the wounded, sinking the dead in the river, and re-organizing the pack train. Then they marched unopposed toward the heart of the Cherokee country, reaching Etchoe at nine o'clock that night.[54]

[51] *Maryland Gazette*, Aug. 13, 1761.
[52] French, *loc. cit.*, Bk. II, 103.
[53] *Maryland Gazette*, Aug. 13, 1761.
[54] Grant's Journal, June 10, 1761, Amherst Papers, B.P.R.O., W.O. 34/40.

The town was deserted. Chilled by the loss of twenty or more dead and many wounded, the Cherokees had fled from their settlements to the woods and mountains.[55] Grant's army had come through practically intact, for it lost but 10 killed and 53 wounded.[56] So skillfully had the Scot handled his force that the Cherokees had been unable to come solidly to grips with it.

At Etchoe, Grant carried out his orders with efficiency. He tore down the houses Montgomery had allowed to stand. The men built fires from the debris, rested and cooked their suppers under the summer night. But their respite was short. Between ten-thirty and eleven o'clock, leaving the Carolinians to guard the wounded and the pack train, Grant marched against Tassee and Nequassee. He burned deserted Tassee and took an old woman prisoner. Then crossing the Cullasaja and the Little Tennessee, the troops marched through the dark to empty Nequassee. Near dawn of the eleventh Grant called a halt. Since early on the tenth his men had marched twenty-one miles with full packs, fought a five-hour battle, and destroyed two towns. Now under strong guard they slept on their arms at Nequassee. Middleton with the pack train and the wounded joined them in a few hours.

The British remained at Nequassee three days. They tore down the houses and from the wreckage constructed rough shelters for themselves. The town house, "a large dome surrounded with resting places of cane and pretty enough," in which thirty-one years before Alexander Cuming had induced the Cherokees to seek the great alliance, they converted into a hospital.[57] When a wounded officer died, they buried him beneath a house and burned it to conceal the grave. Detachments destroyed the young corn in the fields. They pulled up peas and beans and left the vines on the ground to wither. They turned their horse herd

[55] Stephens to Fauquier, Sept. 7, 1761, Amherst Papers, B.P.R.O., W.O. 34/37; French, *loc. cit.*, Bk. II, 62; Laurens Papers, No. 49, p. 18.

[56] Grant's Journal, June 10, 1761, Amherst Papers, B.P.R.O., W.O. 34/40.

[57] French, *loc. cit.*, Bk. II, 105.

loose to crop the knee-high corn. They cut down peach trees, brought into the Cherokee economy from Carolina.

While his soldiers ruined crops, Grant's Indians ranged the countryside seeking scalps. They met no opposition and took but one trophy. The two villages, Neowi and Canuga, built by the refugee Lower Townsmen, they burned.[58] On their return to Nequassee, a disappointed Catawba brained and scalped the Cherokee old woman taken at Tassee.

On June 12, learning that a large party of Cherokees gathered four miles away at Joree, Grant sent five hundred men—the Indian corps and a crowd of volunteers bent on excitement—by a back route to surprise them. The soldiers climbed steep hills, only to find Joree empty.[59] Discouraged, some of the Chickasaws and Catawbas left for Charlestown to sing their achievements, prophesy disaster for the army, and collect the provincial bounty for two scalps.

But Grant's work had hardly begun. He intended to destroy every house, every cornfield, every orchard, and every vegetable plot in the Middle Settlements. To extend his supplies he cut the daily ration. On the fourteenth he marched to Watoga, a town of fifty houses, three miles down the Little Tennessee and on the same side as Nequassee. His soldiers burned the houses and uprooted the corn.[60] Then they advanced to Joree, which they occupied for the night and sent up in flames in the morning. After destroying the corn at Joree, Grant scouted the countryside to ruin isolated houses and crops.

On June 16 the army marched again westward through the closing mountains and soon reached Cowee flats. Cowee was the largest of the Middle Settlements, and Grant made it his base for operations against the Out Towns on Tuckaseigee. Sparing the Cowee houses, the troops devastated the fields and orchards and crossed the river to spend the night in the wretched village of

[58] Grant's Journal, June 12–13, 1761, Amherst Papers, B.P.R.O., W.O. 34/40.
[59] French, *loc. cit.*, Bk. II, 127.
[60] Grant's Journal, June 14, 1761, Amherst Papers, B.P.R.O., W.O. 34/40.

Ussaneh. There they encountered hostility for the first time since the battle. A lone Cherokee attempted to throttle a sentry and drag him off. The desperate man raised an alarm, but in the confusion his assailant escaped.

From Ussaneh, the army marched three miles west to Coweeshee where it was marooned for four days by torrential rains and the flooded river. After destroying Coweeshee and Burning Town, the troops withdrew to Ussaneh to dry their equipment and luxuriate in the wild strawberries. Scouting parties ranged over Cowee Mountain into Tuckaseigee Valley and brought back two scalps and a tale of escape from several hundred Cherokees. One of the scalps was that of Ocayula, who had served the English well against the French at the forks of the Ohio. By the Tuckaseigee he fought his last battle; his weapons, a bow and arrows.

Preparing for a campaign beyond the mountains, Grant placed 80 wounded and sick in Cowee town house, encamped his pack train near by, and detailed 1,000 provincials and rangers to guard them under the command of Lieutenant Colonel Henry Laurens, provincial commander after Middleton had left the expedition in anger over the method of the campaign. On the night of June 25, with 1,500 regulars and the Indian corps, the Scottish Colonel crossed the 4,800-foot-high Cowee range. To Grant and his officers the march seemed one of the most hazardous a military force had ever made. Captain Christopher French described it vividly in his journals:

> . . . we began to ascend Stickowe [Cowee] Mountain which is upwards of two miles to the top and extremely steep which made it a fatigue beyond description to get up it . . . after our halt we marched again through the strongest country ever I saw, anything we had yet passed being nothing in comparison to it . . . . Stickowe mountain which was so very steep and made so slippery by some rain . . . that it was nearly as difficult to get down as up. From here our march was either through deep valleys in some places almost dark or upon the sides of immense mountains with steep precipices on one side and the remaining part of the mountain a great height

252

above the path so narrow as to render it very dangerous . . . we expected to be attacked any moment. In short it was the most fatiguing march that ever was made.[61]

Grant was no less impressed than his young Captain. He reported to Amherst:

About half an hour after one the moon got up and we mended our pace a very little but we were obliged to make frequent halts on account of a number of creeks and narrow defiles we passed. At daylight we found ourselves in the most difficult country that can be imagined, the only practical road commanded everywhere by inaccessible mountains and at the same time so bad that the men could hardly march in an Indian file and if their feet had slipped, they were in danger of falling down a precipice. No troops were ever in so dangerous a position and they continued so till we got to the top of the Catouche [Stickowe or Cowee] Mountains, one of the highest and perhaps steepest in America.[62]

After this adventure the destruction of the Out Towns was tame. In the next four days Grant devastated the Tuckaseigee towns of Stecoe, Conutory, Kithuwa, Tuckareetchee, and Tessuntee. The Indian women and children had hidden in the mountains, and the men had gone to the Overhills.[63] Only seven prisoners were taken, one of whom Grant's Mohawks killed by ramming a stick down his throat. After cleaving a tomahawk into his head and thrusting arrows through his neck, they left his body for the Cherokees to contemplate. From Tessuntee the task force crossed the mountains to Cowee, via burned-out Coweeshee. The night of their return three vengeance-seeking warriors rushed a group of soldiers cooking their evening meal by the river. But the assault failed without casualty to either side, the Indians escaping in the darkness.[64]

[61] French, *loc. cit.*, Bk. II, 130, 133, 141.

[62] Grant's Journal, June 26, 1761, Amherst Papers, B.P.R.O., W.O. 34/40.

[63] *South Carolina Gazette*, Sept. 19, 1761.

[64] French, *loc. cit.*, Bk. II, 145–46.

253

For three days the force rested at Cowee while the Carolina rangers scavenged the countryside burning isolated houses and destroying remote corn patches. On July 2, Grant sent Cowee up in flames and retired to Joree. His expedition had nearly spent its strength. Most of the soldiers had worn out their shoes in the rough country, and each day large numbers reported sick.[65] The Tuckaseigee task force was so weary that Grant could not rely on them for further action. Retreat must be made soon. Though he had no word of a Virginia attack on the Overhills, Grant thought that he must act as if it were a possibility; so, to pin the Valley Cherokees to their homes or to draw them toward himself, he feinted with several hundred men toward the Valley. On July 3 under cover of a thunderstorm the Mankiller of Nequassee and three warriors killed a sentry on the horse lines at Joree and took his scalp.

The next day Grant hurried his forces twenty-five miles up the Little Tennessee, past Etchoe, past the bottoms where Montgomery had fought the year before, across the river at the ford where his own men had battled Seroweh, along the narrow way where the Cherokees had tried to smash him, to the savannas of Estatoe Old Fields, where he encamped. On July 6 from Stecoe Old Fields he made another feint toward the Valley; and on July 9, after thirty-three days in the center of the Cherokee nation, he arrived at Fort Prince George. He was none too soon, for a thousand of his men were shoeless and three hundred were sick. He had burned fifteen Cherokee towns, ruined fifteen hundred acres of corn, and destroyed the Cherokee appetite for war. But it was an unnecessary campaign. The same peace which eventuated could have been had without it.

[65] Grant's Journal, July 2, 1761, Amherst Papers, B.P.R.O., W.O. 34/40.

254

CHAPTER EIGHTEEN

Straightening the Path

In July the Cherokees knew they must ask for peace. The war faction's boasts had died in the flames of the Middle Settlements.[1] The entire Cherokee nation was crowded into the westernmost towns, and meagerly subsisted upon a food supply hardly sufficient to support a third of their numbers.[2] Daily its economy drifted nearer the Stone age level while that of its neighbor rivals, the Creeks, flourished on British goods. The Cherokees had lost heavily in their Virginia and Carolina raids and in their actions against the British army.[3] They were ringed with enemies. From down the Tennessee their former allies, the Chickasaws, warred upon them.[4] The Shawnees, having made peace with the English, had turned against them, and the Six Nations were hostile. Byrd's Virginians threatened from the north, and Grant's force still hung on their eastern flank. Many Cherokees must have feared that just as the French had destroyed the Natchez thirty years before, so the English and their red allies would destroy the Cherokees. Facing these hard facts, Osteneco, Standing Turkey, and Oconostota yielded to the Little Carpenter. Near July 1 a meeting at Chota of headmen from all parts of the nation agreed to sue for peace.[5] They determined,

[1] S. C. Commons House Journals, Sept. 17, 1761.

[2] S. C. Council Journals, Dec. 18, 1761.

[3] Laurens Papers, No. 49, p. 11.

[4] *South Carolina Gazette*, June 20, 1761.

[5] Laurens Papers, No. 49, p. 103.

however, to direct their appeal to Byrd in southwestern Virginia, and the Little Carpenter set out to deliver it.

Though throughout the spring fear of the Virginians had pinned the Overhills to their towns, Byrd had no enthusiasm for marching against Chota. He apparently did not want the assignment. He had been slow in getting on the job in the spring, slow to concentrate his forces, and slow to advance. He did not believe a Virginia assault upon the Overhills practicable with the forces assigned him, and Amherst had denied him the right to make peace.[6] On June 23 with Grant already at Cowee, Byrd, having experienced a succession of frustrations, loitered three hundred miles from Chota. He had but 684 effectives and awaited word of promised North Carolina reinforcements.[7] The grapevine reported Grant halted, as Montgomery had been, by battle before Etchoe. When Amherst, annoyed at his delays, prodded him, he cautiously advanced one hunded miles in two weeks to Stalnaker's where he halted in foreboding at what lay in the gloomy forests ahead.[8] There on July 16 the Little Carpenter came to him. Though the Colonel offered his visitor the usual presents and entertainment, he had to tell him that for terms he must go to Carolina.[9] On August 1, writing resentfully to Amherst, the Virginian resigned his command.[10]

Meanwhile, Grant had launched his own peace overture. On July 14 from Fort Prince George, he sent the Mankiller and the White Owl of Toxaway to the Overhills with a threat that unless they sent emissaries to him by the twenty-ninth, he "would re-enter the country and destroy their town." But already Oconostota, uneasy over Grant's intentions, had dispatched a talk by Old Caesar of Chatuga who, meeting Grant's emissaries on

[6] Virginia Burgesses, Apr. 9, 1761; Byrd to Grant, n.d. (Apr., 1761), Amherst Papers, B.P.R.O., W.O. 34/47; Fauquier to Byrd, Apr. 28, 1761, Draper MSS, ZZ 48; Amherst to Byrd, May 11, 1761, Draper MSS, 4ZZ 31 1–2.

[7] Return of Virginia Regiment to Fort Chiswell, June 24, 1761, Amherst Papers, B.P.R.O., W.O. 34/37.

[8] Journals of the Executive Council of Virginia, June 29, 1761.

[9] S. C. Commons House Journals, Sept. 15, 1761.

[10] Grant to Amherst, Aug. 1, 1761, Draper MSS, 4ZZ 36.

the path, persuaded them to turn back and accompany him to the English camp. There the former slave talked earnestly to the Colonel, presenting a pitiful picture of starvation and death among the Cherokee women and of children hiding fearfully in the hills. As evidence of Chota's desire to end the war, he said even Seroweh would not be allowed to fight again: "The nation would kill him if he did the least mischief."[11] Grant sent Old Caesar back to Chota with a demand that Oconostota come down.[12] But Oconostota, hating and distrusting the English because they had once locked him up, refused and deputized Tistoe of Keowee and the Slave Catcher of Tomatly to go in his place.[13] Grant, insistent on treating only with the first voices—Osteneco, Standing Turkey, and Oconostota—sent them back without a hearing. Unmoved, Oconostota turned the negotiations over to the Little Carpenter, in whose sphere they rightfully belonged and who had just returned from Byrd's camp. Prompted by the fear of renewed warfare engendered by news that Grant's Mohawks had just taken three Cherokee scalps and that the unregenerate Seroweh was again taking horses and prisoners in Georgia, Chota discussed Grant's demands.[14] Finally on August 21 the Little Carpenter set out for Fort Prince George with a delegation consisting of Oconostota's brother, Willinawaw, Old Hop's son Cappy, Old Caesar, Moytoy of Hiwassee, the Raven of Tomatly, Half Breed Will of Nequassee, the Mankiller of Nequassee, and a large number of attendants.[15] At their head a warrior bore a large white flag to signify that theirs was an official mission of good will. Oconostota accompanied them as far as Hiwassee, at least. There he halted to lecture Seroweh, who protested that "he did not know that there was to be a peace," and obtained the release of one of his white prisoners.[16] To Grant

[11] *Maryland Gazette*, Sept. 10, 1761.

[12] French, *loc. cit.*, Bk. II, 153.

[13] *South Carolina Gazette*, Aug. 24, 1761.

[14] Laurens Papers, No. 49, p. 104; S. C. Commons House Journals, Sept. 15, 1761.

[15] French, *loc. cit.*, Bk. II, 159–60.

[16] S. C. Commons House Journals, Sept. 15, 1761.

he sent word that he remained at Hiwassee to free the others of Seroweh's captives. Possibly, as Henry Laurens stated in the bitter debate at Charlestown that winter over the conduct of the war, he went with the deputies to within twelve miles of Keowee where he was consulted in the ensuing negotiations.[17]

The next day the Little Carpenter stood once again in his great role as defender of his people. With pipe and tobacco sent by Oconostota, he opened his mission. He was conciliatory, but he did not beg. Implying that some towns still doubted, he talked for Chota, Settico, Chatuga, and Great Tellico. He asserted that the Cherokees, having had "two bad days"—the battles in '60 and '61 near Etchoe—now knew the strength of the English and that only the English could supply them. He asked English tolerance for Seroweh's misbehavior. Some of his countrymen, he said, still had bad thoughts. Others were hungry and stole horses in order to fill their stomachs; but the Great Warrior would prevent further depredations. Bargaining, the Little Carpenter asked the terms on which the Cherokees could surrender the white people they still held and have a good trade. Grant, disturbed that the war leaders, Oconostota, Osteneco, and Seroweh, and the First Beloved Man, Standing Turkey, had not come, tried to dispel Cherokee distrust by reminding the Little Carpenter that he had required Milne to free the headmen so unjustly seized in May of the year before. But the peace, he said, could only be had in Charlestown. Its terms, which he had worked out with Bull in Charlestown in April, he would present the next day. On August 31 he read them to the Little Carpenter:

1. The Cherokees must recognize English superiority by delivering four to eight of their countrymen, one or two from each of the main regions, to be put to death;

2. The Cherokees must deliver immediately all prisoners, horses and cattle they had taken;

3. The Cherokees must give up intact Fort Loudoun and allow the English to build in the nation such forts as they deemed necessary;

[17] Laurens Papers, No. 49, pp. 108–109.

4. The Cherokees should neither receive nor protect Frenchmen;
5. In the future the Cherokees must kill any of their people who murdered Englishmen;
6. The Cherokees must accept a line twenty-six miles east of Keowee to be their boundary toward Carolina;
7. The Cherokees must respect the herds and planting grounds belonging to the English forts;
8. The Cherokees must make peace with the Catawbas and Chickasaws;
9. The Cherokees must make the Little Carpenter their Emperor.
10. The English would return all Cherokees they held;
11. On the establishment of peace Charlestown would renew the the trade;
12. English offenders against the Cherokees were to be punished only by the English.[18]

That the terms were relatively mild was due to Grant, for Bull was under great pressure in Carolina to make the Cherokees pay dearly in land and lives. Grant feared that harshness would prolong the war. Though Bull regarded the first article as "the grand article that must be insisted on to satisfy our honor," on Grant's urging, the demand for victims had been reduced from twenty-four. Article Six also bore hard on the Cherokees, for the land cession cut off more than half the Lower Towns' hunting grounds. Article Nine, elevating the Little Carpenter to the emperorship, disregarded Cherokee institutions and struck at the heart of Cherokee independence. Article Two, if strictly interpreted, offered difficulty; for the hungry Cherokees had eaten the horses and beeves they had taken. Articles Five and Twelve were not new: forfeiture of Indian lives for the murder of Colonials had been provided for in practically every treaty English had made with Indians. It was the principle upon which Lyttelton had acted when he built up the situation which had provoked the Cherokees to make the final break. Articles Three, Four, Seven, and Eight offered no difficult points; while Articles Ten and Eleven offered

---

[18] S. C. Commons House Journals, Sept. 17, 1761.

trade and the return of captured Cherokees as inducements for Cherokee acceptance of the treaty.

The Little Carpenter, however, was under strong compulsion to obtain as mild a treaty as possible, and time was on his side. Grant, after six idle weeks at Fort Prince George, was unhappy. He had stayed to strike the Cherokees again if they failed to make a peace; but by August 30 he realized that he could not remain much longer. The transport train upon which he depended for his day-to-day supply from the far-off English settlements had worn out. The disaffected provincial regiment disintegrated under his eyes; and the Carolina rangers would disband on October 1. He knew now that Byrd would exert no pressure. Under the circumstances, to hasten negotiations, he lightened the terms as much as he dared. Instead of eight Cherokees for execution, he demanded but four. He omitted Article Six, reducing the Lower Towns' hunting grounds; and, perhaps on the Little Carpenter's advice, he dropped the requirement that the Second Man be made emperor.[19]

But these concessions did not satisfy the Little Carpenter. The Cherokees objected to surrendering any of their countrymen to be victims of Carolina vengeance. His reluctant agreement to give up twenty-four warriors in 1759 had been instrumental in precipitating the war. He knew that the nation would never accept the condition, so he stood firm. He hinted that trouble brewed: that the Creeks boasted that the English feared to punish them for the murders they had committed, and that rogues in the Middle Settlements and Creeks at Hiwassee gave bad talks.[20] And he threatened to return to Chota. His firmness brought results.

Grant feared to break off the negotiations. Since he also did not like the vengeance requirement, he promised to write Bull a recommendation that it be dropped. With that the Mankiller of Nequassee suggested that to cement the peace English and Cherokees should join to attack the Creeks, who, after all, had helped

[19] *Ibid.*, Sept. 15, Sept. 17, 1761.
[20] Laurens Papers, No. 49, p. 11.

to bring on the war. But Grant rejected this nicety of Indian diplomacy. He insisted that the actual peace could only be made in Charlestown. Accordingly the Little Carpenter prepared to accompany Lieutenant Colonel Henry Laurens of the provincials down the path.

Then for a day or two it appeared that, the Indians having become nervous, the peace might not be made after all. The trouble stemmed from the return from Charlestown of the renegade McGunningham with a report that smallpox raged in the provincial capital. Rumor coursed among the Cherokees that the deputies were being lured to their deaths.[21] Some, frightened, returned to Chota; but the Little Carpenter, after brief hesitation, determined to go ahead accompanied by Willinawaw, Cappy, Half Breed Will, and the Mankiller of Nequassee. Rumor also had Frenchmen coming into Chota; but Oconostota, fearing a renewed English assault, sent reassurances of his peaceful intentions.[22]

On September 15 the South Carolina Council convened at Ashley Ferry a few miles outside plague-stricken Charlestown, and listened to the Little Carpenter give much the same talk he had given Grant. That afternoon the Commons House heard the talk and Grant's recommendation that Carolina drop its demand for victims. But the Commons, stimulated by the rancorous speeches of Colonel Middleton, who felt that Colonel Grant had insulted him, concluded that the British campaign of house-burning and corn-pulling had been too gentle. They wanted blood and resolved that before peace could be made Cherokees must be delivered up for execution. The Little Carpenter was adamant, and for a day or two negotiations hung in balance. However, continuation of the war meant the continuation of the heavy expenses, which the Commons disliked even more than they disliked Grant and the Cherokees. They agreed to drop the vengeful first article, but altered several other terms and censured Grant's conduct of the campaign. They required that captured Negro

21 S. C. Commons House Journals, Sept. 15, Sept. 17, 1761.
22 French, *loc. cit.*, Bk. II, p. 163.

261

slaves be returned and divested the colony of further responsibility for forts in the Indian country. Carolina would no longer attempt to administer justice in quarrels between Indians and whites; that would be handled at the forts. Carolina would keep the two killers surrendered to Lyttelton in 1759; and, finally, the cession of the Lower Towns' hunting grounds, given up by Grant, was required.

The Little Carpenter accepted the new terms; for with the demand for further victims dropped, they no longer threatened the lives of leading headmen. The only immediate penalty affected the Lower Towns which had precipitated the war; and no Lower Towns headmen were present to protest the sacrifice of their hunting grounds. The really difficult feature of the terms was Carolina's refusal to return the Cherokees she held captive until the Indians should deliver in Charlestown all the whites, Negroes, and cattle they had taken. Even this provision affected the Lower Towns more than the rest of the nation; for those whom Carolina held were Lower Townsmen. The Little Carpenter was apparently willing to leave this matter to time. He had scored his greatest success, for he had gotten the nation off lightly and he had a treaty he believed Chota would accept. He, of course, could not complete the negotiation without making a personal request. This time it was that his friend Captain John Stuart be made representative of the English to the Cherokees. Bull agreed to consider the proposal and then, as of old, gave the deputies presents and invited them to his house for dinner.[23]

The arrival of the Little Carpenter at Fort Prince George in mid-October was a relief to Grant, who longed to end his wilderness stay and had feared for the Second Man's life among the Cherokee-hating whites along the Carolina road. Confident that the peace would be accepted, Grant demonstrated his faith in the Indians by crossing Keowee River and walking alone a dozen miles into the once hostile Cherokee country. On October 15 the Little Carpenter left for Chota, and the next day Grant's force commenced its march toward Ninety-Six.[24]

[23] S. C. Council Journals, Sept. 15–16, Sept. 18, Sept. 22–23, 1761.

But even as the Little Carpenter went toward home, complications developed to dim his triumph. In early October, already depressed by the enmity of the Shawnees and Iroquois, the Overhills received a shock. The Virginians advanced. Adam Stephen, who had succeeded Byrd, had decided to prod the Cherokees toward peace-making by moving his force up to the Great Island of the Holston. There with seven hundred men he built a base from which, when North Carolina forces joined him, he intended to bear down on the Overhills.[25]

Cherokee scouts, posing as hunters, spied on the Virginians. Uneasy Chota sent runners to Stephen to report the Little Carpenter's peace mission to Charlestown.[26] Stephen answered with a demand that one of the headmen come to him with a white prisoner to confirm his talk.[27] In the Little Carpenter's absence the task fell to Standing Turkey, who carried Oconostota's promise that "no more mischief shall be done by any of our people."[28] Neither Oconostota nor Osteneco could dare yet to entrust themselves to English hands; but Osteneco, who had projects for his own aggrandizement and a reputation in Virginia upon which to capitalize, sent privately to Stephen asking that Standing Turkey be not encouraged to go to Williamsburg, that he himself would visit Virginia when the First Man returned to Chota.[29] Standing Turkey, he pointed out, was yet green in office and, in fact, very much subordinate to the older generation of headmen who held over from Old Hop's regime.

Standing Turkey, however, was not without guile. He moved slowly, stalling for time both to hear from the Little Carpenter and to prevent the Virginians from aggression. He was a month traveling two hundred miles, his alleged reason being that such

[24] Grant to Amherst, Nov. 6, 1761, Amherst Papers, B.P.R.O., W.O. 34/47.

[25] Stephen to Amherst, Oct. 5, 1761, *ibid.*

[26] Connetarke, Sept., 1761, Enc. Stephen to Amherst, Oct. 5, 1761, *ibid.*

[27] Little Carpenter's son to his brother, Enc. Stephen to Amherst, Oct. 5, 1761, *ibid.*

[28] Oconostota, Oct. 17, 1761, Enc. Stephen to Amherst, Oct. 24, 1761, *ibid.*

[29] Judd's Friend's letter, Oct. 17, 1761, Enc. Stephen to Amherst, Oct. 24, 1761, *ibid.*

a large party needed to hunt to provision itself on the road.[30] On the way, Willinawaw overtook him with a copy of the Little Carpenter's peace terms, and he reached the Great Island as winter was about to set in.

When the Little Carpenter arrived at Chota, none of the headmen who should approve the peace were at home to join the delegation to go to Charlestown for ratification. Probably by design, and perhaps for prestige and traditional reasons, neither of the two Overhill leading warriors ever set their marks to the peace treaty; nor did Standing Turkey. For that task, they had delegated their assent to the Prince of Chota. With the Little Carpenter the Prince went about the towns gathering a deputation to meet Bull's requirements for ratification. But with Grant's departure and Standing Turkey's mission holding off Stephen, the Cherokees had lost their urgency about a Carolina peace.[31] Many had gone hunting. Seroweh expressed his contempt by continuing to hunt in the white man's beef herds, though he did promise that in meeting his needs he would be careful not to hurt anyone. In a few days after Grant's departure, half the black cattle left to the Fort Prince George garrison disappeared.

The Little Carpenter, perceiving that he would not meet Bull's deadline, sent his wife and some of his relatives to Fort Prince George as pledge of his intentions.[32] Tistoe and the Wolf brought the Keowee people home from the Middle Settlements "to dance all night for coming home again."[33] But they were unhappy over the land cession. They hurried to McIntosh to protest and to insist on forty miles between themselves and the whites instead of the twenty-six proposed in the treaty. McIntosh sent the compromise to Bull, who, having already corresponded with Grant on the subject, made the adjustment.

The Little Carpenter, arriving at Fort Prince George on November 14, was nervous and irritable. He had been dealing with

30 Stephen to Amherst, Oct. 24, 1761, *ibid.*
31 S. C. Commons House Journals, Dec. 3, 1761.
32 *South Carolina Gazette*, Nov. 7, Nov. 14, 1761.
33 S. C. Commons House Journals, Dec. 3, 1761.

doubt and intransigence. He had gathered deputies of lower caliber than Carolina expected. Attempting to round up all the Cherokee-held whites for delivery, he had obtained but eight, and for these their masters expected ransoms which Carolina no longer provided.[34] The women he had entrusted to the fort were also upset, for they had heard a rumor that Grant had prepared a trap for him and his deputies at Ninety-Six.[35] Confronting McIntosh, the Little Carpenter complained of the food allotted his people and presented the case for ransoms. When McIntosh was cold, he exploded. Taxing the commander and all Carolina with deception, he angrily told the story he had heard from the women. McIntosh discreetly quieted him and asked him to go away and reconsider.[36]

Around the fire that night the Second Man persuaded the women that they had been misinformed, and the deputies to withhold their demands for ransoms until they reached Charlestown.[37] In the morning he calmly listened to McIntosh's rebuke for his having credited "women's stories," but he made the Ensign write Bull excusing the Cherokee delay.[38] He himself sent Bull an apology and warned him the ransom matter would come up for discussion. Finally near December 1, with nine deputies and eighty attendants, he left for Charlestown to hold his last conference with Carolina.

While the Little Carpenter delayed at Fort Prince George, Standing Turkey with four hundred warriors and several captives from the Fort Loudoun garrison arrived at the Great Island of the Holston where Stephen, his force augmented by Colonel Waddell and 256 North Carolinians and 52 Tuscaroras itching for action, impatiently awaited him.[39] On the basis of the terms

[34] Laurens Papers, No. 49, p. 10; S. C. Commons House Journals, Dec. 3, 1761.

[35] Grant to Amherst, Nov. 19, 1761, Amherst Papers, B.P.R.O., W.O. 34/47.

[36] Laurens Papers, No. 49, pp. 8–9.

[37] S. C. Commons House Journals, Dec. 3, 1761.

[38] Laurens Papers, No. 49, pp. 8–9.

[39] Journals of the Executive Council of Virginia, Dec. 10, 1761; Return of Troops, Great Island of the Holston, Nov. 28, 1761, Amherst Papers, B.P.R.O., W.O. 34/47.

he had from the Little Carpenter he concluded a peace with the Virginians which included the Tuscaroras.[40] Then about December 1 with Ensign Timberlake of the Virginia regiment to attest the peace, he set out for Chota.[41]

Stephen regarded his conference with Standing Turkey on November 17–19 as concluding the war.[42] On his report of the terms Fauquier consented to his withdrawal, and before the end of January the Virginia threat to the Overhills marched back over the long road Byrd had built from Fort Chiswell to the Great Island of the Holston.[43]

The Overhills also regarded the peace as completed. On December 26 and 27 all the Overhills headmen except Oconostota, who was said to have gone off to Fort de l'Assomption or Fort Chartres, and the Little Carpenter, then in Charlestown, met in Chota to hear the terms Stephen had approved, and to proclaim the peace. A few days later Chilhowee and Telassee feted Timberlake, whom Osteneco entertained at his home.[44] As a result of Timberlake's visit Virginia was to rate Osteneco highly and to honor him with a trip to England to see George III. But the Overhills' acceptance of the Virginia peace made difficult the Little Carpenter's task of implementing the Carolina terms.

The Overhills by playing both sides had again won an advantage. The parchment had not yet been formally ratified in Charlestown; and, according to the Carolina terms, war would not officially end until the Cherokees had delivered all the white prisoners, all the Negro slaves, and all the horses and cattle they had taken. Then only would the trade be resumed and the Cherokees held in Charlestown be returned. But since the English armies had withdrawn, the Indians knew they could take their time in fulfilling the terms.

[40] *South Carolina Gazette*, Sept. 27, 1761.

[41] Timberlake, *op. cit.*, 10.

[42] Journals of the Executive Council of Virginia, Dec. 10, 1761; Fauquier to Amherst, Dec. 11, 1761, Amherst Papers, B.P.R.O., W.O. 34/47.

[43] Journals of the Executive Council of Virginia, Mar. 11, 1762; Fauquier to Amherst, Jan. 8, 1762, Amherst Papers, B.P.R.O., W.O. 34/47.

[44] Timberlake, *op. cit.*, 31.

The Little Carpenter's peace delegation disappointed the Carolinians.[45] Its members though high in rank were, save for the Little Carpenter, unfamiliar names: Kittagusta, Prince of Chota and Oconostota's brother; Shalleloski of Stecoe, Osteneco's brother; Cappy, adopted son of the dead Old Hop; Onotony, the dead Round O's brother; Teetateloski of Settico; Otacite, the Mankiller of Keowee; Half Breed Will, the First Man of Nequassee; and the Old Warrior of Estatoe. The anti-Cherokee Carolinians were wrong in believing that Tistoe, Seroweh, Standing Turkey, Osteneco, and Oconostota had remained aloof because they intended the war to go on. All but Osteneco and Standing Turkey had been victims of Carolina's violated faith in 1759. Their failure to appear was a just judgment upon Carolina.

The usual amenities were missing from the meeting. Not only had Bull because of illness delegated his duties to lesser figures, chief among them Othneil Beale, but the Carolina assembly had refused money for presents, and merely in charity had supplied the plainest clothing for the peace emissaries. The sessions were austere and businesslike. They opened on December 15 with Carolina difficult on the subject of white persons still captive. Under the Little Carpenter's pressure, however, the Carolina commissioners allowed him three more months in which to return the captives and the horses, slaves, and cattle. But the Little Carpenter protested that the horses and cattle having been eaten could not be returned. He tried also to obtain ransoms for the eight captives he had delivered at Fort Prince George. The commissioners inferentially gave up the demand for the cattle but would give nothing for the prisoners save the renewal of the trade. The final terms, however, granted Tistoe's request for a forty-mile breadth to the Lower Towns' hunting grounds on condition that the Little Carpenter should return in three months.

Ratification took place on December 18. To the whites the signing was everything, the ceremonies nothing. To the Cherokees, who had an immemorial ritual for such occasions, the cere-

[45] S. C. Council Journals, Dec. 16, 1761; *South Carolina Gazette*, May 24, 1762.

monies were essential. All the Cherokees—the deputies and their eighty attendants—entered the chamber, "and after going through certain ceremonies expressing their joy" they shook hands with the Carolinians and sat down. Beale asked if they had anything to say. The Little Carpenter reminded him that they should smoke first; so Beale produced the pipe the Second Man had brought in September, lit it, and passed it to the councilmen and then to the Indians. The Prince of Chota then took the floor and drew out a pipe of "a very special character" with two strings of beads hanging from it. Lighting it, he said, "This pipe was given me by my brother, the Great Warrior, to bring hither. I deliver it as a token to have everything made straight between the white people and the Cherokees." He passed it among the deputies then to the whites. Now the Little Carpenter rose to speak. Though he still held his high position as Second Man and spoke for the nation, the authoritative voice of the Fire King of Chota was no longer in him. "Old Hop," he said, "is gone to sleep and the Standing Turkey is come in his room, but has little to say being just come to the government." The war had made Oconostota the power in the nation, but the Little Carpenter no longer ruled the Great Warrior's mind. He, therefore, could only speak from positional prestige as he went through the great rite of treaty-making to end the war he had opposed:

> I am now come here to confirm the peace. I am sorry that it has pleased the Great Man Above to make the Governor unable to speak to us on this occasion; but I shall speak the same as if he were present.
>
> It is so long a time since I heard the talk of the Great King George over the great water that I cannot say whether any of the nation remember it, but I have always kept that talk and I will to the end of my days; and there is none now in the nation alive but myself of those present when the treaty was concluded with the Emperor of Tellequoh, our then headman; and the paper it was wrote upon is still in the nation. We make use of feathers on such occasions and what I now say may be depended upon.

Here he bent down and with feathers in his hands ceremonially cleaned the path, and then continued:

> Before I came down here last, a great deal of blood was spilt in the path, but it is now wiped away; and I will leave these feathers with the Governor as a sure token that no more will be spilt by us and I hope all will be light and clear again.[46]

Here he gave a string of wampum and an eagle's tail to the commissioners. They expressed the spirit of peace that was in him in his high office.

With this introduction, he gave a talk and presented white beads for each of Tellico, Chatuga, Chota, Tanase, Toquo, Tomatly, Chilhowee, and Telassee. He did not mention the Valley towns of Hiwassee and Nottely, where anti-English Creeks still talked big and from which Seroweh conducted his semi-hostile forays, but only the peripheral towns of Valley Tomatly, Cheoah, Connechetie, Neowi, and Ustanali. The people of the Middle Settlements he made heard only through the Valley towns he had mentioned, where, Grant having extinguished their council fires, they had spoken. From the Lower Towns he had no beads, merely the presence of the Old Warrior of Estatoe, who, he indicated, brought the peace sentiments of those towns.

After the Little Carpenter, Oconostota's deputy, the Prince of Chota, spoke for the nation. From Chota he had brought an eagle's wing. As he displayed it, he said, "It is a token and the highest mark of the sincerity of our desire for peace and friendship that the nation can send; therefore I have brought it to this place where talks are given and will leave it here together with a rattle box and pipe." Having delivered these, he continued. Colonel Grant, he said, had given him a powerful symbol of peace, a great white flag. The Cherokees would keep it safe in return for the honor of receiving it. Then he held out an eagle's tail and said, "As a token of our thanks, the nation have sent the greatest present they can, namely an eagle's tail through which they hope

[46] S. C. Council Journals, Dec. 16–18, Dec. 24, 1761.

269

light will ever shine between the English and them, whom they now regard as their own people."[47]

With the Prince of Chota's graceful speech and his presentation of the tokens, the Cherokees had completed their ceremonials. The Little Carpenter then made his customary closing request. Reminding that he had delivered eight whites and one slave to Fort Prince George, he asked that Carolina deliver to him two of the nearly twoscore Cherokees held prisoner in Charlestown. Beale coldly replied that there was no reward for the delivery of prisoners. The Little Carpenter quietly answered that he had not been talking of rewards and ransoms, that the delivery of two or three Cherokees would give the nation great satisfaction. When at Bull's house the Lieutenant Governor on his sickbed signed the treaty in the presence of the Little Carpenter and the Prince of Chota he gave the Second Man permission to select two of the imprisoned Cherokees to take home with him. The Little Carpenter chose two women.

When the time came for presents, the Cherokees disdained the small heap of clothing offered them and requested instead ammunition for hunting. This was granted. Not expected at Chota until February 15 when most of their countrymen would be returned from their winter hunts, they lingered in Charlestown, eating at the outraged assembly's expense until the provincial commissary finally told them they were needed in the nation to execute the treaty provisions.

Leaving Charlestown on January 2 under escort of Aaron Price, they were long on the road. Carolinians retaliating on the Cherokees for their thefts in wartime stole the deputies' horses, and Price had to go back to Charlestown for more while the deputies awaited his return. Some of the replacements were also stolen.[48] February was well advanced before the Little Carpenter reached Fort Prince George, and by then the headmen had begun to worry over his absence.[49] From the fort the Little Carpenter

[47] *Ibid.*, Dec. 18, 1761.
[48] *Ibid.*, Dec. 18, Dec. 28, 1761, Jan. 1, Jan. 11, Feb. 24, 1762.
[49] Timberlake, *op. cit.*, 87.

sent word to Bull that he forgave the theft of horses, knowing that there were rogues among both nations. Thus he excused Seroweh's activities and the obstacles which lay ahead of him to the delivery of the remaining whites, slaves, and horses. Courteously he commended Price's care of him on the road but sent word to Bull not to expect him at the end of the three stipulated months.[50]

So little interest did important Overhills have in implementing the Carolina treaty, and so low had the Little Carpenter's prestige sunk, that nearly six months elapsed before the Indians complied with the treaty terms. Not many white prisoners remained in the nation—perhaps twenty or thirty, of whom eleven or twelve were children.[51] A few, accustomed to the Cherokee way and liking it, did not wish to go home. Some, though released by their masters, could not obtain transportation or provisions. Others were detained to guarantee the return of captive Cherokees. One Indian master, hearing that the Prince of Chota and Willinawaw demanded the release of all whites, killed the two he held.[52] Though in this act the Indian hoped to stir the war anew, Governor Boone, who had succeeded Bull, decided to forget the murders.[53] Twice in the spring of 1762 the Little Carpenter came to Fort Prince George with apologies and promises but no prisoners.

Carolina hoped that by continuing the trade embargo and retaining some thirty Cherokees taken in the war, she could force the nation to comply. But she was deceived. The Overhills had already broken the blockade by dealings with Virginia and North Carolina traders.[54] Georgia caravans fitted out at Augusta, where Seroweh had gone to proclaim the war's end, traveled into the nation to establish trading camps in the Cherokee forests remote from the surveillance of Fort Prince George.[55] The Caro-

[50] S. C. Council Journals, Feb. 24, 1762.
[51] S. C. Commons House Journals, Apr. 2, May 26, 1762.
[52] S. C. Council Journals, May 5, May 28, 1762.
[53] S. C. Commons House Journals, May 7, 1762.
[54] S. C. Council Journals, May 3, 1762.
[55] *South Carolina Gazette*, June 5, 1762.

lina assembly could now do little about it, for the crown controlled Indian affairs. They voted to confine the trade to but a single store at Keowee.[56]

Final implementation of the treaty was brought about by the Lower Towns and not by the Little Carpenter. The Cherokees held by Carolina were all Lower Townsmen. The Lower Towns enjoyed the least of the illegal trade. Therefore, in May, Captain McIntosh called Tistoe and the Wolf of Keowee to Fort Prince George and, mentioning Overhill indifference to the penalty clauses of the treaty, said that the Lower Towns could quickly have their relatives home and a very big trade if they caused their countrymen to surrender their white prisoners. Seroweh and Tistoe thereupon went to the Overhills and in June brought into the fort all the prisoners and escorted them to Ninety-Six.[57] Already the Carolina council had ordered the new "Board of Directors for Carrying on the Trade" to start trade at Keowee.[58] But the old Carolina monopoly of Cherokee trade was dead, as was the Carolina influence on Cherokee policy. The Cherokees under the leadership of Chota would accept the guidance of the crown's new Superintendent of Indian Affairs, Captain John Stuart, the Little Carpenter's friend. The battles which the Little Carpenter fought for a unitary nation under the supremacy of Chota were not in vain. When early in the nineteenth century the Cherokee republic was founded in northern Georgia, significantly its capital was named New Echota, the new home of the traditional primary fire of the Cherokees. Greatest of Cherokees was Attakullaculla, who stood for traditional nationalism, peace, and civilization.

56 S. C. Commons House Journals, Feb. 20, 1762.
57 *South Carolina Gazette*, June 19, July 3, July 10, 1762.
58 S. C. Council Journals, June 21, 1762.

Bibliography

A. BASIC REFERENCE MATERIALS

1. Comment on Principal Sources

The Cherokee Frontier: Conflict and Survival, 1740–62 was built up from a study of well over two thousand items of contemporary information. These items comprise letters, committee reports, news stories, and records of Indian conferences—most of which are authoritative according to some point of view, some of which are misguided or deliberately misrepresentative, but all of which are pertinent to an understanding of the Indian or white mind and action.

Fundamental to the study of the Cherokees in the period 1740–62 are the "Indian Books of South Carolina," which include the "talks" or messages of the local, regional, and tribal headmen of the Cherokee, Creek, Catawba, and Chickasaw nations. (Books 2, 3, 4, 5, and 6 of the "Indian Books of South Carolina" covering the period 1750–65 have been published as follows: *Colonial Records of South Carolina*, Series 2, *Documents Relating to Indian Affairs, May 21, 1750–Aug. 7, 1754*, edited by William L. MacDowell, Jr. [Columbia, S. C. Archives Department, 1958]; *Colonial Records of South Carolina*, Series 2, *Documents Relating to Indian Affairs, 1754–1765*, edited by William L. MacDowell, Jr. [Columbia, S. C. Archives Department, 1962].) These are on-the-spot accounts of the moods and events in the tribe. Those of the Indians, usually the product of discussions in council, are dressed for the white man's purview and represent the undercurrents of Indian policy about as fully as the face-to-face bargaining of union and management agents represents the private discussions of the separate parties. The traders' reports are also those of interested persons and frequently state what the traders thought Charleston should believe in a given situation. Each report received in Carolina must be read against what George Croghan wrote from the Shawnees and Mingos; what Sir William Johnson heard among the Six Nations; what Lachlan McGillivray, Sam Pepper, White Outerbridge, Thomas Bosomworth, and Edmund Atkin gleaned from the Creeks; the correspondence of French officials in Louisiana, Illinois, and Canada; the letters of John Watts, Nathaniel Gist, the Smiths (Richard and Abraham); and what the various Cherokee headmen said. The intersections of these threads usually indicate the Cherokee pattern.

For better or worse much of the Carolina story on the Cherokees until 1758 lies in the reports of the Carolinians James Beamer of Estatoe, Robert Bunning of Tuckaseigee, Cornelius Dougherty of Hiwassee, Anthony Dean of Toquo, Ludovic Grant of Cheoah, and occasionally James May of Cowee and John Elliott of Tanase and New Keowee. Despite the unsavory reputations some of these men won in various episodes, their testimony cannot be ignored. Bunning, Dougherty, and Grant were generally considered the most reliable; but like the others they were traders and Carolinians before they were friends of the Cherokees. Unfortunately the "Indian Books" are fragmentary for 1758 and end with the May, 1759, entries.

No less important than the "Indian Books" are the journals of the South Carolina Assembly: the Commons House Journals, 1748–1762; the Council Journals, 1745–1762; the Council House Journals, 1750, 1754, 1756, 1758; and the Journals of the Upper House of Assembly, 1747, 1751 (all in possession of the Historical Commission of South Carolina, Columbia, S. C.). These journals contain letters from the Cherokee country which sometimes, for one reason or another, were not copied into the "Indian Books"; the reports of such special commissioners as George Pawley, sent to the nation in 1746—colored by his distress over a brawl with visiting Senecas and the views hostile to the Cherokees in 1751; petitions from the frontier; and reports of committees of action and investigation. The Council Journals of Indian conferences are most valuable. The Journals are now in the course of publication.

The Historical Commission of South Carolina also has in its possession the Sainsbury Transcripts, copies of letters, Board of Trade papers, and other documents in the Public Records Office of Great Britain. Volumes XIV, XX, and XXII–XXVI contain materials on the Cherokee affairs of this period. Where these sources fail, the files of the *South Carolina Gazette* at the Charleston Library Society, supplemented where issues are missing by the *Maryland Gazette* (microfilm in the Yale University Library), which contains excellent exchange material from the South Carolina publication, frequently yield illuminating material. Much of the Cherokee news in the *South Carolina Gazette* appears to have been reported directly from the Indian country either by the publisher's correspondents or by traders and Indians visiting in Charleston. Some of it may be official or unofficial leakage by the Carolina authorities. In the Cherokee war the reporters did not always agree with the official point of view, for they depicted the British officers Stuart, Demere, Coytmore, and Milne as fomenting an unnecessary war.

The Henry Laurens Papers in the Charleston Library Society throw further light on the Cherokee War. Number 49, "Commentaries of Philoceiles in Reply to Philopatrios," Laurens' heated answer to the detractors of Colonel James Grant, defends the conduct of the war and the peacemaking against the assaults of the partisans of Colonel Thomas Middleton, whose command had to be rescued at Second Etchoe. Its partisanship does not detract from the usefulness of its pictures of the Cherokee settlements and of events. It appears not to have been referred to by modern scholars.

The Virginia aspects of Cherokee affairs are treated in the following works: R. A. Brock, *Official Records of Robert Dinwiddie . . . 1751–1758* (2 vols., Richmond, 1883–84); Louis Knott Koontz, *Robert Dinwiddie: Correspondence Illustrative of His Career in American Colonial Government and Western Expansion* (Berkeley and Los Angeles, 1951); John C. Fitzpatrick (ed.), *The Writings of George Washington from the Original Manuscript Sources* (Vols. I and II, Washington, D. C., 1931); Stanislaus M. Hamilton, *Letters to George Washington and Accompanying Papers* (Vols. I and II, Boston and New York, 1898); The Virginia Gazette of Williamsburg (issued on microfilm by the Institute of Early American History and Culture, Williamsburg, Va., 1950); H. R. McIlwaine (ed.), *Journal of the House of Burgessses of Virginia* (Vol. VI, Richmond, 1909); Journals of the Executive Council of Virginia, 1752, 1756–62 (in MacGregor Library, University of Virginia, Charlottesville); W. P. Palmer, S. McRae, and W. H. Fleurnoy, *Calendar of Virginia State Papers* (11 vols., Richmond, 1875–93); the Draper Manuscripts (in the State Historical Society of Wisconsin, Madison); the Amherst Papers (University Microfilm, Ann Arbor, Mich.); and the Loudoun Papers (Huntington Library, San Marino, Calif.), which contain the letters of Edmund Atkin.

Brock and Koontz supplement each other, the latter being rich in Cherokee materials, containing many of Andrew Lewis' reports and several important "talks" from Osteneco, the rival of Attakullaculla. The letters of Nathaniel Gist, Richard Pearis (whose popularity with the Cherokees disturbed official Virginia), and the wily Richard and Abraham Smith detail Cherokee vacillations toward Virginia. The Washington letters present the young provincial Colonel's struggles with Cherokee intransigence, and his ultimate appreciation of their fortitude and their contribution to Virginia defense. The Preston diary in the Draper Manuscripts is the best account of the Big Sandy expedition of 1756 by a participant; while in the same collection the hitherto unnoted letters of John Watts set forth the troubles of the young Emperor in the winter of 1752–53, which contributed to his collapse as a Cherokee power. The *Virginia Gazette* for 1751 and 1752 gives the familiar story of the Cherokee missions to Williamsburg in those years, though one should also consult the 1751 diary of Virginia Council President John Blair (in William and Mary *Quarterly*, Vol. XVII (1900–10) for further details of the Little Carpenter's visit. The Amherst Papers (W.O. 34/35) contain Clement Reed's important dispatch on the Cherokee disorders in Virginia in 1757. Atkin's meticulous accounts of his handling of the Cherokees appear in W.O. 34/47 of the Amherst Papers. For his views on the Indian question and the Virginia Indian problem there are two substantial papers in the Loudoun materials, the first having been published under the title *Indians of the Southern Colonial Frontier*, edited by Wilbur R. Jacobs (Columbia, S. C., 1954).

For the more northerly excursions of the Cherokees essential collections are: *Correspondence of Governor Sharpe* (2 vols., Baltimore, 1890), governor of Maryland; the *Maryland Gazette*; the Pennsylvania *Archives* (First Series, 12 vols., Philadelphia, 1852–56; Fourth Series, 12 vols., Harrisburg, 1900–1902); "The Papers of Colonel Henry Bouquet" (typescript edited by Sylvester K. Stevens and Donald Kent, Harrisburg, Pennsylvania Historical Commission, 1940–43); Alfred Porter Jones, *Writings of General John Forbes Relating to His Service in North America* (Menasha, Wis., 1938); and James Sullivan, Alexander C. Flick, Alma W. Lauber, et al., *The Papers of Sir William Johnson* (9 vols., Albany, 1921–   ). The entanglement of Virginia and Maryland over the Cherokees is depicted in the Atkin-Sharpe-Croghan and the Pearis-Armstrong correspondence in the Pennsylvania *Archives* and in the Sharpe-Denny-Dinwiddie exchanges in the Sharpe correspondence. The Johnson papers treat of Cherokee matters at second hand save in the details of the Cherokee–Six Nations conference at Johnson Hall in 1757 and 1758, and in the reports of Cherokee efforts in the spring of 1761 to organize the northern and western tribes against the English. The Forbes and Bouquet letters of 1758 reveal British impatience with the Cherokees accompanying the Forbes expedition against Fort Duquesne and misunderstanding of Attakullaculla's northern mission to heal the breach between Virginia and the Cherokees. Neither man understood the Cherokees nor made an effort to prevent the Cherokee war. The letters in the Lyttelton Papers (in Clements Library, Ann Arbor, Mich.), of Captain John Stuart and Captains Raymond and Paul Demere, of Lieutenant Coytmore and Ensigns Lachlan McIntosh and Alexander Milne, British commanders of the posts in the Cherokee country, give fort's-eye views of the attitudes and events which led to the Cherokee break with Carolina. In the November-December, 1759, letters of Stuart and Paul Demere these men appear as obtuse as true Britons could be to Cherokee compulsions—Stuart optimistically believing that to disregard Attakullaculla would be to halt the storm. Milne's reports from Fort Prince George give a good picture of Cherokee behavior under the stress of wartime. Also in the Lyttelton Papers are Edmund Atkin's thorough and literal accounts of Creek affairs in 1759. The Superintendent of Indian Affairs for the Southern District emerges a diplomat of heroic proportions who stemmed the war fever of the Creeks with fearless negotiations beneath threatening hatchets.

The British campaigns of 1760 and 1761 in the Cherokee country are officially covered in the reports of Lieutenant Colonel Archibald Montgomery and Lieutenant Colonel James Grant, Governors Fauquier, Lyttelton, and Bull, and Colonel William Byrd in the Amherst Papers. Grant's reports in W.O. 34/47 for the campaign of 1761 state the opinions and observations of a man who did his duty well despite a lack of faith in the wisdom of the course he was required to pursue. Perhaps the most interesting document relating to the 1761 campaign is the unpublished and hitherto unconsulted journal of Captain Christopher French (3 vols., MSS in Library of Congress, Washington, D. C.). French, who as a major had the unenviable distinction of being the highest-ranking British officer captured in 1775 by the Americans, was in 1761 a captain in the Twenty-second. In the

Cherokee campaign he sketched and made notes along the way—briefly when action was intense, at length when the crisis had passed. With his account, Grant's, and Laurens' the campaign comes to life.

Cherokee tradition of the war as retold by John Ross and Charles Hicks in 1825 to John Howard Payne in the Payne Manuscripts (Ayer Collection, Newberry Library, Chicago) tells the story in general outline but adds no significant detail beyond the account of Oconostota's assassination of Coytmore. Their tale is that of things done heroically in the faraway past, Attakullaculla and Oconostota seeming dimly to be epic heroes. One suspects the Carolina point of view to have crept in from the assimilation into the nation of so many whites and mixed breeds. Certainly the English point of view of the war as originating from horse-stealing in Virginia rather than from Carolina murders on the Little Saluda is attuned to the ideas of the contemporary whites.

Of previous studies in this area, the earliest based on sound research is P. W. Hamer's comprised in two articles in the North Carolina *Historical Review* (Vol. II, 1925): "Anglo-French Rivalry in the Cherokee Country" and "Fort Loudoun in the Cherokee War." Hamer, in accepting Carolina alarms, credits the French with a much larger hand in Cherokee affairs than they actually had. Mary U. Rothrock's *Carolina Traders among the Overhill Cherokees, 1690–1760* (Knoxville, Tenn., 1929), gives brief biographical accounts of some of the traders of the period, the abuses in the trade, and a picture of the Pearis-Gist squabble over their mission to the Cherokees in 1754. W. Neill Franklin's *Virginia and the Cherokee Trade* (Knoxville, Tenn., 1933) treats of trade relationships in the period 1753–61 without reference to their bearing on Cherokee or English policy. Chapman J. Milling's *Red Carolinians* (Chapel Hill, N. C., 1940) presents the Cherokee war entirely from Carolina sources. Robert Meriwether's *Expansion of South Carolina, 1729–1765* (Kingsport, Tenn., 1940) deals with Carolina trade relationships with the Cherokees, her land accessions from the Indians, and the war from the point of view of his Carolina sources, accepting as valid Thomas Middleton's bitter attitude toward Grant's 1761 campaign. John R. Alden's *John Stuart and the Southern Colonial Frontier* (Ann Arbor, Mich., 1944) is standard for the Cherokee war. Despite the facts that his treatment of the period 1745–54 is superficial and that his presentation is colored by the English point of view, his book is a good manual for the period 1755–61. His bibliography, compiled before the Lyttelton Papers became available, is a model of its kind. Volumes IV and V of Lawrence H. Gipson's *The British Empire before the American Revolution* (Caldwell, Idaho, 1936–   ) contain an extensive treatment of the Cherokees. Though inaccurate in some details because of the limitations of his sources, Gipson's general picture follows the conventional pattern.

For the Georgia approach, Allen D. Chandler's *Colonial Records of the State Of Georgia* (26 vols., Atlanta, Ga., 1904–1909; Vols. XXVII–XXXIX [typescript] in Georgia State Department of Archives and History, Atlanta) is the source. Volumes VII, XXIII, XXV, XXVII, XXXIII, XXXV, and XXXVI contain the relevant material. W. L. Saunders (ed.), *The Colonial Records of North Carolina* (6 vols., Raleigh, N. C., 1886–1907); Adelaide L. Fries (ed.), *Records of the Moravians in North Carolina* (Raleigh, N. C., 1922); and William Richardson's journal of his abortive evangelizing mission to the Cherokees in 1758–59 ("Report to the Rev. Samual Davies . . . ," in Southern Historical Collection, University of North Carolina, Chapel Hill) comprise what little there is of North Carolina source material for the period.

From the anthropological point of view, James Mooney, *Myths of the Cherokee* (*19th Annual Report, 1897–98*, B.A.E., Washington, D. C., 1900); W. H. Gilbert, Jr., *The Eastern Cherokees* (B.A.E., Bulletin 133, Washington, D. C., 1943); and John R. Swanton, *The Indians of the Southeastern United States* (B.A.E., Bulletin 137, Washington, D. C., 1946), contain useful matter on the political and social institutions of the Cherokees.

2. Other Primary Sources

Abercrombie Papers. Papers turned over to Lord Loudoun by General James Abercrombie. Huntington Library, San Marino, California.

Adair, James. *History of the American Indians.* Edited under the auspices of the National Society of the Colonial Dames of America in Tennessee by Samuel Cole Williams. Johnson City, Tennessee, The Watauga Press, 1930.

Bartram, William. *Travels through North and South Carolina; Georgia; East and West Florida; the Cherokee Country; the Extensive Territories of the Muscogulges, or Creek Confederacy, and the Country of the Choctaws.* London, 1792.

British Public Records Office (B.P.R.O.). Transcriptions and photostats of C.O. 5/14, 5/16, 5/17, 5/20, 5/57, and 5/58; correspondence of governors of South Carolina, North Carolina, Georgia, and Virginia relating to Indian affairs; and reports of Amherst to Pitt relating to affairs in the Southern Colonies. Library of Congress, Division of Manuscripts, Washington, D. C.

Bruce, Peter Henry. *Memoirs of Peter Henry Bruce.* Dublin, Printed by J. and R. Byrn, 1783.

Cuming, Alexander. Sir Alexander Cuming's "Journal" in Williams, *Early Travels in the Tennessee Country, 1540–1800.* Johnson City, Tenn., The Watauga Press, 1928.

De Brahm, William. *Philosophico-Historico-Hydrogeography of South Carolina, Georgia, and East Florida.* Edition of 1853. [Original in Widener Library, Harvard University, Cambridge, Mass].

Gage Papers. "Papers of General Thomas Gage relating to his command in North America, 1762–1776." Clements Library, Ann Arbor, Mich. [Vol. LXXI has material relating to the Cherokee War].

Gentlemen's Magazine. London, 30:442 (Sept., 1760).

Hanna, Charles A. *The Wilderness Trail; or, the Ventures and Adventures of the Pennsylvania Traders on the Allegheny Path.* New York and London, G. P. Putnam's Sons, 1911.

Harris, Thaddeus Mason. *Biographical Memorials of James Oglethorpe, Founder of the Colony of Georgia in North America.* Boston, 1841.

Heyward, John. *The Natural and Aboriginal History of Tennessee up to the First Settlements Therein by the White People in the Year 1768.* Nashville, 1823.

Kimball, Gertrude Selwyn. *Correspondence of William Pitt when Secretary of State with Colonial Governors and Military and Naval Commissioners in America.* 2 vols. New York, Macmillan Company, 1906.

Lawson, Cecil P. *A History of the Uniforms of the British Army.* London, 1941.

Long, Alexander. "A Small Postscript to the Ways and Manners of the Nashon of Indians Called Cherikees." MSS in papers of the Society for the Propagation of the Gospel. Vol. IV: "North and South Carolina, 1715–1761." Library of Congress, Division of Manuscripts, Washington, D. C.

Mooney, James. "The River Cult of the Cherokees," *Journal of American Folklore*, Vol. XIII (1891).

New York Council. "Minutes of the New York Council." Vol. XXV. New York State Library, Department of Manuscripts, Albany, N. Y.

New York Mercury (Gaines), 1757. New York Public Library, New York, N. Y.

O'Callaghan, E. B., ed. *Documents Relating to the Colonial History of the State of New York. Procured in Holland, England, and France by John R. Brodhead.* 11 vols. Albany, 1856–61. [Vol. VI was useful].

Orme, Robert. *Captain Orme's Journal.* In Sargent, Winthrop, ed., *The History of an Expedition against Fort DuQuesne in 1755 . . . from the Original Manuscripts.* Philadelphia, for the Historical Society of Pennsylvania, 1858.

Owen, Narcissa. "Memoirs of Narcissa Owen, 1831–1907" (typescript). Sondley Reference Library, Asheville, N. C.

Paris, France. Archives des Affaires Étrangères, Memoires et

Documents, Amérique 2:198, Memoire pour la Louisiane, 1746.

————. Archives Nationales Colonies. B78, 81, 83; A.C. C11, 81, 85, 97, 99, A104; A.C. C13, 26, A28, A38, A39, A40, A42: Correspondence between Louisiana and Canadian officials with the French ministry. Photostats and transcripts in Library of Congress, Division of Manuscripts, Washington, D. C.

Pease, Calvin, ed. *Collections of the Illinois State Historical Library*. Vol. XXIX. Springfield, Ill., The Trustees of the Illinois State Historical Library, 1940.

Pennsylvania. *Minutes of the Provincial Council of Pennsylvania*. Pennsylvania Colonial Records. First Series. 10 vols. Harrisburg, 1838–60.

Plowden, Charles Jennet Weston, ed. *Documents Connected with the History of South Carolina*. London, 1856.

Post, Christian. *Journal*, in R. G. Thwaites, ed., *Early Western Travels*. Vol. I. Cleveland, O., 1905.

Rowland, Dunbar, and A. G. Saunders. *Mississippi Provincial Archives*. 3 vols. Jackson, Miss., 1927–32. [Vol. III was useful].

Setzler, Frank M., and Jesse D. Jennings. *Peachtree Mound and Village Site, Cherokee County, North Carolina*. Smithsonian Institution, Bureau of American Ethnology, Bulletin 131. Washington, D. C., United States Government Printing Office, 1941.

South Carolina Historical and Genealogical Magazine, Vol. X (1910).

Timberlake, Lt. Henry. *The Memoirs of Lt. Henry Timberlake*. London, printed for the author, 1765.

Treaty Held with the Catawba and Cherokee Indians, A. Williamsburg, W. Hunter, 1756. [MacGregor Library, University of Virginia, Charlottesville, Va.].

United States. National Archives. Archives Building, Washington, D. C.

Virginia Historical Register and Literary Notebook, Vol. IV, No. 3 (July, 1751).

Waddell, Joseph. *Annals of Augusta County, Virginia.* Staunton, Va., C. R. Caldwell, 1902.

B. Background Materials

Alden, John R. "The Eighteenth Century Cherokee Archives," *American Archivist,* Vol. V. No. 4 (Oct., 1942).

Andrews, Charles M. *Guide to the Materials for American History, to 1783, in the Public Record Office of Great Britain.* 2 vols. Washington, D. C., Carnegie Institution of Washington, 1912–14.

————, and Frances G. Davenport. *Guide to the Manuscript Materials for the History of the United States to 1783, in the British Museum, in Minor London Archives, and in the Libraries of Oxford and Cambridge.* Washington, D. C., Carnegie Institution of Washington, 1918.

Brigham, Clarence S. *History and Bibliography of American Newspapers, 1690–1820.* 2 vols. Worcester, Mass., 1947.

Brown, John P. *Old Frontiers: The Story of the Cherokee Indians from Earliest Times to the Date of Their Removal to the West, 1838.* Kingsport, Tenn., Southern Publishers, Inc., 1938.

Corry, John P. *Indian Affairs in Georgia, 1732–1736.* Philadelphia, 1936.

Cotterill, R. S. *The Southern Indians: The Story of the Civilized Tribes before Removal.* Norman, University of Oklahoma Press, 1954.

Crane, Verner W. *The Southern Frontier, 1670–1732.* Durham, N. C., Duke University Press, 1929.

Davidson, Donald. *The Tennessee.* [Rivers of America Series]. New York, Rinehart and Company, 1946.

Filson, John. *The Discovery, Settlement and Present State of Kentucke.* Wilmington, Printed by James Adams, 1784.

Freeman, Douglas Southall. *George Washington*. Vols. I and II. New York, C. Scribner's Sons, 1948– .

Grant, Lt. Col. James. "Military Journal, June–July, 1761," Florida Historical Society *Quarterly*, Vol. XII (1933).

Griffin, G. G. *A Guide to Manuscripts Relating to American History in British Depositories Reproduced for the Division of Manuscripts of the Library of Congress*. Library of Congress, 1946.

Hewatt, Alexander. *An Historical Account of the Rise and Progress of the Colonies of South Carolina and Georgia*. London, 1779.

Hodge, Frederick Webb, ed. *Handbook of American Indians North of Mexico*. Smithsonian Institution, Bureau of American Ethnology, Bulletin 30. Washington, D. C., United States Government Printing Office, 1910.

Koontz, Louis K. *The Virginia Frontier, 1754–1763*. Baltimore, The Johns Hopkins Press, 1925.

Logan, John Henry. *A History of the Upper Country of South Carolina from the Earliest Periods to the Close of the War of Independence*. Columbia, S. C., 1859.

McCall, Capt. Hugh. *The History of Georgia*. 2 vols. Savannah, 1811.

Mereness, Newton Dennison. *Travels in the American Colonies*. New York, The Macmillan Company, 1916.

Myer, William E. *Indian Trails of the Southeast. 42nd Annual Report*, Bureau of American Ethnology. Washington, D. C., 1921.

Parker, David W. *A Guide to the Documents in the Manuscript Room at the Public Archives of Canada*. Ottawa, 1914.

Peckham, Howard H. *A Guide to the Manuscript Collections in the William L. Clements Library*. Ann Arbor, 1942.

Pendleton, William C. *History of Tazewell County and Southwest Virginia, 1748–1920*. Richmond, Va., W. C. Hill Printing Company, 1920.

Rand, James Hall. *The North Carolina Indians*. [The James

Sprunt Studies in History and Political Science, Vol. XII, No. 2]. Chapel Hill, University of North Carolina, 1913.

Rice, Otis K. *The Sandy Creek Expedition of 1756.* [West Virginia History, Vol. XIII]. Charleston, W. Va., State Department of Archives and History, Oct., 1951.

Romans, Bernard. *A Concise Natural History of East and West Florida.* Vol. I. Second edition. New York, 1776.

Spiller, Robert E., Willard Thorp, Thomas H. Johnson, Henry S. Canby, et al. *Literary History of the United States.* New York, Macmillan, 1948.

Stevens, Benjamin F. "Catalogue Index of Manuscripts in the Archives of England, France, and Holland Relating to America, 1763–1783." MSS in Library of Congress, Washington, D. C.

Surrey, N. M. Miller (Mrs. F. M. Surrey). *Calendar of Manuscripts in Paris Archives and Libraries Relating to the History of the Mississippi Valley to 1803.* Carnegie Institution of Washington, Department of Historical Research. Washington, 1928.

Swanton, John R. *Early History of the Creek Indians and Their Neighbors.* Smithsonian Institution, Bureau of American Ethnology, Bulletin 73. Washington, D. C., United States Government Printing Office, 1922.

Volwiler, Albert T. *George Croghan and the Westward Movement, 1741–1782.* Cleveland, 1926.

Williams, Samuel C. "An Account of the Presbyterian Mission to the Cherokees, 1757–1759." *Tennessee Historical Magazine,* Second Series, No. 1 (1931).

――――. *Nathaniel Gist, Father of Sequoyah.* The East Tennessee Historical Society's Publications, No. 5 (Jan., 1933). Knoxville, Tenn.

Index

Abeikas (Creek Indians): 96, 99

Abraham (Negro slave): 140, 196, 217

Acorn Whistler (Creek headman): attacks Cherokees, 22; assassinated, 36

Adair, James: 9, 25, 216

Adamson, Lt.: 131, 219f.

Alabama River: 109

Albany, N.Y.: 156

Allegheny Mountains: 119

Allegheny River: 112

Allen, John (Va. agent): 102

Amherst, Lord Jeffrey: 235, 256; plans for Montgomery expedition of 1760, 207; orders punishment of Cherokees for Fort Loudoun massacre, 245

Ammonscossittee (Young Emperor of the Cherokees): 13, 16, 18f., 22, 32, 78, 81, 88; seeks Virginia trade, 39; discredited, 40; ignored by Little Carpenter, 83; see also Hiwassee-Tellico coalition

Anderson, John: 34

Anderson, Lt.: 218

Atkin, Edmund (Superintendent of Indian Affairs for the Southern District): 118; organizes Indian affairs, 120–21; encounter with Wawhatchee, 121–24; jurisdictional dispute, 126; collapse of his organization, 128; takes over Carolina Indian affairs, 144–45, 148–49; treaty with Choctaws, 173; frustrates Creek rising, 172f.; assaulted by Creeks, 176–77; summons Cherokees to Augusta, 173

Attakullaculla: see Little Carpenter

Atwood, Isaac: 176

Augusta, Ga.: 26, 193, 203, 271

Augusta, Va.: 71, 103, 150

Aurora (bootleg trading settlement): 34

Baldridge, James (trader): 191

Ball Play Creek, Tenn.: 220f.

Beale, Captain (commander of Fort Frederick): 118

Beale, Othniel: 267f., 270

Beamer, James (trader at Estatoe): 11, 30f., 46, 86, 159

Beamer, "Young": 158–59

Beaver's Son (Delaware warrior): 119

Bedford, Va.: 116, 151, 158–59

Belestre, Ens.: capture of, 125; foments anti-English sentiment among Cherokees, 163, 171, 232

Benn, Samuel (trader at Toquo): 77–78, 113, 140

Bethabara, N.C.: 148, 196, 203

Betania, N.C.: 196

Big Sandy expedition: 66–67

Big Sandy River: 67

Black Dog of Chatuga: 131

Index

Teedyuscung (Delaware chief): 147, 156

Teetateloski of Settico (Cherokee deputy): 267

Telassee (Overhill town): 35, 112, 114, 183, 266, 269

Tellico (Overhill town): 146, 269; ties with the Valley, 3; rivalry with Chota, 16; trader Goudy leaves, 37; rise of pro-French sentiment, 72; mission to Charlestown (1756), 78; opens correspondence with the French, 88; Raymond Demere at, 88; mission to the French, 93, 99–101, 111–12, 113; Lt. Wall visits, 106; role of trade in unrest at, 107; Carolina subordinates it to Chota, 110; renews French contact, 130; English attack Shawnees at, 132; white woman murdered at, 136

Tennessee River: 18, 21, 61f., 73, 144

Tessuntee (Cherokee Out town): 253

Tessuntee Old Fields: 212f., 225; see also Etchoe

Thigh, the (Tellico warrior): 135, 137

Thompson, Maj.: 231

Timberlake, Ens. Henry: 266

Tistoe (headman of Keowee): 83, 154, 162, 204, 206, 241ff., 257, 264; feted in Charlestown, 87; takes peace stand, 164; released from Fort Prince George by Little Carpenter, 188; makes peace offer, 199; suggests evacuation of Fort Prince George, 200f.; seized by Milne, 206; released by Montgomery, 210; leads Cherokees at battle of Etchoe, 212

Tobler, Ulric: 194

Tomatly (Overhill town): 95, 269

Toogaloo (Cherokee Lower town): 25

Toquo (Overhill town): 269

Torrens (smuggler): 234

Totscadater (Creek warrior): 176–77

Toxaway (Lower town): 35f., 173, 201, 209

Trade: 22, 42, 44, 78–79, 81, 90, 93, 97f., 109, 114, 130, 144, 165, 170, 180, 233–34; importance of to Cherokees, 6, 14–15; abuses in, 26, 29, 111; Carolina-Virginia rivalry for, 30–31, 32, 53; 1751 regulation of, 33–34; illicit, 34; Dinwiddie encourages Virginia traders, 39; high prices, 45; weakness of French trade, 51; Cherokee debts, 54; Glen promises improvements, 60; credit difficulties, 63, 69; Virginia agrees to enter Cherokee trade, 70, 78; emphasis of Tellico-French mission upon, 100; basis of Tellico trouble, 107; wartime difficulties of, 133; end of Carolina monopoly of, 271–72

Traders: important traders, 11–12; influence on Cherokee policy, 22; flee Cherokee country (1760), 176; murder of Creek traders, 205

Treaty of Aix-la-Chapelle: 22

Treaty of Lancaster (1744): 61

Treaty of 1730: 13, 26, 30, 38f., 44f., 51f., 109, 160, 164, 178, 187, 189

Treaty of 1751: 32

Treaty of 1755 (Saluda): 59–61

Treaty of 1759 (Fort Prince George): 189

Treaty of 1761: 257–62, 267–69

Tuckareechee (Cherokee Out town): 253

Tuckareetchee Old Fields: 214

Tuckaseigee (Cherokee Out town): 26

Tuckaseigee River: 3, 26, 53, 63, 251

Tug Fork: 66

Turner, George (Atkin's agent to Cherokees): 153

Turner's Fort, S.C.: 197

Turtle Creek, Pa.: 124–25

Tuscarora Indians: 265

Tuscoloso (warrior of Settico): 174, 175–76

Twelve Mile Creek, S.C.: 185, 238

Twightwee Indians: 138, 170

THE CHEROKEE FRONTIER

has been planned for maximum comfort in reading and handling. The type is eleven-point Old Style Number Seven, set on the Linotype with two points of spacing between lines. This face is transitional and has more "modern" than "old style" characteristics. It exemplifies the evolution of letter forms toward simplicity that has been in progress during the past fifty years.

UNIVERSITY OF OKLAHOMA PRESS

Norman